DEVELOPING
A HIGH SCHOOL
CORE PROGRAM

THE MACMILLAN COMPANY
NEW YORK · CHICAGO
DALLAS · ATLANTA · SAN FRANCISCO
LONDON · MANILA
BRETT-MACMILLAN LTD.
TORONTO

DEVELOPING
A HIGH SCHOOL
CORE PROGRAM

LUCILE L. LURRY

Supervisor of the Core Program
Prince George's County, Maryland

and

ELSIE J. ALBERTY

Associate Professor of Education
The Ohio State University

The Macmillan Company · New York

© The Macmillan Company 1957

Printed in the United States of America

First Printing

Library of Congress catalog card number: 57-6357

PREFACE

One of the most significant problems facing the American high school is that of reorganizing general education to meet the needs of youth. In a culture characterized by rapid and fundamental change, it is no longer possible to assume that the conditions under which one generation lives can be passed on substantially unchanged to the next generation. Change is a major aspect of our age. The understandings, skills, and appreciations which might have enabled the citizen to live successfully a decade or two ago are no longer adequate. Youth of today are confronted by problems not even contemplated by their parents. These problems must be solved if our democracy is to survive. To provide a program of general education which will meet the needs of youth and help them live successfully in an ever-changing society is the challenge of the American high school.

The writers believe that general education in the high school should be reorganized on the basis of a core program. As used here, core refers to that part of the total curriculum which is basic for all students and which consists of broad preplanned areas of living in which youth usually have problems. From these problem areas, learning units are developed cooperatively in the classroom by teacher and pupils.

This volume is designed to give some direction to those concerned with developing a core program in the high school. It is hoped that the treatment of principles, problems, and practices in reorganizing general educaton on the basis of a core program may prove of value in pre-service education courses and in graduate courses in colleges and universities as well as in in-service programs. The detailed accounts of how schools in several sections of the country are developing core programs should be both reassuring and helpful to superintendents, curriculum directors, supervisors, principals, teachers, parents, and other laymen.

Although those who plan and develop a core program as described here may not always approach their problems in the order in which they are dealt with in this volume, the writers believe that it is necessary to analyze the tasks involved in this order to make clear some possible procedures to use at each step, and throughout, to emphasize the need for continuous working together of the total faculty of a school. The writers hold that all those persons affected by curriculum change—pupils, teachers, parents, administrators, supervisors —must share in deciding the direction of change and the implementation of these cooperative decisions. This feeling for the worth and dignity of the individual, for the value of the cooperative process in the solution of our common problems, and for the method of intelligence as a way to work on our problems is indeed the essence of the core program in action.

The writers take the position that a program of general education should play a significant role in developing effective citizenship. In Chapter I the traditional concept of general education is examined critically and the need for reorganization is established. The assumption is that the ideals of democracy and an analysis of the common needs, problems, and interests of young people provide a sound basis upon which to organize a general education program. In Chapter II the term core is defined. Specific purposes of the core program and the general characteristics which might identify such a program in action are presented. The problem of designing the core program is discussed in Chapter III. In this chapter the writers discuss what is involved in a problem area study and present in detail one formulation of problem areas. Accounts of how problem area studies were made in two actual situations are presented in Chapter IV.

Chapter V suggests a technique which teachers might find helpful as they work together on developing resource guides for use in the core. An illustrative resource guide is also presented in this chapter. The question of how to use a resource guide in developing a learning unit is considered in Chapter VI. More specifically, this chapter deals with the kind of preplanning a teacher does when he is committed to teacher-pupil planning in the classroom and how the teacher plans, develops, and evaluates a learning unit cooperatively with pupils. The latter is illustrated by means of detailed descriptions of core classes in action. The purpose of Chapter VII is to explore the role of the special-interest areas in the core program. Some guiding principles for the participation of special-interest-area teachers are presented and two levels of participation, i.e., the pre-planning level and the action level are discussed and illustrated. In Chapter VIII the writers attempt to analyze the tasks involved in reorganizing general education on the basis of a core program. Also included in this chapter are several examples of *how* groups actually have worked in specific situations to develop core programs; and, finally there is a brief summary statement. The Appendix includes resource materials related to the fifteen problem areas presented in Chapter III and suggestions for use of the core block of time.

The writers wish to acknowledge the help and inspiration they have received from leaders in the field of curriculum development, core teachers, secondary school principals, and other administrators. They also wish to acknowledge their indebtedness to the individuals who prepared materials for use in this book. They are listed in the index and at appropriate points in the text. Finally, the writers wish to express their appreciation to the various publishers who have granted permission to quote from their published works.

L.L.L.

E.J.A.

TABLE OF CONTENTS

I

GENERAL EDUCATION
IN THE HIGH SCHOOL

The present is an era of rapid and fundamental changes. Within the past few decades many aspects of our culture have changed at a rate unparalleled in history. Our society is no longer characterized by the intimate communities of an earlier day but by urban communities and large metropolitan areas. From slightly less than 76 million people at the turn of the century, our population in 1950 had risen to approximately 151 million. We have moved from an agrarian to an industrial economy, from hand labor to automation. Our foreign policy has shifted from one of isolationism to internationalism, and we have been placed in a position of world leadership which has never before been ours.

On every side the old is being replaced by the new. Frequently the rate of change is so rapid that both the old and new elements exist side by side, often in competition with one another. In such a period there is likely to be considerable confusion as to the direction which change should take. This decision should not be left to mere chance. In a democracy the responsibility for directing change rests squarely upon the individual working in concert with his fellows. The notion that the common man through the use of the method of intelligence is capable of making the "best" decisions is basic to our democratic way of life.

Even a casual survey of the contemporary scene clearly indicates that our society is faced with profound decisions as to the direction which change should take. The American people are confronted by unprecedented and vitally urgent problems. Our way of life is in the balance. The threat of world conflict is constantly hovering over

1

us. What does this threat of total destruction mean in terms of military preparedness and civil defense? What effect does this state of affairs have upon the security of people all over the world? How can the instruments developed by science and technology be used to build a better world? Can the ideal of a united world be realized? What is our responsibility for world leadership? How can our standard of living be raised? What is the government's responsibility for social welfare? How can our natural resources be conserved? How can our various minority groups attain their full rights as citizens? Such problems must be solved if our way of life is to survive.

In today's world, the American high school is presented with a difficult challenge. Our young people are growing up in an age in which the nature of our society and the position of the individual in it are changing rapidly. Life is becoming more and more complex. It is no longer possible to assume that the conditions under which one generation lives can be passed on essentially unchanged to the next generation. Youth of today are faced with problems not even contemplated by their parents. The quality of the decisions they make will influence the future of democracy. Clearly, if the high school is to become a dynamic force in preserving, interpreting, and refining our democratic way of life, it must deal realistically with the problems that confront youth in an ever-changing society.

Is the High School Keeping Pace with the Times?

For many years after its inception, the high school went complacently about its business of providing a program of secondary education for a small, highly select group of American youth. There was relatively little criticism of its efforts. Most people were satisfied that the high school was carrying out its proper function—preparation for college. In the last half century, however, as a result of the increase in the number of youth attending high school, there has been considerable agitation to change this emphasis in secondary education. The struggle has been a long and difficult one, but changes are gradually taking place.[1] During the years when our society has

[1] For a more detailed discussion of the present status of secondary education—problems, issues, and trends, see Harold Alberty, Reorganizing the High-School Curriculum (Revised). New York, The Macmillan Company, 1953, Chapter I.

been changing most rapidly, the high school has been changing from an institution designed to educate college-bound youth to a more broadly conceived institution designed to provide a program of secondary education for all youth. The responsibility of the high school has grown from preparation for college to preparation for life.

To the extent that the high school is helping *all* youth develop to the fullest possible extent as citizens of our democratic society, it is keeping pace with the times. It seems appropriate, therefore, to center this discussion on two inseparable aspects: (1) the progress we have made toward providing for all youth in the high school, and (2) the provisions we have made for common citizenship education.

Providing a Program of Secondary Education for All Youth

To appreciate the progress we have made toward providing a program of secondary education for all, it is helpful to look at the phenomenal increase in high-school enrollments since 1890.[2] At that time the total high-school population was approximately 212 thousand pupils, a ratio of one high-school pupil to 312 persons of the general population. By 1915 the total high-school population was slightly over 1,300,000 pupils, an increase of over 500 per cent in just twenty-five years. By 1926 the ratio of high-school pupils to the general population was one to thirty-one. In 1940, it was estimated that out of a population of nearly 19½ million youth aged twelve to nineteen years, approximately seventy per cent were in school. Ninety-four per cent of youth in the age group twelve to fourteen attended school. Seventy-five per cent of the fifteen to seventeen year olds were enrolled in high school, and twenty-seven per cent of the eighteen to nineteen year old youth were attending high school, junior college, or some kind of post high-school institution. During World War II many youth dropped out of school to work, but after the war high-school enrollments again spiralled upward, and by 1950 the number enrolled in the high school had increased to something over eight million. The secondary school population had increased nearly 4,000 per cent since 1890. It is estimated that more than four

[2] The statistics in this discussion are based upon the 1950 report of the United States Census Bureau.

out of five adolescents of school age are in school now, and there is every reason to assume that this figure will increase in the next decade.

This rapid growth in the high-school population gives some indication of the importance that the American people attach to education and the tremendous responsibility of education for meeting the needs of youth. But how nearly have we achieved the ideal of providing a program of secondary education for all? Recent studies indicate that the high school is still a rather selective institution.[3] Financial status and mental ability continue to rank high among the most selective factors. Contrary to popular belief, high-school attendance is financially impossible for many young people. Usually, those of low mental ability do not get into high school, and when they do they are likely to drop out before graduation. Furthermore, it has been estimated that only about half of all those who enter school actually continue until graduation from high school. Of the fifty per cent who have dropped out of school prior to graduation, almost all have withdrawn during the secondary school years.

Admittedly, the fact that more than eighty per cent of the school-aged adolescents are now in school has created problems that did not exist when only the select few who were preparing to enter college attended high school. A wider range of interests and abilities has to be provided for. One might well expect that this change in the character of the school population would have precipitated basic changes in the curriculum, but unfortunately such is not the case.[4] A comparison of today's high-school curriculum with that of twenty or even thirty years ago reveals that while there has been an increase in the number and variety of courses offered, greater emphasis on guidance, more attention to extra-curricular activities, improvement

[3] Several studies of the high school population are summarized in *General Education in the American High School*. North-Central Association of Colleges and Secondary Schools. Chicago, Scott, Foresman and Company, 1942. Chapter I. Also see W. Lloyd Warner, Robert J. Havighurst, and Martin B. Loeb, *Who Shall Be Educated?* New York, Harper & Brothers, 1944. Paul B. Jacobson, "The Cost of Attending High Schools," *Bulletin of the National Association of Secondary School Principals*. XXXVIII, 3-28 (January, 1944); Harold Hand, "For Whom Are High Schools Designed?" *Educational Leadership*. VI, 359-365 (March, 1949).

[4] See Alberty, *op. cit.*, pp. 6-9.

in textbooks and audio-visual aids, and the like, there has been relatively little basic change in the curriculum. For the most part, the requirements for graduation remain the same. Academic courses continue to hold their time-honored position. All in all, studies of the needs, problems, and interests of young people growing up in our culture seem to have had little impact on the high-school curriculum. Thus, while the gains have been gratifying, it appears that we have a long way to go before we can claim that we are providing secondary education for all.

Developing Effective Citizenship

With the influx of pupils and the broadening of the responsibility of the high school has come an indictment on the part of laymen and educators alike that the high school is not meeting the challenge of the times. More and more attention has been focused on the role of the high school in our society. Numerous committees and commissions have been formed,[5] and literally thousands of man hours have been spent in a critical examination of the curriculum.

Much of the concern has centered in the area of general education.[6] This is only natural since this part of the curriculum has been charged with the responsibility for maintaining our democratic society as a closely knit and well-integrated unit. Recognition of the continuous threat to our way of life by forces within and without our democracy has made us even more aware of the consequences of neglecting basic citizenship education.

As a result of this widespread concern, high schools began to reexamine the purposes and procedures that characterized the program required of all. The content of subjects such as English, mathematics, science, and the social sciences was enriched, and teaching procedures were improved. In science classes, for example, the use of the project method was extended. Pupils went on field trips, consulted resource persons and made use of a variety of audio-visual aids.

---

[5] See J. Paul Leonard, *Developing the Secondary School Curriculum* (Revised). New York, Rinehart & Company, 1955, Especially Chapters VI, VII, and XIII.

[6] Briefly, general education might be defined as that part of the curriculum required of all on the ground that it provides for the understandings, values, and skills needed by all for effective citizenship in a democracy. Adapted from Alberty, *op. cit.*, pp. 163-164.

English classes provided more opportunity for creative writing and recreational reading. Pupils kept a file of their writings together with a record of their errors in grammar and sentence structure and developed word lists. In mathematics classes problem material of a practical nature was emphasized. Boys and girls engaged in projects, both individually and in groups. Studying physical growth trends of adolescents, making scale drawings of the school buildings and grounds, and operating the school store are examples of such projects. Social studies classes spent more time in studying community problems, and the use of the survey technique became very popular.[7]

The departmentalization of subject matter was questioned. Intensive study, focusing on how the high school could more effectively meet the needs of youth was undertaken, and experimental programs designed to make general education more functional began to appear.[8] General courses or "broad fields" courses such as general science, general mathematics, language arts, and social studies became quite common. These courses drew their subject matter from a single field but cut across the lines dividing specific subjects within a field. Unified studies programs were undertaken by some schools. In such programs a number of subjects were unified or fused. The usual combination was English and social studies, but experiments aimed at unifying mathematics and science were also fairly common. Other schools deviated even farther from the traditional approach to general education and attempted to develop programs which were based on the common problems of adolescents using the organized bodies of subject matter as resource materials in the solution of the problems.[9]

[7] For a discussion of the changes in traditional subjects see Roland C. Faunce and Nelson L. Bossing, Developing the Core Curriculum. New York, Prentice Hall, Inc., 1951, pp. 49-51.

[8] The Eight-Year Study carried on by the Commission on the Relation of School and College of the Progressive Education Association was one of the most significant of the studies undertaken. For a description of the study and the findings see Wilford M. Aikin, The Story of the Eight-Year Study. New York, Harper & Brothers, 1942; H. H. Giles, S. P. McCutchen and A. N. Zechiel, Exploring the Curriculum. New York, Harper & Brothers, 1942. Thirty Schools Tell Their Story. New York, Harper & Brothers, 1942.

[9] For a discussion of the emerging design of general education see Alberty, op. cit., Chapter VI; J. Galen Saylor and William M. Alexander, Curriculum Planning for Better Teaching and Learning. New York, Rinehart & Company, Inc., 1954.

In spite of these evidences of progress, high schools continue to be
dominated by a traditional concept of general education. Little
more than a casual examination of most high school programs indicates that the program required of all on the ground that it provides
for the common needs, problems, and interests of youth consists
largely of logically organized subjects.[10] The usual practice is to
require English, social studies, mathematics, and physical education
at both the seventh and eighth grade levels. In addition the pupils
may elect one or more courses from among such possibilities as
music, fine arts, industrial arts, home economics, and science. The
program is much the same at the ninth grade level except that the
student has more opportunity to choose electives. In many schools
mathematics becomes an elective in the ninth grade. In grades ten,
eleven, and twelve, there is a marked decrease in the number of
courses required of all (English, social studies and physical education
are usually the only requirements at these levels) and a corresponding
increase in the electives offered.[11]

The courses required of all for citizenship education have serious
shortcomings. Among their major shortcomings are these:[12]

1. **They are not designed to deal with the common needs, problems and interests of youth.** Each subject area is organized in terms
of its own logic. There is no particular attempt to identify and make
a direct attack upon the common problems of young people growing

---

Chapters 8-10; Nelson L. Bossing, *Principles of Secondary Education*. New York,
Prentice-Hall, Inc., 1955 (Second Edition), Chapter XII.

[10] The United States Office of Education reports that the general education
programs of approximately 96½ per cent of the high schools in the United States
consist of separate subject-matter classes. See Grace S. Wright, *Core Curriculum
in Public High Schools, An Inquiry into Practices, 1949*. Bull. 1950, No. 5.
Washington, Federal Security Agency, Office of Education, 1950.

[11] For a description of the program of studies in accredited high school see
Grace S. Wright, *State Accreditation of High Schools Practices and Standards of
State Agencies*. Bull. 1955, No. 5. Washington, U.S. Department of Health, Edu-
cation, and Welfare, Office of Education, 1955.

[12] Other appraisals of the subject-centered curriculum may be found in: Alberty,
op. cit., Chapter V; Saylor and Alexander, *op. cit.*, Chapter 8; Earl C. Kelley,
Education for What Is Real. New York, Harper & Brothers, 1947. Chapter 2.
For a discussion of the need for a new general education program in the high
school see Harold Alberty, et al., *Preparation of Core Teachers for Secondary
Schools*. Washington, Association for Supervision and Curriculum Development,
1955, Chapter I.

up in our culture.[13] Problems are treated but incidentally as they serve to enrich the subject-matter field. The assumption apparently is that once the pupil has mastered the subjects required of him he will then be able to deal adequately with the problems he faces.

The noted English philosopher Alfred North Whitehead touches on this point in his statement: "Education is the acquisition of the art of utilization of knowledge."[14] In a longer statement Whitehead expanded this:

> The solution which I am urging is to eradicate the fatal disconnection of subjects which kills the vitality of our modern curriculum. There is only one subject matter for education, and that is life in all its manifestations. Instead of this single unity, we offer children algebra, from which nothing follows; geometry, from which nothing follows; science, from which nothing follows; history, from which nothing follows; a couple of languages, never mastered; and lastly, most dreary of all, literature, represented by plays of Shakespeare, with philological notes and short analyses of plot and character to be in substance committed to memory. Can such a list be said to represent life, as it is known in the midst of living it? The best that can be said of it is, that it is a rapid table of contents which a deity might run over in his mind while he was thinking of creating a world and had not yet determined how to put it together.[15]

The implications of these remarks are clear. The school must provide experiences that have pertinence to the lives of pupils and to the society of which they are members. This, of course, is not to say that knowledge of subject matter is not essential, for the citizen cannot deal effectively with his problems without adequate knowledge. It is only to say that the school must deal more directly with the needs, problems, and interests of young people growing up in our culture.

[13] For a description of recent studies of the school's responsibility for personal-social problems see Kenneth B. Henderson and Harold C. Hand, "To What Extent Is the General Public in Sympathy with the Current Attacks on the Schools?", *Progressive Education.* XXIX, 110-115 (January, 1952).

[14] Alfred North Whitehead, *The Aims of Education.* Mentor Ed., New York, The New American Library, 1949, p. 16. (published originally by the Macmillan Company, 1929.)

[15] *Ibid.*, pp. 18-19. Also see John Dewey, *Experience and Education.* New York, The Macmillan Company, 1938; C. Lester Anderson, Gertrude Whipple and Robert Gilchrist, "The School as a Learning Laboratory," *Learning and Instruction,* Forty-Ninth Yearbook of the National Society for the Study of Education, Part I. Chicago, The University of Chicago Press, 1950, Chapter XIII.

2. **Frequently they are merely the first in a series of highly specialized courses.** One group of educators analyzes the situation as follows:

The impact of specialism has been felt not only in those phases of education which are necessarily and rightly specialistic; it has affected the whole structure of higher and even secondary education. Teachers, themselves products of highly technical disciplines, tend to reproduce their knowledge in class. The result is that each subject, being taught by an expert, tends to be so presented as to attract potential experts. This complaint is perhaps more keenly felt in colleges and universities. . . . Even an elementary course is devised as an introduction to a specialism within a department; it is significant only as the beginning of a series of courses of advancing complexity. In short, such introductory courses are planned for the specialist, not for the student seeking a general education.[16]

As the Committee points out, the trend toward specialism is most pronounced at the college level. Its impact on the secondary school is becoming increasingly evident. Elementary courses which lead toward specialization in a subject field are frequently required of all on the ground that they are essential for effective citizenship. The senior high school, as might be expected, is particularly vulnerable here. The junior high school has not entirely escaped the pressures in this direction, however.

3. **Too often the learning experiences are planned and carried on without sufficient regard for what is now commonly accepted concerning the learning process.** The learner is looked upon as a passive organism that responds more or less mechanically to stimuli. Fixed bodies of subject matter are imposed upon him without taking into account his needs, nature, and previous experiences—this despite the fact that learning is now generally held to be an active process which involves the interaction of the dynamic learner with his equally dynamic environment.[17] Similarly, *much of the current practice is*

[16] *General Education in a Free Society.* Report of the Harvard Committee. Cambridge (Mass.), Harvard University Press, 1945, pp. 56-57.
[17] See William Heard Kilpatrick, *Modern Education: Its Proper Work.* New York, Hinds, Hayden and Eldredge, Inc., 1949, pp. 10-17. For a comprehensive treatment of learning and learning theories see: Boyd H. Bode, *How We Learn.* Boston, D. C. Heath and Company, 1940; *The Psychology of Learning,* Forty-First Yearbook of The National Society for the Study of Education, Part II.

inconsistent with the findings in research on adolescent growth and development.[18] Those primarily concerned with covering ground and passing on the accumulated knowledge in their field of specialization are not likely to be stimulated by the latest developments in this area—except as they may be used to achieve conventional purposes. It is those who are genuinely concerned with making the school an effective instrument in helping young people solve their problems and live successfully in a confused society who are most likely to utilize every means at their disposal to gain an understanding of their pupils.

4. **The fundamental skills are narrowly conceived.** Seldom are they broadly defined and taught in terms of the use made of them. Pupils are expected to master the "essentials" defined by the subject-matter specialist and somehow to make the inner logic of the area a part of their everyday lives. All too often the so-called fundamentals are defined in terms of the 3 R's. Little attention is given to developing skill in areas such as human relations. Hanna points up the inadequacy of the common concept of the fundamentals in this statement:

> Because we live in a power age with its increasing interdependence and complexity, we are forced to develop competencies in our children far greater than those required of previous generations. What we and our children need is greater mastery over an expanded list of 3 R's. On this point there can be no argument.[19]

Subject matter and tool skills often become the end rather than the means to the end—the development of well-rounded individuals.

5. **Guidance is commonly looked upon as something apart from the instructional program.** Pupils' common personal-social problems are usually referred to the guidance specialist. Seldom, if ever, do

Chicago, The University of Chicago Press, 1942; E. R. Hilgard, *Theories of Learning*. New York, D. Appleton-Century-Crofts, 1948; *Learning and Instruction*, Forty-Ninth Yearbook of the National Society for the Study of Education, Part I. Chicago, The University of Chicago Press, 1950.

[18] See Saylor and Alexander, *op. cit.*, pp. 257-258; Lindley J. Stiles and Mattie F. Dorsey, *Democratic Teaching for Secondary Schools*. New York, J. B. Lippincott Company, 1950, Chapter 7.

[19] Paul R. Hanna, "The Three R's Have Changed," *The School Executive*. LXX, 78 (October, 1950).

these problems have any effect on what goes on in the classroom. Furthermore, the student is continually shuttled from one class to another, from one teacher to another throughout the school day; and, therefore the continuous pupil-teacher relationships basic to effective guidance are unlikely to develop.

Educators today find it helpful to think of teaching as a process of guiding learning. Stiles and Dorsey provide amplification of this point of view in the following statement:

> Teaching is guidance to the extent that it functions as a process of helping the learner make adjustments. In a very real sense, however, guidance may be thought of as the democratic approach to teaching. . . . The key to the interrelatedness between instruction and guidance is found in their common purpose. The aim of each is to help the individual to acquire capacity for self-direction, and each seeks to help the individual maintain satisfactory adjustment. . . . Teaching is a process of *guiding* the learning of others.[20]

In schools which operate in harmony with this point of view, the instructional program is flexible. Teachers operate in a framework which enables them to help young people deal directly with their common problems. Classroom teaching is regarded as inseparable from guidance. Of course, not all guidance services needed by youth can be supplied by the classroom teacher. There is a definite place for specialized guidance counselors and for a planned guidance program.

6. **The use of democratic practices in the classroom is not encouraged.** Fixed quotas of subject matter to be covered are not conducive to cooperative planning. In a compartmentalized program pupils all too seldom find themselves in situations in which they are called upon to make choices, put plans into action, and take the consequences of their action—practices which are the essence of the democratic process. The decisions concerning what to study, how and when to study, and how to evaluate progress are usually made by the teacher and/or the textbook-writer. The net result is that there are very few significant opportunities for pupil-pupil or

[20] Stiles and Dorsey, *op. cit.*, pp. 235-236. Also see *Guidance in the Curriculum*. 1955 Yearbook of the Association for Supervision and Curriculum Development. Washington, D.C., National Education Association, 1955.

pupil-teacher planning. Teachers, too, tend to work in isolation from one another rather than engage in cooperative planning. There is little reason for them to do otherwise as they go about the business of imparting the so-called fundamentals in their fields of specialization. Actually, *what is now known about groups and their behavior in different kinds of environments is largely ignored.* Recent studies of group behavior which show that a group engaging in an activity of common concern operates most effectively when democratic principles are utilized in planning and carrying forward the activity have had little effect upon current practices.[21]

To put it briefly, the concept of perpetuating and refining our democratic way of life through active participation in democratic living is not making itself felt sufficiently as high schools develop programs for common citizenship education. In a framework such as that described above, youth are likely to gain few insights into the problems they face as they go about the normal processes of living, for life is not composed of problems which can be channeled into subject-matter compartments. Generally speaking, life confronts the individual with problems whose solutions are dependent upon knowledge from many fields and which require the use of a wide variety of resources.

If the major problems of youth are to be dealt with realistically, the traditional subject-matter approach to general education must give way to an approach based on broad units of work which know no subject boundaries. This calls for a drastic reorganization of the general education program.

[21] See Herbert A. Thelen and Ralph W. Tyler, "Implications for Improving Instruction in the High School," *Learning and Instruction.* Forty-Ninth Yearbook of the National Society for the Study of Education, Part I. Chicago, The University of Chicago Press, 1950, Chapter XII; Herbert Thelen, *The Dynamics of Groups at Work.* Chicago, The University of Chicago Press, 1954. Also see Kenneth D. Benne and Bozidar Muntyan, *Human Relations in Curriculum Change: Selected Readings with Special Emphasis on Group Development.* New York, The Dryden Press, 1951; Ronald Lippitt, Kenneth D. Benne, and Leland Bradford, "The Promise of Group Dynamics for Education," *Journal of the National Education Association.* XXXVII, 350-352 (September, 1948); L. Thomas Hopkins, "Classroom Climate Can Promote Creativeness," *Educational Leadership,* XIII, No. 5, 279-282 (February, 1956).

REORGANIZING GENERAL EDUCATION

To be effective, a program of general education should be based on the common needs, problems, and interests of youth. Thus any reorganization of general education calls for reflection on the ideals and values of democracy and an analysis of the needs, problems, and interests of youth as they arise from the matrix of democracy.

Democratic Values and Their Implications for Education

It is assumed that there is common agreement that the basic ideal of democratic living is the optimal development of the individual. Democracy is not merely a form of government but a way of living together. It exists to the degree that it is reflected in the attitudes, values, and behavior of men as they go about the business of everyday living in a complex society which is undergoing rapid change. Very briefly, democracy might be interpreted as "associated living conducted on the basis of respect for personality."[22] This means that all forms of social arrangements in every sphere of activity should foster the fullest and most complete development of all individuals.

This concept of democracy involves, on the one hand, the active aspect of individual freedom—the freedom of self-direction, the freedom of every person to develop his potentialities to the fullest possible extent; and, on the other, the moral responsibility not only to regard every other person as a free individual—free to grow and develop his potentialities, but to seek the common good. That is, personal freedom exists in so far as it is in harmony with the basic value of democracy—the extension of the welfare of all people. The individual cannot develop through the violation of the personality of others. Each man must recognize his dependence upon every other man, the similarity of their problems and purposes, and be willing to cooperate in planning and working together toward goals for the common good. Cooperation implies more than a sense of team play and a recognition of common concerns, however. It involves group action based on thinking. This calls for faith in the

[22] Kilpatrick, *op. cit.*, p. 8.

method of intelligence as the method for solving problems in all areas of living. In a democratic society there is faith in the intelligence of the common man—faith that he can recognize and define his problems, set up hypotheses, marshal and organize data, arrive at conclusions and act upon them. We have faith in the ability of the common man to make a good decision and to carry out a program of action on the basis of reflective thinking.

To put it briefly, the basic ideals of democracy are:

1. The optimal development of the individual.
2. The use of cooperative means in achieving the highest possible development of all individuals.
3. Faith in intelligence as a method of solving the problems of living.

These ideals might be further clarified by analyzing some of the personal characteristics essential to democratic living which they imply; for example, social sensitivity, tolerance, cooperativeness, the ability to think reflectively, creativeness, and self-direction.[23] Such characteristics are relatively simple to define and illustrate and as a result are frequently used in attempts to elaborate the meaning of democracy. For example, in attempting to define democracy in operational terms, The Ohio State University School uses democratic values as "threads of continuity" that give unity to curricular experiences at all levels in the school program. The statement of these threads is as follows:

1. **Developing social sensitivity.** Experiences which develop an awareness and responsiveness to human values should be the concern of the school. Democracy is based upon the mutual respect for personality, by which is implied that each person will respect differences in social or racial groups and strive to elicit the unique contributions of others to the common good.

2. **Developing cooperativeness.** The school program should provide continuous opportunities for young people to work together toward common needs. This includes cooperative planning of programs in every area of school life, and the carrying out and evaluation of such programs.

---

[23] See the report of the Committee on the Function of Science in General Education, *Science in General Education*. New York, D. Appleton-Century Company, Inc., 1938, pp. 35-52.

3.   Developing the ability and zeal to utilize the method of intelligence in solving all problems of human concern. The method of intelligence in a narrow sense includes the following factors: (a) recognizing problems, (b) formulating hypotheses, (c) discovering and organizing data, (d) arriving at tentative conclusions and acting upon them. In a wider sense it also means that the individual will strive to extend thinking to as many areas of living as possible, to develop a consistent pattern of behavior, and to regard truth as tentative and experimental, rather than as absolute.

4.   Developing creativeness. In so far as possible the school should provide experiences which demand normal adjustments to situations rather than those which emphasize routine and repetition. Good citizenship calls for individuals who have the ability to synthesize elements of experience, which seemingly are unrelated, into unified wholes. Such experiences are not confined to the arts but should characterize every area of school life.

5.   Developing skills in democratic living. Students should learn to choose leaders in terms of qualities needed for the particular job at hand. All students should have opportunities for leadership at their level and all should be able to cooperate with leaders. All should have a growing understanding of how to enlist effective participation for common ends by enabling all to take part in defining goals and in selecting their own part in working toward goals. Leaders should become increasingly skillful at distributing responsibilities so that all may participate effectively. Before the end of the high-school years these experiences in democratic participation should have reached out beyond the school into the community at many points.

6.   Interpreting democracy. It is not enough that young people should live democratically. They should know what they are about, in the sense that they should become increasingly aware of the value of such living, not only within the school but in life outside of the school. This does not imply dreary "talks" by the teacher on the meaning of democracy, but rather that the democratic life of the school shall be so dynamically related to life outside that the students will be led to understand its meaning, and seek to extend it to all situations in which they are involved.

7.   Developing self-direction. All experiences should be such as to aid in the process of "growing up," by which is meant the gradual development of mature relationships with others; that is, the cultivation of a growing sense of responsibility for one's own development in the light of a consistent set of values.[24]

[24] *The Philosophy and Purposes of The University School*, Columbus, Ohio, The Ohio State University, 1948, pp. 9-10.

There are, of course, numerous formulations of the characteristics of behavior that define effective democratic citizenship.[25] The illustration merely represents the highest level of agreement reached by one school staff. The important point here is that there must be some kind of agreement upon the characteristics of a democratic personality if the basic ideals of democracy are really to give direction to the reorganization of general education.

In light of the discussion of basic democratic values, it should be clear that the *purpose of education in a democracy is to promote the optimal development of all individuals.* Actually, this means that the school should foster those social arrangements which are most likely to provide the conditions conducive to the continuous development of the individual.[26] The school should provide for rich and varied experiences in all aspects of living directed toward:

1. Helping the individual to meet his needs and to reconstruct and clarify his values.
2. Cultivating a sense of responsibility for behaving in such a way as to promote continuous development on the part of all citizens.
3. Helping the individual to become increasingly more competent as a contributor to the welfare of all, through working with his fellows on common problems and developing his capacities and interests in specialized fields.
4. Developing an understanding of the techniques and values of group action in solving human problems.
5. Developing a faith in intelligence as a means of solving individual and group problems.[27]

An analysis of this concept of the role of education indicates that there are two interrelated aspects of education which must be taken into account if the notion of the optimal development of all is taken seriously. First, there are those understandings, values, and skills needed by all citizens if they are to participate effectively in our democratic society (general education); second, there are those

[25] See, for example, *Democratic Citizenship and Development of Children.* Citizenship Education Study. Detroit, Mich., Detroit Public Schools, 1949. See also *Science in General Education.* op. cit., Chapter II.

[26] The following draws heavily upon Harold Alberty's discussion of the emerging design of the general education program, *Reorganizing the High-School Curriculum* (Revised). New York, The Macmillan Company, 1953, pp. 160-166.

[27] *Ibid.,* p. 161.

special needs, interests, and abilities which are unique to the individual (special-interest education). Obviously, the high school must provide opportunities for developing general citizenship (common understandings, values, and skills) and for the cultivation of special interests and abilities. What this means in terms of designing a curriculum is not so obvious, however. In this volume, the writers are primarily concerned with the development of an effective program for common citizenship education. Succeeding chapters will outline a rather specific proposal for reorganizing general education in the high school and offer some concrete suggestions for moving toward the proposed program.

The Adolescent Learner

Effective reorganization of general education necessitates agreement not only on the values basic to democracy, but also on a concept of needs. It is the problem of defining needs which has been a center of controversy in efforts directed toward such reorganization.

Perhaps the most common interpretation of needs is that they are drives, tensions, biological urges in the individual that determine action. In elaborating this interpretation, Alberty states:

> Some of the tensions or urges are vague and poorly defined by the individual, others are clear-cut and definite, dominated by a goal or purpose. The need for food is an example of a basic elemental need. A dominating purpose to become a lawyer is a more complex and comprehensive need, but both are characterized by a biological tension or urge. Between the indefinite restlessness that may characterize at first the need for food, and the organized feeling of need to become a lawyer, is a complete range of drives that often are spoken of as problems, interest, whims, wishes, desires, longings, or purposes.[28]

Such needs are usually referred to as psycho-biological needs. Schools which base their programs on the expressed wishes, wants, or desires of students lean heavily upon this interpretation.

In contrast to this psycho-biological concept, many people refer to the needs of the adolescent as the lacks or deficiencies that must be eliminated if he is to become the sort of adult that is looked upon

[28] *Ibid.*, p. 91.

as desirable. As Alberty points out,[29] needs defined in this manner have no necessary connection with what is felt by the adolescent at any given time. Needs of this sort are discovered by an analysis of society rather than the behavior of adolescents.

A third interpretation rejects both of those briefly described above. Needs are held to be personal-social in character. That is, they are the product of the interaction of the individual and his environment. The Committee on the Function of Science in General Education described this quite clearly:

To speak of a need without including both its *personal and social* aspects is to leave out an indispensable element. Merely to say that Johnny wants something or that teacher X believes Johnny needs a particular piece of knowledge, is to leave out the element of interaction between the two necessary components.

Now when the term *need* is used in this manner, it is evident that in any need as it exists at any given moment the two aspects will be present in varying degrees. Indeed, the emphasis shifts back and forth from one aspect to the other. Some needs, such as the "need for self-assurance," are more personal in character, whereas others such as the "need to participate with others in social-civic life" show more obviously their involvement in the social scene. But in the case of both of these illustrations, the two aspects are present. Self-assurance cannot be attained except with reference to situations involving the environment, particularly other persons; if it were possible for a person to exist in a vacuum, the problem of self-assurance would never exist for him; on the other hand there would be no participation in social life except because of the needs of individuals. . . .[30]

The Committee goes on to classify the basic personal-social needs of the adolescent (usually referred to as "adolescent needs") in terms of four interrelated aspects of living: *Personal Living,* the development of the individual as a person; *Immediate Personal-Social Relationships,* the adolescent's relationship with persons and groups in his immediate environment; *Social-Civic Relationships,* the adolescent's relationships with wider social groups in the immediate and wider community; and, *Economic Relationships,* the

[29] *Ibid.,* p. 92.
[30] *Science in General Education. op. cit.,* p. 26.

effective participation of the individual in economic life.[31] This formulation is not fixed or final. It is merely suggestive of the basic personal-social needs of the adolescent.

An eight-fold classification of common needs was utilized by the Illinois Secondary School Curriculum Program.

1. Earning a living
2. Developing an effective personality
3. Living healthfully and safely
4. Managing personal finances wisely
5. Spending leisure time wholesomely and enjoyably
6. Taking an active part in civic affairs
7. Preparing for marriage, homemaking, and parenthood
8. Making effective use of educational opportunities[32]

Schools which attempt to utilize the adolescent-needs concept in developing a curriculum find such formulations helpful but usually find it necessary to make a thorough-going analysis in terms of the conditions peculiar to their situation.

In a more recent classification of needs Havighurst abandons the term "need" and refers to the "developmental tasks" of youth. These tasks which represent personal-social needs that must be met are as follows:

1. Accepting one's physique and accepting a masculine or feminine role
2. New relations with age-mates of both sexes
3. Emotional independence of parents and other adults
4. Achieving assurance of economic independence
5. Selecting and preparing for an occupation
6. Developing intellectual skills and concepts necessary for civic competence
7. Desiring and achieving socially responsible behavior
8. Preparing for marriage and family life
9. Building conscious values in harmony with an adequate scientific world picture[33]

[31] *Ibid.* pp. 27-32.
[32] Harold C. Hand, *Problems of High School Youth.* Springfield, Illinois, Department of Public Instruction, 1949.
[33] Robert J. Havighurst, *Developmental Tasks and Education.* New York, Longmans, Green, and Co., 1950, pp. 30-56.

A third term frequently introduced in discussions of the adolescent learner is "problem" or "problem area." The term "problem area" is commonly used to designate a broad category around which a large number of adolescent problems cluster. Lists of problem areas usually include broad areas such as *Personal and Community Health*, *Values and Beliefs*, *Vocations and Employment*, *Government*, *Home and Family Living*, *Leisure Time*, and *Intercultural Relations*.[34] Presumably, the problems which fall in these categories reflect the needs of adolescents in our culture, stemming from the interaction of the individual and his environment.

Terms such as "need," "developmental task," and "problem" have been the center of considerable controversy in recent years. Like many other terms in educational literature they are used by people in many different ways. Confusion is the usual result. Those who are trying to understand the adolescent are apt to question whether the different interpretations can be reconciled or even whether the needs concept can be utilized in curriculum development.[35] A careful examination of the work of authorities in the field of adolescent development may relieve some of their anxieties, however. Actually, there is considerable agreement concerning the behavior of adolescents. In the first place, the adolescent period is the period between childhood and adulthood which is characterized by continuous physical, emotional, intellectual, and social change. Contrary to much that has been written on the subject these changes are not abrupt but are gradual.[36] There are, of course, extreme variations among individuals, but there are certain characteristics (frequently classified in terms of three levels of adolescent development, i.e. Early Middle, Late) reported in various studies[37] that are sufficiently

[34] For a more detailed discussion of problem areas see Chapter III.

[35] For a helpful discussion of the use of the concepts of needs by teachers and curriculum workers see Camilla M. Low, "Determining the Nature of the Needs of Youth," *Adapting the Secondary School Program to the Needs of Youth*. Fifty-Second Yearbook of the National Society for the Study of Education. Chicago, The University of Chicago Press, 1953, Chapter II.

[36] Gesell and his associates, however, take the position that the stages of growing up fall into a very definite pattern and that a stage of turmoil inevitably follows a stage of calm. See Arnold Gesell, Frances L. Ilg, and Louise B. Ames, *Youth: The Years from Ten to Sixteen*. New York, Harper & Brothers, 1956.

[37] See, for example, *How Children Develop*. A Report of the Faculty of the University School. Columbus, The Ohio State University, 1946; *Adolescence*.

common to allow one to reach at least tentative conclusions about adolescent behavior.

For example, early adolescents are primarily concerned with discovering themselves: who they are, what they are becoming, why certain characteristics develop at certain times, what their abilities are. Learning how to adjust to the physiological and emotional changes that are occurring and comprehending what is "normal" in their growth are vital to this process of discovery. This too, is a period of revolt against authority. As most children reach early adolescence they experience a desire to become independent of those who exercise any authority over them—parents, teachers, older brothers, and sisters. At the same time they have a tendency to conform to the standards of their peer groups. They want to be well-liked by others and have full status as members of the group. In this period, boys and girls are striving to establish themselves as individuals who are capable of assuming responsibility for their own acts.

During middle adolescence, young people are primarily concerned with social adjustment. They are striving to adjust to the standards and demands of the groups to which they belong. At this stage, too, they are faced with the responsibility for abiding by the rules and regulations that apply to adults. Frequently this process of developing behavior that is acceptable to themselves and to their elders results in confusion and frustration. In this period of increasing independence, most boys and girls become concerned about their effect upon others. They want to know whether the perception they have of themselves is the same as others have of them. Opinions of the opposite sex become increasingly important. During middle adolescence young people usually are well along in their transition from the dependency of childhood to the self-reliance of adulthood. They

---

Forty-Third Yearbook of the National Society for the Study of Education. Chicago, Department of Education, University of Chicago, 1944, Part I; Lindley Stiles and Mattie E. Dorsey, *Democratic Teaching in Secondary Schools*. New York, J. B. Lippincott Company, 1950, Part II. Some researchers prefer to classify the characteristics of adolescent development in terms of a particular age level. See, for example, Gessel, Ilg, and Ames, *Ibid*, and Robert J. Havighurst, "The 13-Year Old," *Journal of the National Education Association*. **XLV,** 10-12 (January, 1956)

are increasing in their ability to plan and make choices and many are beginning to make progress toward their life goals.

Later adolescents are seeking to establish complete self-direction and independence. Dependence upon parents for security has disappeared almost entirely. At this stage individuals are capable of managing their own affairs. Many have established almost complete economic independence. Boys and girls are equally concerned about developing socially acceptable behavior, and the choosing of a wife or husband becomes a motivating factor in relationships between the sexes. There is usually a pronounced growth in interest in civic affairs, social issues and the like during late adolescence. Interest in the comon welfare often overshadows self-interest. This is the period during which young people who develop normally usually complete the transition from childhood to adulthood.

Generalizations such as those sketchily presented above should be regarded as tentative and subject to further examination. They may, however, gives clues that will be helpful in developing an understanding of adolescent behavior.

It is the position of the writers that the adolescent-needs concept provides a sound basis for reorganizing general education. As was pointed out earlier, nearly everyone gives lip service to the idea that the high school should help all youth develop to their fullest possible extent as citizens of a democracy. If this idea is to become a reality, groups concerned with reorganizing the high school curriculum will have to give considerable attention to developing an understanding of the adolescent in our confused culture. Several accounts of how studies of the adolescent were carried out in actual school situations are included in Chapter IV.

A Look Ahead

The writers take the position that the need for reorganizing general education has been sufficiently well established and that a promising proposal for such reorganization has been devised through careful study and experimentation on the educational frontier. In short, it would appear that the American high school is in a favorable position to move ahead in reorganizing general education.

The part of the curriculum which is basic for all should consist of learning activities that are organized without regard to conventional subject-matter lines. More specifically, the general education program should be organized in terms of problem areas, broad preplanned areas of living in which young people usually have problems rather than in terms of logical systems of knowledge. From these problem areas, learning units could be developed cooperatively in the classroom by teacher and pupils. Such an organization would make available a large block of time (from one-third to one-half of the school day). This factor in itself has many possibilities for making guidance an integral part of the life of the school. It also makes possible a great variety of firsthand experiences such as field trips and community surveys which cannot be dealt with in a single class period. It provides for the development of democratic values as teachers and pupils work together on problems of common concern. And, it provides for an attack on problems in all their related aspects rather than in a piecemeal fashion.

This chapter has stressed the point that a program of general education should play a significant role in developing effective democratic citizenship. The ideals of democracy and an analysis of the needs, problems, and interests of youth growing up in our culture were held to be a sound basis upon which to organize a general education program. Succeeding chapters will be concerned with taking a look at a proposal for organizing general education on the basis of a core program and how it might be implemented.

SELECTED BIBLIOGRAPHY

Adapting The Secondary School Program to the Needs of Youth. Fifty-Second Yearbook of the National Society for the Study of Education. Chicago, The University of Chicago Press, 1953.

Adolescence. Forty-Third Yearbook of the National Society for the Study of Education. Chicago, The University of Chicago Press, 1944.

Alberty, Harold, *Reorganizing the High-School Curriculum.* New York, The Macmillian Company, 1953 (Revised). Especially Chapters I-VI.

———, et al, "Progressive Education: Its Philosophy and Challenge."

Report of the Committee on Philosophy of the Progressive Education Association. Progressive Education. XVIII, 1-28 (May, 1941).

———, "What Is Progress in Secondary Education?" An Editorial. Educational Leadership. X, 466-470 (May, 1953).

Bode, Boyd H., How We Learn. Boston, D. C. Heath and Company, 1940. Chapters XIV-XVI.

Dewey, John, Democracy and Education. New York, The Macmillan Company, 1916.

———, Experience and Education. New York, The Macmillan Company, 1938.

Faunce, Roland and Nelson Bossing, Developing the Core Curriculum. New York, Prentice-Hall, Inc., 1951. Chapters IV and V.

General Education in a Free Society. Report of the Harvard Committee. Cambridge (Mass.), Harvard University Press, 1945. Especially Chapters I, II, and IV.

Gesell, Arnold, Frances L. Ilg, and Louise B. Ames, Youth: The Years from Ten to Sixteen. New York, Harper & Brothers, 1956.

Havighurst, Robert J., Developmental Tasks and Education. New York, Longmans, Green and Company, 1950.

How Children Develop. A Report of the Faculty of the University School. Columbus, The Ohio State University, 1946.

Kilpatrick, William Heard, Modern Education: Its Proper Work. New York, Hinds, Hayden, and Eldridge, Inc., 1949.

Learning and Instruction. Forty-Ninth Yearbook of the National Society for the Study of Education. Chicago, University of Chicago Press, 1950. Part I.

The Philosophy and Purposes of the University School. Columbus, The Ohio State University, 1948.

Saylor, J. Galen and William M. Alexander, Curriculum Planning for Better Teaching and Learning. New York, Rinehart & Company, Inc., 1954, Parts 1 and 3.

Science in General Education. Report of the Committee on the Function of Science in General Education. New York, D. Appleton-Century Company, Inc., 1938.

Stiles, Lindley J. and Mattie F. Dorsey, Democratic Teaching in Secondary Schools. New York, J. B. Lippincott Company, 1950. Parts 2, 3, and 4.

Thelen, Herbert, The Dynamics of Groups at Work. Chicago, The University of Chicago Press, 1954.

What Shall the High Schools Teach? 1956 Yearbook of the Association for Supervision and Curriculum Development. Washington, D. C., National Education Association, 1956. Especially Chapters III, IV, and V.

II

DEFINING THE
CORE PROGRAM

The need for a reorganization of general education in the American high schools and the philosophical and psychological bases of such a reorganization were presented in Chapter I. It was suggested that this reorganization might proceed along the lines of a core program. The writers hold that when the part of the curriculum basic for all is thus organized, general education will bridge the gap between educational philosophy and action.

The term core means many things to many people. Like all educational terminology, it is subject to the usual confusion. It also suffers the further curse of being relatively different because people assume, not being used to it, that it has no relationship to good practices of the past and is, therefore, entirely experimental and completely new. In this light, they reason, it could be a very good idea or it could be a very bad idea—but who knows? The six current conceptions of the core prevalent in American education theory and practice have been carefully defined and illustrated by Harold Alberty in the Fifty-Second Yearbook, Part I of the National Society for the Study of Education. Alberty says:

> There seems to be one common element in programs that are referred to as the core. The term is applied in some fashion to all or part of the total curriculum which is required of all students at a given grade level. In other words, the core is used to designate all or part of the program of general education. This important concept is utilized as the point of departure in presenting the six designs.
> The various interpretations, presented in the order of their deviation from the conventional curriculum organization, are as follows:

I. The core consists of a number of logically organized subjects or fields of knowledge each one of which is taught independently.
   Example: English, world history, and general science are required at the ninth grade level. They are taught without an organized attempt to show relationships.

II. The core consists of a number of logically organized subjects or fields of knowledge, some or all of which are correlated.
   Example: American history and American literature are required of all twelfth grade students. When the history teacher is dealing with the Civil War, the English teacher introduces literature of that period.

III. The core consists of broad problems, units of work, or unifying themes which are chosen because they afford the means of teaching effectively the basic content of certain subjects or fields of knowledge. These subjects or fields retain their identity, but the content is selected and taught with special reference to the unit.
   Example: Living in the Community is selected as a unit of work for the tenth grade. The unit is then organized in terms of science, art, social studies, etc., and taught by specialists, or by one teacher.

IV. The core consists of a number of subjects or fields of knowledge which are unified or fused. Usually one subject or field (e.g., history) serves as the unifying center.
   Example: American history and American literature in the eleventh grade are unified through a series of epochs such as *The Colonial Period, The Westward Movement, The Industrial Revolution.* The unification may be extended to include other fields such as the arts, science, and mathematics.

V. The core consists of broad, preplanned problem areas, or resource units from which are selected learning experiences in terms of the psychobiological and social needs, problems, and interests of students.
   Example: A unit on Healthful Living, in the twelfth grade, stresses the health of the group, and how these problems are related to the immediate and wider community. The unit is teacher-student planned, but in terms of basic curricular structure.

VI. The core consists of broad teacher—student planned units of work, or activities, in terms of the expressed wishes or desires of the group. No basic curricular structure is set up.
   Example: An eighth grade group, under guidance of the teacher, decides to landscape the school grounds. The activity meets all the criteria decided on by the group.[1]

[1] For further elaboration see Harold Alberty, "Designing Programs to Meet the Common Needs of Youth," *Adapting the Secondary School Program to the*

The reader will note that as one progresses from Type I as described by Alberty through Type VI one experiences a progressively different concept of scope and sequence of the program designed to meet the common needs of youth. The scope gradually moves from the logical organization of subject matter in a textbook to the common problems, needs, and interests of boys and girls. The concept of sequence in program development moves from page to page assignments and predetermined plans on the part of a teacher to the more psychological arrangement of the consideration of the growth and development of individuals—their experience background, their hopes, desires, longings, and needs. As one moves from a Type I concept of the core through the various stages, one recognizes that each concept brings into play more and more of the research in how people learn and an adequate philosophy of education. Education, like medicine, nutrition, warfare, transportation, to name but a few areas, has put into action some of its valid research in a core program.

The Position of the Writers

To clarify the position of the writers the specific concept of core to be described in this book should be stated. Succeeding chapters will assume this same concept to be operative as insight into a step-by-step development is gained. It is believed that if anything like an effective job is to be done in general education in the secondary school, a complete reorganization of the basic purposes and curricular structure is in order. The reader will note that in the Alberty analysis, core Types I-IV, inclusive, provide progressively a more functional approach to general education. No more can be claimed. The content is a subject-centered one and the sequence of activities is predicated upon what adults see as lacks and needs of adolescents in our society. If we intend anything really serious in the way of core program development, in our opinion, a concept approximating Alberty's Type V will need to be developed. Therefore, the purposes and general characteristics of the core described here will assume that *core consists of broad, preplanned problem areas defined by the faculty in terms of the common personal-social*

Needs of Youth. Fifty-Second Yearbook of the National Society for the Study of Education, Part I. Chicago, The University of Chicago Press, 1953, Chapter VII.

needs, problems, and interests of adolescents in this society. The reader may question why a Type VI core is not chosen here for further clarification. It is the position of the writers that a program lacking a preplanned basic curricular structure is unrealistic in face of existing conditions in teacher shortages, the lack of pre-service education for core teaching, and the dearth of instructional materials suited to the needs of such teaching. Furthermore, to leave the complete choice of areas of study to teachers and pupils with neither total faculty planning nor certain limitations would seem to invite lack of continuity in the learning experience, and needless repetition and/or severe gaps in the general education experiences of boys and girls. From this point on, the term core will mean: a development consisting of broad preplanned problem areas, or resource guides from which are selected learning experiences in terms of the psychobiological and societal needs, problems, and interests of students.

It seems wise to attempt to spell out the specific purposes of the core program and the general characteristics which might identify such a program in action. In Chapter VI of this book these general characteristics will be made much more specific as the stories of the development of two learning units in an actual core classroom are described.

The Purposes of the Core Program

The following discussion of the purposes of a core program does not necessarily imply that such purposes are achieved only in a core program. The discussion will seek to point out that the organization, the process, and the scope of the core program do serve these purposes in a somewhat unique fashion. Any simple statement of purposes usually turns out to be an oversimplification. For that reason the characteristics of the core program are elaborated after the statement of purposes.

The core essentially is designed to help the adolescent:

1. Grow in understanding and in competent performance of his obligations as a member of the family, the community, the state, the nation, and the world.

2. Grow in understanding of democratic principles; in skillfully thinking through his own problems and helping to think through problems common to his group, and in appreciation for and willingness to improve democracy as a way of life.
3. Grow in the skills and knowledge of social and moral principles involved in getting along with himself and other people.

The reader will recognize that the stated purposes of the core have a one-to-one relationship with those problems and needs, common to all people regardless of the vocational choice or the particular specialized interest of an individual. The validity of such purposes in education today seems quite apparent. Schools have perhaps always hoped that such purposes were, at least, the by-products of their efforts. Chapter I dealt with some of the weaknesses of conventional secondary education in achieving the purposes stated here. Therefore, it would seem fruitful to analyze the characteristics of the core program which seem to promise more in this respect.

Characteristics of the Core Program

What are, then, the unique characteristics of a core program which should succeed in accomplishing our purposes? Let us now list and elaborate them. A core program in action will evidence some, if not all, of the following characteristics:

1. **A block of time ranging from 1/3-1/2 the total school day is allotted to the core.** This time will be spent with the guidance of one teacher. Most schools familiar to the writers require a 3 hour block of time per day for the core in grades 7 through 9 and a 2 hour block of time in grades 10-12 (inclusive). Practices do vary, however, from school to school in terms of the local situation.

What are the advantages of this block of time with one teacher? How is this characteristic of the core program related to the stated purposes? The guidance factor as it relates to teacher load is perhaps the most obvious advantage. In a subject-centered organization a teacher could meet as many as 200 different pupils per day. In such an arrangement a teacher could hardly be expected to come to know pupils beyond the procedure of associating names and faces and of noting such evidence as the grade book evoked by each pupil's name. How can we help pupils to understand themselves and others when all we know about them from our brief contacts is a name and a face? The longer block-of-time helps to make provision for individual conferences with pupils. It gives opportunity for wider participation in group activities and for supervised study where teachers may observe study and work habit skills. This added time allows for more individual help for those who need additional guidance because of certain lacks as well as those who need teacher challenge to spur them on to more stimulating understandings.

Now let us consider the research-honored principle of how people learn as related to the nature of experience. People learn best when they have worthwhile purposes which they have shared in setting-up and when their vicarious experiences are strongly implemented by direct, firsthand experiences. A 2-3 hour block-of-time facilitates learning in these respects. Groups have time to plan what they are going to do without the interruption of bells. Field trips may be taken by a small group or the whole class without causing the pupils to miss several of their other classes. An idea can be developed until a reasonable grasp is had by pupils. If some pupils need a practice session it can be scheduled immediately. Other pupils can go on with activities needed in their particular cases. The longer block-of-time promotes better interpersonal relationships. It seems necessary to provide experiences in human relations in the classroom if we expect to achieve growth in this area as a desired outcome.

2. **Teacher-pupil planning as well as teacher-teacher and pupil-pupil planning is a characteristic method of the core.** It was Boyd H. Bode who said that history merely proved that the common man was never given a chance to think and then blamed because he didn't think. Almost all statements of the purposes of secondary education include the development of critical thinking as a desirable outcome. Our results may show achievement in this area to be one of the weakest links in public education. The core program stresses planning in terms of significant purposes. It presupposes a basic curricular structure in the form of broad, preplanned problem areas and a learn-

ing unit developed from these problem areas through teacher-pupil planning. Through teacher guidance, pupils learn to make choices, to put their plans into action, and to take the consequences of their actions. If they are going to attain personal and civic competence this seems a necessary experience. Particularly through pupil-pupil planning around their selected interests related to the core unit they learn to communicate their ideas, to compromise a position from time to time in order to get consensus, and to understand themselves and others. This cooperative planning on the solution of common problems is an essential of democratic living. It is the essence of personal and civic competence. The proper development of a core program means that teachers are going to have to do much cooperative planning among themselves and with principals, supervisors, consultants and other resource people. When a wide variety of resources must be shared, when evaluation devices must become creative, when human growth and development processes must be taken into account in scope and sequence planning, when the problem-solving approach is considered of top priority, and when resource guides have to be developed, teachers have to plan together. To provide maximum continuity, grade level and departmental meetings are necessary and careful records need to be kept on what is done in each learning unit. When teachers, pupils, and others in the educational process get the habit of planning and thinking together to solve their common problems the next step logically follows. People must be helped to see the relationship of in-school planning to out-of-school experiences. When this relationship is internalized it appears that transfer of learning is more likely to take place.

3. **The problem-solving approach is paramount as a process of democratic living as the core program is developed.** Could it be that we are so perplexed with the complex problems which face us at the mid-century mark because, as a people, we are not "at home" with the problem-solving approach? This skill is not something one is born into nor is it one acquired overnight. As one seventh grader expressed it: "It hurts to think!" In a democracy we believe that all people have the capacity to learn to use more effectively the problem-solving approach if afforded meaningful situations which require

the use of the process. People do little thinking unless faced with a real problem. Why should they? However, life persistently puts before us situations in which creativity—the life-blood of the problem-solving process—is essential. The core program deals with life's common problems. In the solution or even in the further exploration of these problems we perceive a quest for new answers and a willingness to abandon outmoded ones. Problem-solving involves a careful appraisal of present status in relation to a goal and an attitude of "What are our possible next steps" in terms of this goal. A core program is getting into action when pupils first conceive that they want to accomplish a certain thing—something which they hold to have value. Next we should see a plan being formulated to achieve what is wanted. At this point we should not see trial-and-error approaches or completely fruitless attempts being made. On the other hand, we should see pupils carefully weighing this and that possibility in terms of what they know is their goal. A good group tries a plan out before acting by projecting it in imagination toward the goal. A core class will not stop here. It will put the most promising hunch into action. It will see if the plan works. Some groups end their problem-solving at this point. If the attempt worked—fine! If plans went awry—too bad! A core class at work has just begun to use the problem-solving approach when action results. *Evaluation* takes place. Plans do not always work even with the most careful thinking through. Pupils in a core class should develop a willingness to give up previously held ideas if these ideas are found inadequate. They should learn to analyze plans in terms of weakness and strength and to use this analysis as a new plan emerges. If a plan does work pupils should recognize the elements of success and intellectualize these for new but similar situations. Pupils learn to recognize that the process of evaluating, replanning and trying again is the mark of intelligence. Temporary failures are to be expected. When *achievement* is reached something new has been created. Core classes should point up the fact that in the ability to reconstruct experience is life's most profound significance. All good teaching deals with problem-solving. Pupils in the core should have this rich experience in group planning, trying, evaluating and achieving through these plans.

Teachers should help pupils realize that the use of the problem-solving approach in groups is more satisfying because it brings the imaginations, powers of abstraction, and efforts of several people to bear upon the goal. The problem-solving approach at the group level on real concerns is perhaps one of the most significant characteristics of the core program.

4. **Common needs, problems and interests of adolescents in this society are the content or scope of the core program.** Subsequent chapters of this book will deal in quite some detail with the problem of determining content of the core program through the defining of problem areas, and developing resource guides and teacher-pupil planned learning units. This is a point at which the core has a uniqueness not claimed by other areas of the school's program. The starting point in the core is not the chronological or logical order of a subject-field discipline but rather those problems defined by the group as of common concern. This *does not* mean a "What do you want to do today, kids?" approach. This *does* mean a careful analysis by the faculty of the needs of youth based on the literature, observation, conferences, interviews, surveys, problem check-lists, child study groups, community studies, interest inventories, working with parents, and the like. This means that the faculty has the responsibility for organizing these data and using the data to organize a list of areas in which boys and girls have common problems. These problem areas will become the basic curricular structure of the core program. Learning units will be developed through teacher-pupil planning from the many possibilities of these broad preplanned areas.

Closely allied to the common problems approach is the choice of *contemporary problems* as a basis for exploration in the core class. War and peace are common problems of mankind but how concerned is the average tenth grader with the Punic Wars? The use of leisure time is a common interest of teen-agers, but are the leisure time activities of colonial Americans an immediate-felt need of adolescents? Will we ever get to a unilateral foreign policy if we always feel the urge to begin with ancient trade routes to the Orient? This is not to say that the race experience should not be drawn upon in exploring common problems. What has been learned through ex-

perience is a most valuable resource as pupils effect a plan of action—
define a promising hunch.

The concept of "need" has always seemed to raise the level of
confusion in educational circles. Chapter I explored the psychological aspects of this concept. Chapter III will explore this concept
as it relates to the content of an adequate core program. At this point
let us say that the writers accept needs as personal-social in nature.
The individual has certain urges, longings, desires, wishes, and wants
which arise because the standards, requirements, and conditions of
society impinge upon him. That is, needs arise as a result of the
interaction of individuals and society.

5. **The exploration of common problems, the meeting of common needs and the widening of interests in the core program utilizes
subject matter from all pertinent fields of knowledge.** It is no doubt
apparent by this time that the core program is not a compartmentalized organization of fields of knowledge such as English, history,
geography, music, and homemaking. In most junior high schools
where the core organization is used, however, English and the social
studies and sometimes science are omitted from the regular curricular offerings outside the core. Most senior high schools using the
core as a required area continue to meet the specialized needs of
certain individuals or small groups by offering as many electives in
English and social studies outside of the core as possible. In the
senior high school, physics, chemistry, and biology, as well as other
science courses intended to meet special needs and interests, are most
often offered outside the core though these areas are drawn upon
in their general education aspects to solve problems arising in the
core class.

Since core is defined in terms of the personal-social problems of
pupils at this particular time of living the full exploration of these
problems cannot take place by using ony the logical organization of
one subject-field. For example, an eighth grade core class might be
concerned with problems of living together in their county. These
problems might be the structure and processes of government, the
prevailing tax base, inadequate educational facilities, and health and
safety hazards. If such problems are adequately dealt with several

fields of knowledge will be drawn upon—county history, civics, geography, mathematics, health, art—to name a few. For example, the uses a teacher and pupils might make of art here are legion. Graphs depicting present conditions and murals showing possibilities for improving certain conditions could be used quite effectively. Art as a mental health agent might be shown by the class' organizing an evening art group for adults. Other fine and practical arts have a contribution to make toward helping a county solve its problems of living together.

While the logical organization of subject matter is not the focal point of a core program, it would be entirely fallacious to assume that, therefore, no subject matter is learned. Rather than being taught and learned for its own sake, subject matter is put to work in a core class to help pupils solve real problems and widen expressed interests. Usefulness in living, it is believed, will increase the learning of subject matter rather than decrease it.

6. **The core is required of all pupils regardless of special needs, problems and interests.** This characteristic of the core has been mentioned in the previous discussion. Since the content of core is based upon the *common* problems met by people in this society and since all pupils will work together to effect a better way of life, there seems no reason to deny the experience to some pupils while affording it to others in the same school. Through experiencing a core program, pupils get insight into the worth and dignity of the individual. All types of people live in today's world. The more we realize that *all* people have a significant contribution to make in the solution of common problems and that there is an endless variety of contributions to be made, the less we insist that only certain types of achievement receive status recognition in our schools. One good way to help students recognize that a wide variety of contributions are necessary to the solution of a group's problems is to involve them in a program making use of this idea.

It should be underscored and understood that the core program does not attempt to deal with vocational preparation in its specialized aspects. Typing, bookkeeping, tailoring, geometry, algebra, journalism, agriculture, football, creative dancing, band, choral music, photography, physics, watercolor—to name a few—are taught outside the core as areas which pupils elect with guidance in terms of their particular needs and interests. Core also does not attempt to deal with the special techniques of an avocational interest such as might be found in any subject-field area. This is the job of specialists and much opportunity should be offered for this type of development in a school's program. Further, the core program can promise no panacea for pupils who have reached secondary school with severe reading difficulties and definite reading handicaps in the area of quantitative concepts. These problems will grow more acute as secondary school enrollment increases unless the teacher-shortage and crowded-classroom crises are resolved. School officials and taxpayers must face up to the problem of providing more teachers with specific training in remedial areas. The core program, however, does offer certain kinds of help to students with many such problems. With a reduced load and the block-of-time arrangement, core teachers have more opportunity to know individuals. They can help identify pupils who need such help and make plans with them to get this help. Since the core content deals with the real problems of pupils, care can be taken to see that a variety of projects are chosen within the ability range of individuals. Nothing is more frustrating to those with a reading handicap than a curriculum in which success is based entirely upon one's ability to read and comprehend at a stated level.

7. **Individual and group guidance are integral parts of the core program.** The core teacher is the key guidance person in the school. This is not to say that guidance personnel are no longer needed. Their work takes on more, not less, significance as they bring their expertness to bear in the core program. When an adequate core program is functioning in a school, education and guidance become synonymous. If the function of guidance is to help pupils solve their problems then we find in the core a full scale program dedicated to this approach. If the core concerns itself with a continuous attack on the common personal-social problems of youth as content, the core teacher plays a leading role in guidance and trained guidance personnel become the most valuable available resource.

A core program in action could use guidance personnel to initiate a study of the needs of adolescents. Chapter IV of this book gives details on how guidance personnel functioned in a needs study to select and administer various instruments, to collect other types of data and to summarize these data and make certain interpretations to teachers and parents. Guidance workers have a vast knowledge of suitable pamphlet and bulletin material centered upon personal problems of youth. They are often consulted to make suggestions about the use of this material in the classroom. These specially trained people are used in the preplanning period with teachers to suggest problems and how to deal with them through meaningful experiences. They are particularly helpful as consultants in the in-service program when teachers are developing skill in group guidance techniques. In the core classroom, the guidance worker makes an invaluable contribution in teacher-pupil planning, serving as a resource person from time to time to work with small groups or with the whole class on a problem of common concern. They often function most effectively in helping teachers to identify pupils whose severe personal problems require help beyond the training and time of a core teacher.

The block-of-time arrangement affords time for the core teacher to use the individual conference technique. Before this conference, he may talk over individual problems with the guidance worker. Many core teachers keep individual folders on each pupil, thus accumulating much evidence which helps interpret individual behavior. Guidance workers may be called in on these conferences, or it might seem best for the pupil to leave the core class to have a private conference with the guidance worker or some other specialist who has been asked for advice. As the guidance worker helps pupils solve their everyday problems, he establishes rapport with them and, thus, can handle individual problems more effectively. With this description of guidance in action it should be obvious that the entire field gains a new "place in the sun" as it becomes synonymous with cooperative curriculum development.

8. **Evaluation is a cooperative, continuous, and creative process in the core program.** The concept of evaluation as a cooperative, continuous, and creative process in education has become almost a cliché in educational parlance. This situation arises partly from our

lack of a concept of education in action in the secondary school which lends itself to this rather advanced belief in the area of evaluation. How does the core *problem* help to bring a more adequate evaluation concept into action? The *cooperative* setting-up of goals of the learning unit through teacher-pupil planning and the total school faculty development of resource guides are excellent illustrations of cooperative evaluation. We name our values when we set our goals. What we work for is what we want most—value most. In a less than problem-centered framework, so much time is spent in re-citing, quizzing and examining that little time is left for learning through cooperative evaluation. It is believed that people learn best when they have a share in deciding what is to be learned. If this is so, our learning of knowledge, skills, values, and understandings deemed important, can only be facilitated by cooperative definition of goals, periodic evaluation of progress, and joint determination of new goals. *Continuous* evaluation occurs in the core program because evaluation is inherent in what is being learned. Where the learner is certain that the solution of problems is related to his everyday living homework is self-imposed, activity is not resisted; interest, the greatest motivating factor, is present, and behavior is being changed. Two to three hours per day spent in an atmosphere where goals have meaning to the learner—where he keeps asking himself, "What does this mean to me?" "How am I doing?" should be effective in changing behavior. If he is urged to think not only of himself but of the social situation in which he operates, the evaluative process becomes closely identified with the problem-solving process and with one of the foremost goals of education, i.e., making the learner responsible both for himself and for the general welfare of those around him. Evaluation becomes a *creative* process in the core program because such effort takes on a less objective quality and becomes more intrinsic to the learner. Evaluation in the core program takes a wide variety of forms and is oriented away from subject matter and toward self- and group examination. All evaluation must be made in terms of purposes. Our purposes in the core program are in terms of desirable changes in behavior. Such purposes cannot be evaluated by pencil and paper tests alone, nor can we apply the same standards to every pupil. Much self-evaluation and much group evaluation are used in core classes. The criteria for evaluation are teacher-pupil developed, and the entire process is teacher guided. Teacher abdication is impossible in creative evaluation. Teacher observation of changed behavior plays an important role in the core. Instruments designed both to evaluate critical thinking, changed attitudes, basic communication skills in use in real situations, and ability to apply principles of logical reasoning and to interpret data are widely used. Teachers often make use of the individual pupil conference method of evaluation and of the group discussion technique. Adequate core programs keep parents well-informed of goals to be achieved, and often use their suggestions in setting-up goals. Therefore, parents, from time to time, cooperate in evaluating progress through letters, questionnaires, personal conferences and group discussions.

The block-of-time arrangement for core, the content defined in terms of the common problems of youth, and the concept of guidance as an integral part of the program all help to put into action an adequate concept of evaluation.

9. **The fundamental skills are broadly defined and taught in terms of the use made of them in the core program.** There are at least 4 R's operating in a core classroom—reading, 'riting, 'rithmetic and relationships. The authors consider this 4th R all-important when we face realistically the fact of world conditions. The situation today is not due to non-readers and poor handwriting or misspelled words and miscalculations in quadratic equations. It is due to a failure in human relationships. Research shows that the schools are doing a better than ever job of teaching the traditional fundamentals.[2] The reasearch in the area of human relationships as they

[2] See Archibald W. Anderson, "The Charges Against American Education," *Progressive Education.* XXIX, 91-105 (January, 1952); William S. Gray, "What Is the Evidence Concerning Reading?" *Progressive Education.* XXIX, 105-110 (January, 1952); Louis E. Raths and Philip Rothman, "Then and Now." *Journal of the National Education Association.* 41, 214 (April, 1952); William Van Til," Research Affecting Education," *Forces Affecting American Education.* 1953 Yearbook of the Association for Supervision and Curriculum Development. Washington, D. C., National Education Association, 1953, pp. 119-141; "High Schools: Are They Doing Their Job?" *Changing Times.* The Kiplinger Magazine. 7, 27-32 (July, 1956).

relate to class-room teaching is not extensive. That published, however, points to the value of teacher-learning situations created through a core program.[3] The core program sets up situations to help pupils: (1) improve their reading ability; (2) spell correctly the most used words in the English language; (3) use the language effectively to communicate their ideas; (4) write a legible hand; (5) develop skill in critical thinking; (6) use individual time and the time of the group to accomplish worthwhile purposes; (7) widen interests, and (8) understand themselves and others. Provision is, therefore, made for developing the range of skills needed by youth to cope with life's real problems. Skills are developed when they are needed in activities and drill is used largely as an individual or small group matter as the need for more practice to clinch a process is evidenced. Research in the learning process seems to indicate that skills are learned best in situations calling for the use of the skill being sought. Pupils in core classes use the language to communicate ideas by writing letters for materials and information, keeping diaries, writing articles for the school and local papers, and writing a creative story. Their oral communication is developed through class-planning sessions, discussions of issues and problems, interviews with outside resource people, and making oral reports to the class. They have adequate opportunity to develop skill in interpreting number values and symbols by tabulating poll results, planning poster and window displays, constructing various types of equipment for core activities, using sampling techniques, and keeping class accounts.

In addition to the 3R type skills, the pupil in a core class gains experiences which develop his skills in the fourth R—relationships. In this area, he uses the language to communicate ideas in conference, to hold to the point of discussion, to make contributions that further thinking, to be a good listener, and to cooperate in making decisions. He achieves effective social and working relations needed for sound leadership as he secures cooperative participation of group members, identifies needs and concerns of individuals in the group, and outlines preliminary plans needed to carry out responsibilities. He learns

[3] *Ibid.*

effective group membership by keeping informed about group activity, helping to formulate group policy, selecting leaders, and evaluating the work of those delegated a responsibility. The pupil in core classes uses problem-solving skills in deciding on and clarifying purposes, projecting the consequences of alternative procedures to achieve purposes, planning a wise use of his time and energy, locating and evaluating resources, and testing held beliefs against new findings. Yes. the fundamental skills receive *the* major emphasis in a core program.

10. **A wide variety of resources in men, materials and techniques are used to promote learning in the core program.** The characteristics of the core program discussed in the previous pages make the use of many and varied resources a logical conclusion. Life's common problems cut across the conventional organizations of human knowledge. No one textbook would suffice. The best textbooks could serve only as valuable basic resources. The problem or the situation determines the particular resource to be used. If a community social problem is being explored, data are collected from original sources. The interview technique is widely used to get these data. There are many people—sometimes parents—living in the immediate community who have lived abroad. These people are very effective resources when core classes study how people live in other countries. Survey and sampling techniques are used frequently to get information on the present situation, for example, in slum area housing or to determine what action the public would support for the improvement of housing in certain areas. Since current personal-social problems form the content of the core, much bulletin, pamphlet, and leaflet material is used. Not all books are quite up-to-date as to the problems of just yesterday and the tomorrow ahead. Television and radio are particularly useful in keeping informed for discussion around current problems and issues.

In addition to audio-visual aids, resource persons, surveys and opinion polls, the community as a laboratory, art media, textbooks, other books, pamphlets, bulletins, leaflets, magazines, newspapers, radio and television, there are important techniques of teaching and learning used as resources in the core program. The method used is often as vital as the material obtained. How to get information, how to judge propaganda and fact, and how to organize data and to present it in a meaningful form are stressed as a basic communication skill. A field trip taken by a core class is not a sight-seeing excursion. It is taken because it accomplishes some definite purpose implicit in the learning unit. Time is spent helping pupils learn to use the interview technique to secure needed information. When surveys are made, an adequate sampling is assured by drawing upon mathematics and our recorded experiences in sampling procedures.

Perhaps, more than anything else, the emphasis put upon group process techniques and individual guidance and evaluation should be valued as a resource in the core class. If properly released, our greatest resources are most often inherent in our own group. Core teachers, with a reduced pupil load, a content based upon common personal-social needs, and a cooperative goal-setting in learning units through teacher-pupil planning have a more than even chance to know the resources among the pupils in the class. The continuous effort to recognize individual worth and its contribution to the common goal guarantees a wider use of group resources.

The group concern that is engendered for learning in new and meaningful situations is a vast energy in itself. The most vital resource in the nature of a technique used in the core program is the problem-solving approach which was discussed earlier. This "going at" all endeavors with a clarity of purpose, willingness to withhold judgment, careful collection of data, analysis of consequences of the most reasonable hypothesis before acting, and the continuous evaluation which leads to changed behavior is one of the most valuable assets pupils develop. This is a resource that serves them throughout life.

11. **The democratic value system is the basis of the core program.** Education for democratic living has been of paramount concern to school people for many years. The core program is perhaps the one effort insisting that the development of these values is inherent in its organization, process, and content. In Chapter I and elsewhere in the discussion of the characteristics of the core program, the writers have emphasized concern for the optimal development of the individual

for the value of the cooperative process in the solution of common problems, and for the problem-solving approach as the method of the core program. Understanding the individual, thus helping him to plan in terms of clarified purposes is one of the major advantages of the block-of-time with one teacher. The content of the core program is based upon those personal-social problems common to the group. These problems are chosen through teacher-pupil planning and upon a basis of what we know about young people in early, middle, and later adolescence. Care is taken to help individuals make wise choices as to projects selected for committee work. The reader will remember that the stated purposes of the the core program emphasized understanding oneself and others. As people work with others, they soon begin to realize that some of the same pressures which impinge upon them affect the behavior of others. Cooperativeness—its hows and whys—is one of the major outcomes of the core program thus far. When students work for several years in such an atmosphere, an indelible impression is made. Cooperativeness is a learned response. It does not just happen because a need arises. The problem-solving approach used as the method in the core program has profound implications for democratic education. Because individual growth and development is of major concern to teachers, faith in the belief that all people can be taught to think through proper experiences is exercised. The full and free participation of all in the problem-solving process, the wide variety of experiences offered, and the personal-social nature of the content of core help to insure significance in terms of real life situations outside the environs of the school.

Photographs found on the following pages will, to some extent, furnish a pictorial account of the characteristics of the core described in the previous pages.

Transitional Steps or a Word of Warning

The reader could get the impression that this indicated change in over-all philosophy, curriculum framework, and the scope and sequence of learning activities must all take place at one time, and that this, if it so happened, would be necessarily good. Not so. In most schools experimenting with the core program, an English-social studies fusion has been the initial effort. It has been the experience of the writers that regardless of initial steps in reorganizing the general education program, those who experiment need to keep in mind "Where do we go from here?" Too many school faculties have tinkered with a few new ideas only to bog down in the process. These people usually return, with some regret, to a subject-centered framework for lack of a basic understanding of what is involved in developing an adequate core program. It is wise to make only the changes which at any given time can be understood and made functional. Needless to say, all of these people should be involved in the change from the very beginning. In fact, the closer to grass roots initiative the change comes, the better prospect there is for real change to take place. Any sign is promising that indicates teachers and administrators are becoming more concerned about how humans grow and develop and that school people are interested in making education consistent with what we know about democracy. Schools will start their needed changes in different ways but their goals will be essentially the same. The research listed in the selected bibliography at the end of this chapter will indicate many ways a school might approach the problem of initiating and developing a core program.

Core Is Not All of the Curriculum

A word of reminder should be noted here after the lengthy discussion of the characteristics of the core program. There are other aspects of the curriculum which must come under scrutiny as a group reorganizes to help youth meet their needs and solve their problems. Any adequate high school curriculum provides for (1) a common learnings program required of all (core), (2) physical education and recreation, (3) special services (cafeteria, health, guidance), (4) special interests (precollege, prevocational) and (5) a wide offering in the arts—both practical and fine. Many a core program has failed because these other aspects of the program did not enter into the rethinking of the school's philosophy and purposes and the follow-up in curriculum development. A pupil's education would be sadly lacking if only his general education within the core were adequate. A pupil's education in the areas of his special interests should be given the same careful consideration as that given to his general education. Therefore, the total faculty of the school should share in deciding the purposes both of the core program and of that part of the curriculum outside the core. At the same time, careful thought should be given to the ways in which each area

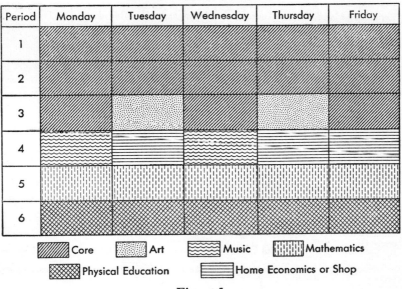

Figure 1

contributes to the other as each works to help pupils grow and develop. Figures I, II, and III are sample daily schedules for pupils in the junior and senior high school. The reader will note that the time scheduled outside the core is allocated in terms of the particular pupil's needs, problems and interests.[4]

[4] Junior high school schedule, Greenbelt Junior High School, Prince George's County, Maryland, contributed by Allan I. Chotiner, formerly principal. Junior-senior high school schedule, Fairmont Heights Junior-Senior High School, Prince George's County, Maryland, contributed by G. James Gholson, Principal.

The Use of the Core Block-of-Time

One of the problems in core program development centers around the use of the extended block-of-time. Most secondary school teachers have not experienced preservice education for use of more than a fifty minute period with one group of pupils. There is also a seeming confusion concerning the core unit and the core block-of-time.

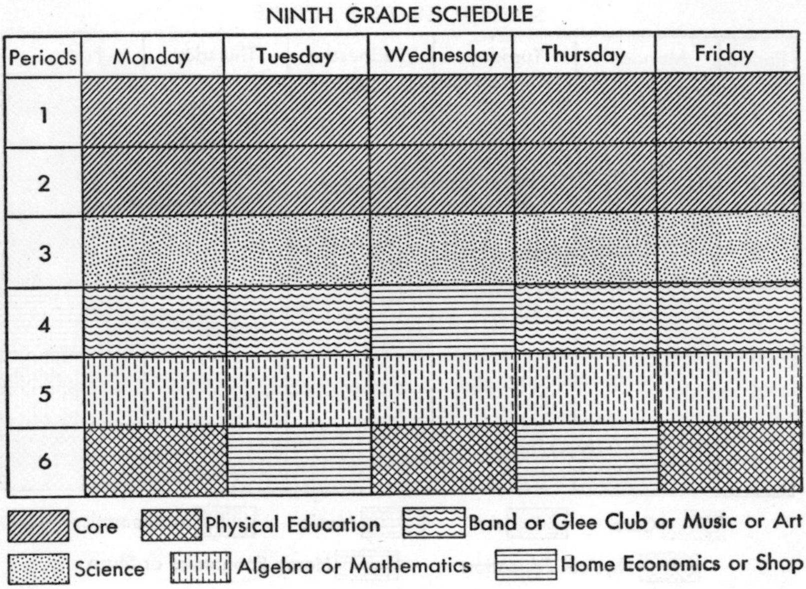

NINTH GRADE SCHEDULE

Periods	Monday	Tuesday	Wednesday	Thursday	Friday
1					
2					
3					
4					
5					
6					

Core   Physical Education   Band or Glee Club or Music or Art
Science   Algebra or Mathematics   Home Economics or Shop

Figure 2

When a school reorganizes its general education program on a core framework, the core assumes certain responsibilities otherwise taken care of in the various phases of the more departmentalized approach or in the extra-curricular activities. In Chapter VI of this book the function of core as it relates to the core unit is discussed in detail as two learning units carried on in a core classroom are described. Therefore, little need be said on this point except that the core is responsible for organizing, developing, and evaluating with pupils learning units drawn from preplanned problem areas representing the common personal-social needs of the pupils in a particular core class.

The core unit activities occupy the major part of the block-of-time, but let us look to other activities which need be carried on in an adequate core program.[5] If a core class is to be a good example of democracy in action several other types of activities might be brought in which are planned to widen and deepen appreciations, gain insight into individual needs, further knowledge of school and community problems, and provide for the development of creative abilities at the optimum level. Such planning adds to the warmth— the human element—that should pervade. The type of activity used in the core block-of-time will depend upon the particular situation. Some of those most often included are remedial work, free reading, creative writing, special school and community projects, individual guidance related to more personal problems of a pupil, and activities usually associated with the home room in a subject-centered organization.

The core class is most often considered the home base or home room for a group. Business is sometimes limited to administrative routines of attendance taking, announcements and the like. At other times, home room parties and certain traditional occasions, e.g., the Christmas dance, are planned. This is the time when the student council representative reports and further action is discussed for this body's consideration. Collection of funds for crippled children, the Red Cross, and the Community Chest are handled through the core class as homeroom business. Planning and carrying through on matters of this type help pupils realize the complexities of modern day living—the need for good time management and better human relations.

There seems to be some difference of opinion as to the extent to which the core program should be responsible for remedial work. Ideally, it is perhaps best to have this work done in the core class in order that pupils may be helped to use materials related to the core unit. Further, this being with his group at all times engenders

[5] For a graphic presentation of "How to Use the Core Block-of-Time" see Appendix, pp. 290 to 295.

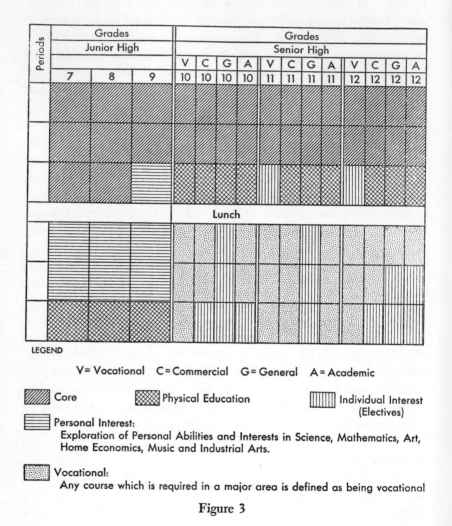

LEGEND

V = Vocational   C = Commercial   G = General   A = Academic

▨ Core   ▨ Physical Education ||||| Individual Interest
                                                     (Electives)
⬓ Personal Interest:
    Exploration of Personal Abilities and Interests in Science, Mathematics, Art,
    Home Economics, Music and Industrial Arts.

▦ Vocational:
    Any course which is required in a major area is defined as being vocational

Figure 3

a feeling of belonging in the pupil which might be lost were he segregated for certain activities. On the other hand, it is only fair to face up to the fact that remedial cases often require teachers with a high degree of skill in a specialized area, e.g., certain aspects of the teaching of reading. At present, most core teachers lack this type of training. Since teaching in the core is, for the most part, an in-service program, we can add to the frustration of teachers by insisting that they bear all of the responsibility for remedial work. Suffice it to say, whenever possible this work should be incorporated in the core block-of-time. When a fairly large group needs help on such things as simple word recognition skills, increasing reading speed, syllabication, and accuracy in quantitative thinking, it is of particular importance that such a goup is handled by a core teacher. There are times when a remedial specialist is needed. If a pupil's reading is retarded more than two grade levels, if some emotional block seems to be hampering his progress, or if his lack of quantitative skill restricts the group's progress, it is perhaps unrealistic to expect the core teacher to help make a satisfactory adjustment.

Quick referral by the core teacher of remedial cases to the guidance worker, the school psychologist, and the research specialist plus the help of a resource person in remedial work and conferences with parents often get good results. Care should be taken to relate remedial materials to the work of the core class. Every effort should be made to help the pupil feel no stigma is attached to those working with the remedial teacher. These cases can move in and out of the core class during the two to three hour block while other individuals are working on their particular problems in the classroom, in other parts of the building, or out in the community. No large group activity should be undertaken during this period.

This discussion of remedial work in the core program is not to be confused with practice sessions used to clinch meaning. The latter is the sole responsibility of the core class.

Often a core class, because of the emphasis on the problem-solving approach and on community living, becomes involved in spearheading or helping to explore the solution of certain school and community problems. Care should be taken here that pupils are not exploited, and, on the other hand, that they are involved in significant tasks. Pupils are quick to catch on when their advice is asked where the answer makes no difference and when they are asked to perform meaningless, superficial small jobs. Core classes have helped to improve a crowded situation in school corridors and cafeterias. They have conducted pupil opinion polls in order that good school policies be determined. Some have helped to involve more parents in the school's program through various media. One produced a film-strip to explain the core program to parents, laymen and other school people.[6] In the wider community, core classes have helped to organize clean-up campaigns, to get-out-the vote on election day, to establish teen-age centers. and to beautify unsightly spots. Recently, a core class known by the writers was influential in the formation of a county-wide youth council to deal with spreading juvenile delin-quency. These are but a few of the worthwhile school and community activities which might find their inception in a core class. Participa-tion in such projects gives teen-agers experiences in democratic living and a sense of achieving adult social status.

Creative writing is an aspect of a pupil's over-all development which could be encouraged through the core program. Because the core is flexible in content and varied in its approach to method, pupils might get hold of some of their most creative ideas here. These would not necessarily be directly related to the core unit. Quite probably these ideas would be an outgrowth of the wide range of experiences offered to individuals in a core class. Not all pupils will wish to join in such an activity nor should this be required. If time is scheduled for creative writing and if the core teacher is careful in his motivating activities in all likelihood more and more pupils will participate. Pupils do not create in a vacuum. Progress can be ascer-tained from time to time by means of individual pupil folders filed in the core classroom. All creative efforts should be carefully read by the teacher and evaluated with the pupil. Sharing periods with an interested small group, the total group, or another core class often affords impetus for further creativity. Pupil efforts can be

[6] This filmstrip was produced by the Bladensburg Junior High School, Bladens-burg, Maryland.

published in the school newspaper and in local papers. One core class published its own newspaper including bits of creative writing from the group. Another undertook quite an ambitious project. The class published a magazine called *Core Capers* made up of the creative efforts of the entire group. This was a major project for an entire year. Some core teachers will feel that to guide such endeavors is not their forte; others interested in such projects will be glad to act as resource personnel. A particularly gifted child should be guided to seek such help and to choose courses in creative writing from the elective offerings.

Free reading was mentioned as an activity core classes might engage in aside from the core unit. Only a brief discussion on this activity will be included here since it is dealt with in detail in Chapter VII.[7] The core teacher has perhaps a better opportunity than other teachers to observe the reading habits of pupils. A wide variety of reading materials is used in the learning units and tendencies toward too little depth, too much breadth, over emphasis on one type of book, and actual dislike of reading become apparent. Free reading periods are not to be misconstrued as a time when no standards and no teacher guidance prevail. This is the time when individuals are helped to raise their own standards, to widen and deepen their appreciation of books, and to experience library facilities as a resource to be used for enjoyment now and throughout adult life. Often, pupils are encouraged to keep a card file on the books they read for pleasure during the free reading period. Sometimes sharing periods are scheduled so pupils may stimulate others to try books they have liked. Skits, role playing, art work, and group reports make this an interesting time for all pupils.

The group guidance factor plays a major role in core program development. The content and method used and the extended block-of-time make this possible. Individual guidance is important. Perhaps no one in the school knows the pupils he teaches better than the core teacher. This knowing pupils does not come about willy-nilly the conducive set-up notwithstanding. Time must be set

[7] See pp. 219 to 226 for the account of "Language Arts in the Core Program" by Jean V. Marani.

aside for individual conferences. One school system known to the writers makes an extra hour available each day for core teachers to schedule such conferences. In this system all core classes meet only two hours each day. Where the three hour block-of-time is allotted to the core, these conferences can be arranged periodically in the core class. In newer buildings, conference rooms with glass partitions are being built into core rooms. If such facilities are not available, the teacher and pupil can talk quietly while the other pupils are at work. Such conferences can deal with academic progress, vocational choice, selection of elective offerings, and matters of a more personal nature. Sometimes this conference leads to referrals to resource people who are specialists in the field of the pupil's problem. At other times the conference may point up the need for parent visitation. All in all, this experience helps pupils obtain a feeling of security in the school situation. It gives teachers a clearer sense of direction as to next steps.

Only a few types of activities used in addition to the core unit have been described. A good core teacher is always on the alert for unique possibilities to make democracy more meaningful to his pupils. The pupils will suggest many ideas, if given the opportunity, to make school *live* for them.

SELECTED BIBLIOGRAPHY

Adapting the Secondary School Program to the Needs of Youth. Fifty-Second Yearbook of the National Society for the Study of Education, Part I. Chicago, The University of Chicago Press, 1953. Chapter VII.

Alberty, Harold, *Developing a Core Program in the High School*. A recording available from Educational Recording Services, 5922 Abernathy Drive, Los Angeles 45, California.

——, *Reorganizing the High School Curriculum*. New York, The Macmillan Company, 1953 (Revised). Chapter VI.

——, "A Sound Core Program," *Journal of the National Education Association*, 45, 20-22 (January, 1956).

Developing Programs for Young Adolescents. Prepared for the Association for Supervision and Curriculum Development by the Department of Supervision and Curriculum Development of the Florida Education Association. Washington, D. C., National Education Association, 1954.

Board of Education of the City of New York, "Practices in Experimental Core Classes." *Curriculum Bulletin*, 1953-54 Series, No. 8, 1954.
————, *Suggestions to Teachers of Experimental Core Classes*. Curriculum Bulletin, 1950-51 Series, No. 2, 1951.
Board of Education of Prince George's County, Upper Marlboro, Maryland, *A Core Program in a Junior High School Curriculum*. A filmstrip in color with recorded script. Produced by the pupils of the Bladensburg Junior High School, Prince George's County, Maryland.
Education, "Core Program in Action Number." January, 1953, Volume 73, No. 5. Massachusetts: Palmer Company, 349 Lincoln Street, Hingham.
Faunce, Roland C. and Bossing, Nelson L., *Developing the Core Curriculum*. New York, Prentice Hall Inc., 1951. Chapters 3-5 inclusive.
Harap, Henry, *Social Living in the Curriculum*. Nashville, Division of Surveys and Field Service, George Peabody College for Teachers, 1952.
Leonard, J. Paul, *Developing the Secondary School Curriculum*. New York, Rinehart & Company, 1953. Chapter 14.
Lewis, Gertrude M., *Educating Children in Grades Seven and Eight*. Washington, United States Department of Health, Education, and Welfare. Office of Education, Bulletin 1954, No. 10, 1954.
Lurry, Lucile L., "The Contribution of Home Economics to Selected Problem Areas in the Core Curriculum of the Secondary School." Unpublished doctoral dissertation, Columbus, Ohio, The Ohio State University, 1949. Chapter 2.
Preparation of Core Teachers for Secondary Schools. Committee on the Preparation of Core Teachers, Association for Supervision and Curriculum Development. Washington, D. C., National Education Association, 1955. Chapters I and II.
Toops, Myrtle Dewey, *Working in the Core Program in Burris Laboratory School*. College Publication 154, February, 1955, Muncie, Indiana, Ball State Teachers College, Muncie.
Wright, Grace S., *Core Curriculum Development: Problems and Practices*. Bulletin 1952, No. 5. Washington, Department of Health, Education and Welfare, 1952.

III

DESIGNING THE
CORE PROGRAM

The question of a valid content for the core program is a major one in the minds of those who wish to proceed in this direction. In Chapters I and II we have said that a rather thoroughgoing reorganization of general education in the high school curriculum is in order if an adequate development is to be achieved. It was further implied that the faculty of a school and/or the teachers and administrators of a school system have the task of defining the basic structure of general education in terms of the adolescents' common needs, problems, and personal-social interests. This basic structure would be defined in terms of broad problem areas. Learning experiences would be drawn from these problem areas through teacher-pupil planning in the classroom:

1. *How does a group organize itself to get this job done?*
2. *What are the processes or tasks involved?*
3. *Who should be involved in the process?*
4. *How is division of labor effected?*

It cannot be over-emphasized that any curriculum change must involve at some point all of the people whom the change affects—pupils, teachers, administrators, parents and other laymen. Further, it is particularly necessary that the professional personnel involved—teachers and administrators—feel a real need for changing the status quo. In most cases the principal of a particular school and/or some qualified person designated by the board of education takes the responsibility for leadership in any proposed change.

Chapter VIII of this book contains a detailed account of how a faculty might work together to develop a core program. The roles of those involved are defined. Suffice it to say here that before a problem area study is launched those participating must have developed a cooperative clear-cut sense of direction or in other words a philosophy of education. If a rather high level of consensus on the aims of education is lacking among a school's faculty the development of a core program might do little more than confuse the issue.

What is Involved in a Problem Area Study?

There is no ready-made blueprint for anyone to use in making a problem area study. The specific examples given in Chapter IV of how two schools went about this task will indicate that several methods hold fruitful possibilities. Much depends upon the time, guidance, facilities, and professional know-how available. Effective use has been made of the case study method, the interview method (with pupils and parents), problem check lists (standardized and teacher constructed), interest inventories (standardized and teacher constructed), informal school contacts, student reactions to existing curricular experiences, cumulative records (scholastic achievement, health and personality development), the published research, and certain types of community studies involving present conditions and needed improvements. Whatever the plan used, the administrator does the spearheading. Trained guidance personnel are perhaps in the best position to administer tests of any nature, and to coordinate and interpret results. The curricular implications of such studies seem best done through a cooperative endeavor involving teachers and administrators and, at times, pupils, parents, and other laymen. Guidance personnel also have a responsibility for the in-service training of teachers in the areas of individual and group guidance techniques. When classroom teachers have a reasonable know-how in these areas, a better cross-section of common problems is obtained than in cases where a guidance counsellor must serve 1200 individuals or 36 home room groups. At this point, it might be well to note that a problem area study is concerned with the identification of the common, everyday problems of pupils, not their serious maladjustments. The latter are matters for professionals in psychology, psychiatry and the like.

The faculty could begin its problem area study by carefully reviewing the published materials on adolescent needs and considering the implications for its local situation. Two frequently used studies of adolescent needs are: *Fostering Mental Health In Our Schools*, the 1950 yearbook of the ASCD (Chapter 6 and 7) and the study done by the faculty of the Ohio State University School, *How Children Develop*. A simple and direct statement of the needs of youth is found in the eighth yearbook of the John Dewey Society, *The American High School*. The chapter on developmental tasks is written by Stephen Corey. Another such statement was made by Robert Havighurst and is published in a later book called *Human Development and Education*.[1]

This study of the published research could best be done by a total faculty group in somewhat of the seminar pattern with leadership roles being assumed by various individuals. Concurrently, or following this study of the literature, the case study method might prove effective. The Institute of Child Study, at the University of Maryland, has pioneered in an effort to help teachers understand children by this means. The American Council on Education's, *Helping Teachers Understand Children*, would be valuable to a group contemplating this approach. As the faculty works together on these basic studies, parents and other laymen might join the group as regular participants, or they might be used from time to time as resource people in respect to a particular problem.

Numerous problem check-lists and interest inventories have been used to identify common problems. These represent a comparatively easy method of collecting data and are, for the most part, quite inexpensive. Such standardized instruments have limitations and

---

[1] See also: *Growing Up In An Anxious Age*. 1952 Yearbook of the Association for Supervision and Curriculum Development, Washington, D. C. National Education Association, 1952; Paul H. Landis, *Adolescence and Youth; The Process of Maturing*. New York, Prentice-Hall, Inc., 1954; Harold Alberty, *Reorganizing the High School Curriculum*. New York, The Macmillan Company, 1953 (Revised), Chapter IV.

should not be used as *the* one way to get at the needs of pupils. Many adolescents are unaware of their problems, or sometimes a particular inventory may fail to enumerate the problems experienced by some individuals. Sometimes adolescents are very wary of revealing their pressing problems to teachers or to any adult. Further, adolescent behavior being what it is, interest indications on inventories cannot be taken as the last word. These indications are useful particularly for exploratory experiences but it should be remembered that some interests expressed at any time are likely to be transitory with some youth. Needless to say, with careful leadership by trained guidance personnel, data collected through the use of such devices can be very helpful in a problem area study. Some widely used instruments are: (1) *The Mooney Problems Check List*, (2) *The Pond's Student Interest Inquiry*, (3) *The Ohio Critical Thinking Check-Up*. (4) *The Science Research Associates Test*, (5) *The Ohio Social Acceptance Scale* (or a teacher-devised socio-metric technique), and (6) *The Scale of Beliefs Test*.[2] Many teachers have used effectively the "free choice" method. Here pupils simply list their problems, interests, and needs out of relation to any structure.

Studying the community can insure a further element of realism as another vital contribution in suggesting needs, collecting and organizing data, and helping a faculty develop insight into the community. Useful data for problem area development have been obtained by giving attention to such community problems as: (1) How do people earn a living here? (2) What kinds of homes are represented by our pupils? (3) What are the recreational facilities of our community? (4) What are the various social, religious, and racial groups represented in our community? (5) Is an optimum health plan provided in this locality? *The Evaluative Criteria*, 1950

---

[2] The *Ohio Critical Thinking Check-Up* and *The Ohio Social Acceptance Scale* are available from the Bureau of Educational Research, The Ohio State University, Columbus, Ohio. *The Mooney Problems Check List* is available from Educational Testing Service, Princeton, New Jersey. *The Pond's Student Interest Inquiry* is available from the National Association of Secondary School Principals, Washington, D. C. *The Science Research Associates Test* is available from Science Research Associates, Evanston, Illinois. *The Scale of Beliefs Test* is mimeographed material, available from The University of Chicago Press, The University of Chicago, Chicago, Ill.

edition, provide an organization for a study of the school community that might be used by faculty and parent groups.

When the data from the pupil population and community study reports have been collected and organized, the group might proceed to investigate the research dealing with problem area studies. Formulations which meet the criteria of a core program such as that described in Chapter II have been made by Bostwick and Reid, Van Til, Alberty and Lurry.[3] The Lurry study will be presented in some detail as an example of what a faculty might develop as a basic curricular structure of its core program. The reader will note that Chapters V, VI, and VII of this book draw heavily on the Lurry statement as a point of departure for the development of resource guides in the preplanning stages of the core program, in describing actual core classroom situations, in the contribution of the special interest areas in several situations, and in listing the possible activities suggested in each problem area in the appendix. The authors' detailed use of the Lurry study should in no way be taken by the reader to mean "This is it" for the design of a core program. It is intended only to suggest how the transition is made from studies of the needs of youth in a particular situation to the basic structure of a core program. An attempt will be made to show why these problem areas are representative of the common needs of youth by relating each to criteria considered adequate in choosing problem areas. This should be construed as a method any faculty could use to make its program defensible in light of its purposes.

The Lurry[4] problem area study was made in 1949. It involved the development of a set of criteria for selecting problem areas, a review of the literature in problem areas used in the core program development for a period of ten years, and the judgments of thirty curriculum workers in the United States who had wide experiences with the development of core programs. As a basis for the develop-

[3] Alberty, *op cit.*; Prudence Bostwick and Chandos Reid, *A Functional High School Program*, New York, Hinds, Hadyn and Eldridge, 1948; William Van Til, "A social Living Curriculum for Post-War Secondary Education." Unpublished doctoral thesis, Columbus, The Ohio State University, 1946.

[4] Lucile L. Lurry, *The Contribution of Home Economics to Selected Problem Areas in the Core Curriculum of the Secondary School.* Unpublished doctoral thesis, Columbus, The Ohio State University, 1949.

ment of the criteria, the writer drew heavily upon Stephen Corey's statement of the common developmental tasks of youth. Corey states in *The American High School* that the principal tasks of adolescents in our culture are: coming to terms with their own bodies; achieving independence from parents; learning new relationships to their age-mates; achieving adult social-economic status, acquiring self-confidence; and acquiring a system of values.[5] The reader will note in studying the criteria that they reflect the concept of core described in Chapter II. At that time it was proposed that a problem area should:

1. Represent persistent problems of a personal-social nature common to adolescents in our culture.
2. Be adapted to the maturity level of the group.
3. Provide experiences for growth in terms of such values as tolerance, social sensitivity, cooperativeness, civic competence, aesthetic appreciations, self-direction, critical thinking.
4. Encourage the use of the problem solving technique to attack problems in all areas of living.
5. Provide opportunity for cooperative planning in the group, i.e., teacher-pupil, teacher-teacher, pupil-pupil planning.
6. Provide opportunity for generalization beyond the experiences of adolescents and their own daily lives.
7. Provide opportunity for meaningful direct experiences and enriching vicarious experiences through a wide variety of resources in men, materials, and techniques.
8. Provide for the integration of knowledge through the use of subject matter as it bears upon the problem at hand.
9. Provide experiences which develop continuity in the emotional, intellectual, and physical aspects of the learning process.
10. Provide opportunity for the guidance functions of teaching, both individual and group, to become an integral part of the curriculum.

[5] Hellis L. Caswell, et al. *The American High School*. Eighth Yearbook of the John Dewey Society. New York, Harper & Brothers, 1947, p. 80.

11. Extend the interests of individuals into the various special-interest areas.
12. Lead to other meaningful learning experiences—suggest new problem areas.

In light of these criteria, a review of the literature in problem area development, and the judgments of thirty curriculum workers, sixteen problem areas were selected as a basis for the scope of an adequate core program. These were:

1. Problems of School Living
2. Problems of Self-Understanding
3. Problems of Finding Values by Which We Live
4. Problems of Social Relationships
5. Problems of Employment and Vocation
6. Problems of Using and Conserving Natural Resources
7. Problems of Education in American Democracy
8. Problems of Constructive Use of Leisure
9. Problems of Family Living
10. Problems of Communication
11. Problems of Democratic Government
12. Problems of Community and Personal Health
13. Problems of Economic Relationships in a Democracy
14. Problems of Achieving World Peace in the Atomic Age
15. Problems of Intercultural Relations
16. Problems of Critical Thinking[6]

It might be helpful at this point to present each of these problem areas in some detail as to possible scope and as to adequacy in terms of the criteria. The scope suggested is not in any way to be considered exhaustive. It is merely intended to be suggestive of possibilities.

1. **Problems of School Living.** How can adolescents get most out of their school experiences? Include such problems as: (a) Making friends with the people in their class and others in the school, e.g., other students,

[6] In this account *Problems of Critical Thinking* is being omitted as a separate problem area. While no basic disagreement was incurred concerning the inclusion of this area in the initial study, the writers' experience in core program development tends to indicate that critical thinking might be treated as an area of method rather than one of possible scope of the core program.

administrators, teachers, custodians, clerical workers; (b) Understanding the contributions of each of these people to school life; (c) Getting acquainted with the physical aspects of the school; (d) Understanding the opportunities offered by the school and how these can best be used by students; (e) Experiencing the values of cooperative planning, i.e., teacher-pupil, pupil-pupil, and small and large group planning; (f) Developing self-direction through self-government; (g) Developing desirable home-school relationships; (h) Evaluating, serving and improving the school together; (i) Developing a relationship with the school which will continue after graduation; (j) Helping to formulate, execute and evaluate objectives of the school.

This problem area is very closely related to the personal-social problems of adolescents in our culture. Since pupils, generally speaking, are "placed'" in a particular school and class because of conditions beyond their control, the element of intragroup relations becomes important. A large portion of the group life of which youth are a part centers in school living. Alberty points to the need of the adolescent as he grows toward maturity to achieve and maintain both a sense of security and achievement. The adolescent seeks to satisfy these needs through developing status with age-mates of both sexes, and developing status in groups in the immediate and wider community.[7] Learning units which might grow out of this problem area would afford an opportunity to provide successful participation in group activities. Experiences here would further provide a sense of security and belonging as the student becomes familiar with and understands the immediate environment. The problem of knowing people and their possible contributions to cooperative living is fundamental in developing democratic values.

This study of human relations could very well start in the core class. This should result in a better program of human relationships in the total school environment. As the process of obtaining better relationships is generalized by pupils with guidance by the teacher, new problems for further investigation in the wider community, e.g., housing, community recreation, sanitation facilities will be more meaningful. If pupils share in formulating, executing, and evaluating the objectives of the school, it may be easier to develop skill in the

[7] Alberty, *op. cit.*, Chapter IV.

use of the problem-solving technique. Genuine planning on common problems gives people something to think about. As the educational resources of the school are explored, the core staff has an opportunity to extend the interests of individuals into various special-interest areas. Thus, another opportunity arises to make a guidance program function as an integral part of the curriculum.

We are not attempting to indicate the maturity level at which problem areas are used. It is proposed in this connection that different emphases might be given at various levels. For example, a learning unit from this problem area might be developed at the early junior high level to provide orientation to a new school. At the senior high school level, a learning unit concerning the evaluation of the objectives of the school in terms of individual and group development would be appropriate. Such a learning unit might lead into a discussion of how alert, responsible citizens may have a part in developing a more adequate school system for democracy.

2. **Problems of Self-Understanding.** How can we know more about ourselves? Include such problems as: (a) Understanding my body; (b) Improving my personal appearance; (c) Realizing my strengths and weaknesses; (d) Gaining insight into my own behavior, e.g., understanding the longings, urges, and desires which drive me to action; (e) Achieving increasingly mature relationships with the opposite sex; (f) Getting along with Dad, Mother, siblings and age-mates; (g) Overcoming inferiority and adjusting to decrease aggression or self-protectiveness; (h) Changing environment and its effect in my life; (i) Doing the right thing at the right time; (j) Making and carrying out plans for improving my personality; (k) Knowing where I can go to get help with my problems; (l) Experiencing the use of the problem-solving method in dealing with individual and group problems; (m) Gaining some insight into the problems of fear and insecurity.

Self-development problems and problems of psychological understanding rank high in all adolescent studies. Stephen Corey, *et al.,* point to development of self as one of the major developmental tasks of youth.[8] Students, perhaps, are much more interested in the application of psychology to self-understanding than with theoretical

[8] Stephen Corey, *et al., General Education in the American High School.* New York, Scott, Foresman and Company, 1942, p. 106.

principles. Their concern is with certain aspects of behavior, e.g., shyness, inferiority, and aggressiveness. These problems are personal, yet are inevitably related to relationships with age-mates, with Mother, Dad, siblings, and to sexual development.[9] Rapid body changes during the period of adolescence cause great concern, and this is a good time for education on the whole subject of sex through frank, honest, straightforward discussions.

Such a problem area has rich opportunities for providing experiences for growth in terms of democatic values. If young people understand their own desires, longings, and urges, if they understand some of the blocks to regarding people as individuals, they may have a greater appreciation of the importance and the difficulty of practicing respect for individual worth. Further, one may move from self-understanding to generalizations about social problems. This is particularly true in problems of fear and insecurity. Such psychological insights are tools of social competence in the analysis of social problems.

In providing experiences which help students understand themselves, thus gaining some insight into the problems of others, there is fine opportunity to develop skill in the use of the problem-solving technique. There is, perhaps, as good opportunity in this problem area as in any for the guidance function of teaching to become an integral part of curriculum. This statement applies to both individual and group guidance. Indeed, guidance is the keynote of any learning unit developed out of this problem area. Personal and social adjustment cannot be met entirely by experiences provided through the school, but school experiences can go a long way in meeting such needs. Many meaningful, direct experiences in school situations can be provided. Of particular importance are those experiences dealing with cleanliness, good manners, taste in selection of clothes, and effective speech. Above all, the area affords experiences which give confidence and success in meeting and working with others to work out hopes and aspirations. Such experiences help to develop emotional maturity. As the core moves toward helping boys and girls

---

[9] *How Children Develop.* A report of the Faculty of the University School. Columbus, The Ohio State University, 1946, p. 50.

understand themselves, it comes closer to satisfying the personal-social needs of youth.

3. **Problems of Finding Values by Which We Live.** What means most to use in life and why? Include such problems as: (a) Considering what I value most and why; (b) Exploring the various souces of our values; (c) Studying the great religions; (d) Understanding the basic tenets of the major conflicting ideologies; (e) Achieving values we cherish in a democracy; (f) Developing skill in using intelligence to arise at values in all areas of living; (g) Understanding the relation of values to action in all areas of living; (h) Changing world conditions and how these affect values; (i) Understanding the problems of living with others whose values may be different from ours; (j) Experiencing many situations in which choices must be made; (k) Intellectualizing the process of making choices as a way of life; (l) Becoming aware of the conflicting values in American life evident in the immediate and wider community.

The exploration of values cannot be separated from other units of work. Since, however, several adolescent studies point to the intense struggle these boys and girls go through in attaining adult status, it seems necessary to make explicit the determination of values in our society and in other societies. Most of the studies on adolescent development point to the need for a satisfying world picture and a workable philosophy of life. They also point out that a philosophy of life is workable only in so far as it reaches from the immediate personal to wider and wider social and economic relationships. Symonds found that "philosophy of life" scored very high in his study of personal problems ranked by youth. Out of fifteen areas of experience in which problems arise, youth ranked philosophy of life, i.e., personal values, ideals, religion, in sixth place. The average rank in this instance was only one point lower that the area ranked in first place.[10]

This problem area offers much opportunity to provide meaningful, direct experiences and rich, vicarious experiences whether the learning unit developed concerns religions, political, social, and economic ideologies, moral codes, or emphasises conflicts in our own value system. In a metropolitan area, field trips to various socio-

[10] Percival Symonds, "Life Problems and Interests of Adolescents," *School Review*, XLIV, 515 (September, 1936).

economic sections could be used to explore environment as a source of values. There are rich resources in movies, film strips, and other audio-visual aids on these subjects. There are opportunities for student and community panels and forums. Most communities in the present day are sufficiently unprovincial to provide, as resources, men of differing points of view on religion, ideologies, and economic and social relationships. The conflicting values in American life can be pointed out by a series of planned experiences in any community. What community repudiates technological know-how? Yet, what community has a satisfactory solution to the distribution of the benefits of science without disturbing other values we cherish? We are in fair agreement as to the value of individual worth. Yet, young people have only to make a cursory community survey on housing to find that we are inconsistent at this point. Through such experiences, it may become obvious that the answer does not reside in the teachers and textbooks. Subject matter from psychology, sociology, ecnomics, home economics, science, philosophy, and the like, is meaningful as it bears upon the problem at hand. Cooperative planning between a teacher and the group is necessary to make these experiences most worthwhile.

The opportunity to intellectualize democratic values—to consider seriously what we mean by democracy—could never be better than as we explore the sources of values. As boys and girls discuss the values they held as young children and the wide scale of values on which they see adults operating, they can be led to examine choice-making as a way of life. In other words, what does it mean in a concrete situation if *I* use tradition, authority, or experience as a basis for making a decision? Such a process can easily be generalized as it applies to the larger social situation.

Experience in this problem area might lead to many other profitable learning experiences—might suggest new problem areas. Certain experiences might lead to an exploration of the arts and how man through the ages has shared insights and appreciations. Other experiences might lead to a problem area centered around intercultural relations—civil liberties, or integration and the public schools. Sharing what each individual has found most worthwhile may help provide a feeling of group unity though a wide diversity of experience and background exists. Functional guidance operates here to lead the interests of individuals into special interest areas.

In the authors' opinion the school can never take its place as an instrument for achieving a better way of life for all people until it faces squarely its responsibility for helping young people learn how to value. Boys and girls must learn to look for the value concepts inherent in any problem. We thus provide experiences which develop continuity in the emotional, intellectual and physical aspects of the learning process. The individual must see the process of valuing as an instrument by which he may bring maximum intelligence to human problems.[11]

4. **Problems of Social Relationships.** What is our responsibility (individual and group) in facing and helping to solve the social problems of our community, state and nation? Include such problems as: (a) Social security; (b) Medical care; (c) Housing; (d) Juvenile delinquency; (e) Legal aspects of family life, e.g., divorce and marriage laws; (f) Civil liberties; (g) Community recreation; (h) Government or private ownership of public utilities; (i) Family and child welfare agencies; (j) Labor-management relations; (k) Cooperatives; (l) City and regional planning; (m) Understanding the conflict between democratic cooperation and so-called "free" enterprise; (n) Consideration of the trend toward economic-social interdependence and the need of a philosophy of democratic cooperation here.

This problem area gives further opportunity for adolescents to generalize beyond the experiences of their own daily lives to the larger meaning of democracy. Young people today are growing up in an age in which understanding the complex interrelationships of achieving the good life for all people is one condition of survival. Alberty says that the maturing adolescent develops concerns about achieving a social outlook on life, that he achieves this social outlook through the development of increasing unity and consistency in thinking and action, increasing ability to deal with related abstractions, increasing ability to recognize and deal with conflicts, and an increasing ability to grasp the nature of truth and the techniques for discovering and

[11] For a further development of this position see: H. Gordon Hullfish, "They Look at Their Beliefs," *Progressive Education*, XXVI, 50-55 (November, 1948). Also see: Bulletin of the California State Department of Education, *Evaluating Pupil Progress*, XXI, No. 6, (April, 1952).

utilizing it.[12] If we recognize that a major responsibility of the school is to develop well-rounded personalities, able and willing to take their place in society, it is evident that we imply social competence. A major factor in social competence is concern about, or at any rate interest in, social, economic, and political problems. The principle which ought to be applied here is the widening of the area of mutually shared interests. Alberty further points out that the maturing adolescent develops and maintains a sense of achievement through understanding of and participation in the solution of basic economic and social problems.

It is conceivable that at some point in secondary school, adolescents with their teachers would develop learning units centered around several of these explicit social problems. As adolescents mature, and give more attention to the outstanding social problems of the community, they should become increasingly able to deal with related problems in the state, nation and world.

It would be laboring the point to show in greater detail how this problem area meets the criteria. The problem will be one of selecting from several possible experiences with materials and techniques, and limiting the scope of meaningful possibilities rather than one of searching for them. The possibilities for special-interest areas to contribute widely in these experiences are important as youth continue to build an adequate social outlook. The leads into other learning experiences and specialized areas that such an area of study offers are numerous.

5. **Problems of Employment and Vocation.** What are our opportunities for employment in the community now? What factors should we consider in choosing a career? Include such problems as: (a) Exploring opportunities for work experiences in the community for us now; (b) Having meaningful work experiences and evaluating these in terms of economic skills developed, interests widened, and social insights gained; (c) Getting and keeping a job, e.g., selecting my job, getting a job, getting along with others on the job, making the most of my job; (d) Exploring vocations in the immediate and wider community; (e) Realizing my vocational aptitudes; (f) Giving attention to the preparation needed for various vocations; (g) Considering the importance of various vocations in

[12] Alberty, op. cit., Chapter IV.

terms of group welfare; (h) Homemaking as a vocation for all; (i) Relating the choice of a vocation to the changing American and world scene; (j) Understanding the social, political, and economic implications of a vocational choice; (k) Gaining some insight into labor-management relationships; (l) Considering the problems of shifting population in relationship to employment; (m) Understanding the importance of and the problems inherent in maintaining high employment; (n) Becoming aware of the fact that some high school students must look forward to unskilled labor; (o) Understanding the guaranteed annual wage.

The testimony that employment and vocations are important to adolescents is borne out consistently by adolescent studies regardless of the angle from which adolescent needs are derived. Evidence that schools and school systems consider this an important area of need was shown by the writers' review of literature in problem area development. The area ranked sixth in frequency as to times listed in the fifty-two areas found. This area was listed by twenty-five schools. *Economic Participation in a Democracy*, which ranked first in this review of the literature was listed only thirty-one times as being appropriate for the core program. It ought to be obvious that these two areas have many inseparable and interrelated aspects. Lurry's study also suggests general acceptance of this problem area as appropriate for the core program. *Employment and Vocations* was one of five problem areas which encountered no rejections by curriculum workers asked to evaluate the Lurry proposal for a core program. The literature points to the need for guidance of adolescents in choosing an occupation and for vocational preparation. Doane emphasizes that vocational guidance is of more concern to youth in high school than vocational training.[13]

As core teachers work with students in efforts to help them discover the particular occupations for which they have aptitude and inclination, the guidance function operates as a major factor. Problems of employment and vocations should have definite implications for extending into the various special interest areas. This problem area lends itself admirably to meaningful, direct experiences as

[13] Donald C. Doane, *The Needs of Youth.* Teachers College, Columbia University, Contribution to Education, No. 848. New York, Bureau of Publications, Teachers College, Columbia University, 1942, p. 73.

students learn about various occupational opportunities through field trips into the community, contacts with many people who are specialists in the various fields, and other resources. Meaningful work experiences might grow out of learning units developed within this problem area. There is opportunity for much cooperative planning by teacher, pupil, and employer as these work experiences are planned, executed, and evaluated. The opportunity for growth in terms of democratic values is particularly significant as students are guided through experiences which point up the social values of the whole area of work. Here the problem-solving technique can be so definitely pointed-up as it relates to choice making. Intelligent education centered in this problem area will relate to gaining insight into such social issues as labor-management relationships, the problems of a migratory population and the importance of the problems inherent in maintaining high employment.

6. **Problems of Using and Conserving Natural Resources.** How can our natural resources be best developed and used? Include such problems as: (a) Exploring the natural resources of our own community and considering their development and use in terms of the common welfare; (b) Meeting our basic needs for food, shelter, clothing, recreation through wise use of resources; (c) Meeting the issue of conservation of natural resources in a democracy through education for self-control; (d) Realizing the importance of producing, building, and growing—without destroying —the bases of the future existence of democracy; (e) Planning jointly for resource use by the citizen and his government; (f) Considering the world-wide social, economic and political implications involved in the need of all people for vital sources of energy; (g) Relating wise use of natural resources to conservation of human resources.

A review of the literature used in the Lurry study, and the responses of curriculum workers to the tentative statement of problem areas in this study, indicate that *Problems of Using and Conserving Natural Resources* should be part of the core program. The area was rejected entirely by no person. Evidence that schools have considered the study of conservation important is based upon the fact that the literature reveals only four problem areas more frequently used. *Science and General Education* points to the need of maturing adolescents for effective action in solving basic economic problems.

In addition, it points to the conservation of exhaustible natural resources as a social responsibility.[14]

Democratic values in relation to the problem-solving technique come into play here as students are guided in finding a principle on which decisions about the use of resources may be made with intelligent regard for the common welfare. Society can destroy itself through disregard for the method of intelligence in the use of its resources. The question is, will we put education to work building a popular will for the conservation of natural resources before it is too late?

A learning unit in this problem area is perhaps best approached through some current conservation issue of the community. Such a unit might be developed around the introduction of a controvesy such as TVA and the Dixon-Yates Contract. Through films, speakers, field trips, student discussion groups, reading materials, and community-school panels youth may be helped to develop an awareness of social and economic problems created by a misuse of resources in agriculture, industry, forestry, mining, and recreational areas. There is a good opportunity to develop meaningful concepts concerning the interrelated and inseparable aspects of human resources and natural resources. The place of democratic planning between the citizen and his government in resource use is a concept which can be emphasized here and generalized into many areas of living. There is opportunity to extend insights of the adolescent to world citizenship as he sees the political, social, and economic implications of conservation in problems of world trade. All people ought to have the vital sources of energy. This may be the time to explore the pros and cons of the protective tariff.

7. **Problems of Education in American Democracy.** Why is education an important factor in our lives as citizens of a democracy? Include such problems as: (a) Exploring the educational opportunities in the immediate community; (b) Studying the historical development of education in America; (c) Perpetuating, yet re-creating democratic ideals through education; (d) Realizing educational inequalities prevalent in the immediate and

[14] *Science in General Education.* Committee on the Function of Science in General Education, Progressive Education Association. D. Appleton-Century Company, 1938, pp. 288-289.

wider community; (e) Using education to help raise the standard of living in the group; (f) Understanding the impact of education on such social institutions as the home, church, government, etc.; (g) Becoming a more intelligent participant in the democratic process through education; (h) Making use of various educational services in the community by members of the family; (i) Differentiating the practical implications of the more important theories of education that effect current school practices; (j) Considering how and why schools should make provisions for individual differences; (k) Understanding the various pressure groups that operate on education; (l) Contrasting values and beliefs and resulting implications for living stressed by American schools and those stressed by Russian schools; (m) Implementing the Supreme Court's decision on segregation and the public schools; (n) Dealing with the attacks on public education.

If public education is to play its proper role with parents and other adults in the betterment of the current social scene, this role will have to be examined and clarified by pupils in the public high schools. A large majority of secondary school pupils do not attend college. There is still an enormous drop-out problem after sixteen years of age. Therefore, this problem should be included both in the junior high school and in the later years of the senior high school. Studies have shown that adolescents manifest concern over problems of education.[15] This area was included in only three accounts of core programs in the literature. In each case "getting an education" was the point of emphasis. The importance of an educated electorate in a democracy was largely ignored.

There is no dearth of problems for pupils in this area. While the completely vicious attacks on public education have somewhat subsided there is no guarantee that they will not rise again. The causes of these unwarranted attacks, how to meet and/or prevent them seem pertinent problems for senior high pupils. Rapidly increasing enrollments are causing a severe tax on our present educational facilities and personnel. Should not pupils be helped to understand the deferred payment plan for school buildings? What are we doing

[15] See the study done by the Commission on Human Relations of the Progressive Education Association on the typical points of focus or concerns of adolescents reported in H. H. Giles, S. P. McCutchen, and A. N. Zechiel, *Exploring the Curriculum.* New York, Harper & Brothers. 1942, pp. 315-328, and William Van Til, "A Social Living Curriculum for Post-War Secondary Education." Unpublished doctoral thesis, Columbus, The Ohio State University, 1946.

through vocational guidance to help pupils explore teaching as a career? Are we engaging in activities which help adolescents recognize their responsibilities as competent citizens to interpret and work for an adequate program of education for all youth? A learning unit in this area might make some real contribution as we struggle to implement the Supreme Court's decision regarding segregation and the public schools. Other educational agencies in the community —home, church, government—might be explored so that the school's role might be further clarified. Some of the studies related to the relation between education and the standard of living achieved might serve to spark discussion. Why not ask the pupils to make such a survey in their immediate community? Informal studies made in Prince George's County, Maryland, showed that pupils wanted to understand the various theories of curriculum development, methods of instruction, and evaluation procedures being used by the school. Perhaps our allegiance to democracy as a way of life could be strengthened if boys and girls clearly saw it as a source of educational objectives. After all, this is one way in which we differ radically from a totalitarian state.

This problem area may seem to include a large order of predicated needs. Some of this gets pretty close to the "here and now" living of pupils. In any case, its social significance should not be lightly taken.

8. **Problems of Constructive Use of Leisure.** How can we become more interesting and better adjusted people through extending individual and group interests? Include such problems as: (a) Extending aesthetic appreciation, e.g., music, painting, literature, nature, science, through participating in experiences in these areas; (b) Having experiences in the special interest areas of the school, e.g., industrial arts, home arts, fine arts, dramatics, physical education; (c) Recreation in the home; (d) Hobbies; (e) Developing, extending, and maintaining adequate community recreational facilities for all citizens; (f) Developing a concept of creative experience as it is related to well-balanced living; (g) Experiencing individual and group activities as constructive uses of leisure; (h) Developing a basis for choice in acquiring recreational interests; (i) Developing a fair degree of skill in several types of recreational activity (individual and group); (j) Having experiences in which individuals and groups engage in creative activity.

Howard Bell's Study in Maryland brought out the fact that from the sociological point of view recreation is a significant youth need. Analysis of the data of this study showed that seven out of every ten young people felt that they were living in communities with inadequate recreational programs.[16] Current reports would not seem to refute these conclusions. *Youth and the Future*, a report of a study sponsored by the American Council on Education, has this to say about relations between recreation and education: "The schools have a responsibility to equip their pupils for fruitful use of leisure which is equal to their responsibility to equip them for useful work. Upon this, much of the quality of our local and national culture in the future depends."[17]

There is an opportunity to make values most meaningful in a learning unit developed from this problem area since recreation is so closely allied to what youth do. The student is perhaps most interested in recreation from the standpoint of what is worth doing. Concrete situations, then, can easily be used to illustrate how recreation is often derived from traditional and authoritarian sources rather than from intelligence. Youth have not been led to the point of intellectualization as regards choice-making in use of leisure time. The problem of constructive use of leisure time promises to become more fundamental as an atomic age bears down upon us.

Such a problem area offers much in the way of direct experiences which might extend aesthetic interests and appreciations while helping youth develop a sense of achievement. The guidance function operates here as teachers help students develop some degree of skill in the creative arts—a feeling for creative experience as it is related to well-balanced living. Except for a favored minority, it is probable that the work of the world has never afforded more than a large element of routine which made limited use of the worker's potentialities. Then, it may be said of a large and increasing number of people that if they are ever to experience the feeling of creating or

[16] Howard Bell, *Youth Tell Their Story*. Washington, D. C., American Council on Education, 1938, pp. 181-189.

[17] *Youth and the Future*. General Report of the American Youth Commission of the American Council on Education. New York, D. Appleton-Century Company, 1942, p. 160.

achieving something worthwhile in itself, it must be outside of work. It is evident, at this point, that this problem area offers many possibilities for extending the interest of individuals into special-interest areas, and that any learning unit developed would perhaps suggest other learning experiences and afford leads into other problem areas.

Wrenn and Harley point out the further implications of such a problem area for cooperative planning between teachers and pupils, pupils among themselves, and likewise, teachers. They say: "It is also true that the creative element in work is not restricted to manipulative occupations, where the effect of technological change has been most severe. For instance, there is something creative in the planned modification of behavior through group experience."[18]

Generalization beyond the experience of adolescents and their own daily lives is provided in dealing with the concept of adequate recreational facilities for all people. Youth have been known to take this situation in hand when the "city fathers" refused to deal with it. There are many examples of youth centers established and carried on by youth themselves. Such an experience could have valuable implications in developing responsibile citizenship if adequate guidance is provided. Learning units developed around this problem area should encourage pupils to develop recreational interests that will carry over into adult life. The school has a major obligation to provide intelligent guidance in the use of commercial recreation which carries over into adult life, e.g., use of newspapers and periodicals, radio, television, and movies.

It would only press the point to add that this problem area meets the criteria in providing for integration of knowledge by cutting across conventional subject matter lines, and providing for continuity in the emotional, physical, and intellectual aspects of learning.

The primary function of education can no longer be considered that of preparing people for college or for jobs—important as this may be. Education is preparation for living; and living is what is happening to youth every moment. Leisure is a part of this living. Learning how to put it to more constructive use is part of learning how to live.

[18] Gilbert C. Wrenn and D. L. Harley, *Time on Their Hands*. Washington, D. C., American Council on Education, 1941, p. XVII.

9. **Problems of Family Living.** How can family living make for happier individuals? Include such problems as: (a) Defining the characteristics of the democratic home; (b) Interpreting these characteristics in terms of behavior of the individual in the home; (c) Sharing in the maintenance aspects of family living; (d) Solving family conflicts through the family council; (e) Making a house a home; (f) Developing a consistent set of values to guide life through family living; (g) Having and rearing children; (h) Understanding myself and others as members of a closely knit group; (i) Creating our own home, i.e., problems of eugenics, courtship, marriage; (j) Considering the family as a unit in a democratic society and its relationship to other social institutions; (k) Planning in family living as to the use of resources such as time, money, energy; (l) Studying the effect of technological development on home life in our society; (m) Developing an understanding among family members of the problems of old-age; (n) Reconciling conflicts between home standards and community standards; (o) Participating as a family unit in developing community standards; (p) Considering similarities and differences concerning family life, in general, in a democracy and in other societies.

Concerns of adolescents which arise in the problems of family living stand out sharply in Keliher's categories "Establishing Independence" and "Establishing Self in Society."[19] Alberty feels that maturing adolescents derive and maintain a sense of security from status within the family group; this includes a feeling of responsibility, feeling that one counts, feeling of "belongingness," satisfaction through contribution to common ends, and gaining gradual independence.[20] Problems of relationships with parents and other members of the family, Doane concluded, are more often the problems of parents and other concerned adults than of the average youth. Doane found,[21] as might be expected, that interest in problems of planning for marriage and a family increases with age. On the other hand, we find this statement in *Youth and the Future*: ". . . every study of youth attitudes and interests makes plain the fact that young people themselves are deeply troubled by questions concerning family and marital relationship. In setting up any series of problem areas for planning in regard to youth and the future, obviously a place must be made for the problems of marriage and the home."[22]

[19] See Giles, McCutchen, and Zechiel, *op. cit.*, pp. 316-319.
[20] Alberty, *op. cit.*, p. 20.
[21] Doane, *op. cit.*, pp. 120-121.
[22] *Youth and the Future. op. cit.*, p. 164.

Regardless of argument, the fact remains that most youth are members of families, and that most youth look forward to establishing their own homes. The fact that in our society individuals reach sexual maturity before reaching economic, emotional, and social maturity produces conflicts in family life. The adolescent strives for independence from the family while still needing the love, affection, and feeling of security and belonging which the family should provide. When 185 high-school students in nine varied American communities were asked, "If your school offered the twenty-eight fields of study in consumer education which are described and you were to choose from them, which six would you most want to take? 'Making your house a home' ranked third with forty-two per cent choosing this area."[23]

Learning units developed from this problem area might provide for group meetings and panels in which were developed good parent-child-teacher relationships. The schools can do much to develop understanding between parents and children as the latter seek to establish independence from the family, yet have a guilt complex about doing so, and the former tenaciously cling to an authoritarian concept of parenthood. There is an opportunity here to intellectualize the meaning of democracy in living together. Such problems as consideration of the effects of scientific discoveries and inventions upon the constitution and functions of the family provide an opportunity to relate these effects to other social institutions, e.g., the school, government, church. This problem area provides for the integration of subject matter. The organized fields of knowledge such as psychology, sociology, home economics, economics, and physical science have a bearing on many of these problems. For instance, a learning unit pointed toward planning the use of family resources of time, money, and energy could well draw upon each of the above mentioned areas in their general education aspects.

Meaningful, direct experiences can be developed in dealing with problems related to planning, executing, and evaluating constructive

[23] Van Til, "Consumer Problems of the High-School Student," *The Bulletin of the National Association of Secondary School Principals,* **XXVIII,** 79-86 (November, 1944).

adolescent participation in family life. There are many opportunities to encourage the problem-solving approach in reconciling family conflicts and conflicts between home and community standards, and in participating as a family in developing community standards. As students consider the family life of other nations, there is further opportunity to reach beyond the confines of one family and one community and to build greater understanding among peoples. For instance, value patterns for family living in Russia, China, Latin America, and Great Britain are important.

Emotional and intellectual continuity in learning may be further developed as young people are guided in their plans for establishment of their own homes. They frequently express a need for special preparation for marriage, a need which is seldom met to their satisfaction. Practical experiences with children might be included in this problem area as the importance of education for child bearing and rearing is made explicit. The use of good reading materials for young people can help make these experiences most meaningful. Visits to various agencies which advance family welfare, e.g., the Children's Bureau, family counseling services, family welfare agency, etc., might help students gain some insight into the various ways society provides for promoting family life. A study of welfare agencies should promote critical thinking on the problem of whether society is conscious enough of the family as its basic social institution. Boy-girl relationships, courtship, marriage, child care, and planning a home, lead to a discussion of mate selection and the responsibilities of the democratic individual in the home.

This problem area might lead interested pupils into sociology and home economics. The area might lead into learning units growing out of such problem areas as *Social Relationships in a Democracy, Achieving World Peace in the Atomic Age, Constructive Use of Leisure Time, Economic Relationships in a Democracy,* and the like.

10. **Problems of Communication.** How can we express our ideas more clearly to others, and how can we understand better the ideas of other people? Include such problems as: (a) Exploring the various media which we have used to communicate our ideas and emotions, e.g., music, painting, dancing, dramatization, arts and crafts, group discussion, writing,

drawing, modeling; *(b)* Developing a pleasing voice; *(c)* Learning to listen, read, and observe with understanding; *(d)* Recognizing advantages that skill in communicating will give individuals in group situations; *(e)* Recognizing benefits and dangers of mass communication in light of democratic values; *(f)* Learning to compute and estimate speedily; *(g)* Utilizing many devices for communicating, such as radio, movies, film strips, slides, pictures, graphs, maps, printed materials, prints, and dramatics.

The problem of communication is central in human relationships. The process of critical thinking is perhaps too complex to suggest the exact part words play in it. The writings of semanticists such as Rudolph Flesch, S. I. Hayakawa, George Salt and others tend to validate the idea that critical thinking is improved as one develops facility in expressing his ideas clearly in words. This problem area offers opportunities to clarify the term "creative" as applicable to any reorganization of experience. Meaningful experiences can be developed as pupils use varied arts in clarifying and interpreting their own feelings and those of other people. The methods of instruction used here can help pupils move away from preoccupation with simple linear thinking about cause-effect relationships in unrelated segments of experience. There is much need for training students to perceive interrelationships among their experience. We also need to recognize the role of music, art, drama, and the dance as media of communication equally significant with the language arts.[24]

The role and problems of communications in international as well as domestic affairs can be pointed up through study of the uses of radio, television, daily papers, and news journals. Proper attention to communications might do much to ease our world tensions.

Learning units in this area offer experiences with a wide variety of resources. Certainly the arts include media to meet many individual differences. Analysis of information presented through mass media such as television, radio, lectures and the like can be a good learning experience. A wiser use of mass media in recreation could result for adolescents. New horizons in vocational possibilities might grow out of such a study. The field of electronics, to name only one, offers exciting new careers for young people.

[24] For further elaboration see: Francis Shoemaker, "Communication Arts in the Curriculum." *Teachers College Record,* 104-111 (November, 1955).

Cutting across traditional subject-field lines is natural in any learning unit drawn from this problem area. So are direct, first-hand experiences. An emphasis on democratic values, it would seem, is an important one in the area. Almost any significant problem chosen for study by young people would logically and psychologically lead into other areas of common need and interest.

11. **Problems of Democratic Government.** How do we share in government in a democracy? Include such problems as: (a) Learning the rights and obligations of citizens by sharing in solution of school and community problems pertinent at this level; (b) Seeing citizenship in a wider perspective by being concerned with current local, national, and international issues; (c) Gaining insight into problems of carrying on city, state, and national government through selected representatives; (d) Seeking understanding of the process of interaction in a group; (e) Studying how group conclusions are formed; (f) Developing a concept of personal responsibility for democratic government through sharing in school government; (g) Experiencing ways to improve school and community through democratic government; (h) Seeing the relationships between school-community problems and problems faced by adults outside the school; (i) Studying conditions under which individuals actually develop attitudes of responsibility, i.e., in sharing situations or relations.

Though Doane's study showed that, generally speaking, students ranked problems with a personal emphasis higher, in every area except two, than those with a social emphasis, he found that they still had much interest in current problems of a primarily social nature.[25]

The faculty of the Ohio State University School believes that adolescents beginning in the middle period (14-16 years) have a concern for how to have a good government. They believe that young people of 16-18 years usually exhibit a growing comprehension of the larger social, economic, and political issues of the day—that they are interested in the problems of government in the school, community, state and nation.[26]

Specific practice in government might be provided in each core group. Representatives might be elected to All-School Councils where students work with those from other core groups in cooperation with teachers and administrators to solve current school problems.

[25] Doane, *op. cit.*
[26] *How Children Develop, op. cit.*, pp. 65, 71, and 73.

In such an activity the problem-solving approach should be of concern. Students should have an opportunity through this problem area to learn the rights and obligations of citizenship in the wider community through their own experiences. Work on such community projects as traffic hazards, a campaign for more adequate recreational facilities, clean-up drives, surveys concerning fire prevention might take youth directly to the City Council, the traffic department, the health department and other governmenal bodies.

As the essentials of "participating" citizenship in a democracy are developed, students gain insights into the meaning of democracy. Respect for the opinions and civil rights of others grows, ability to take part in self-governing groups, and an awareness of the concept of the general welfare are developed as well as a willingness to be guided by this concept.

The interests of individuals can be extended in several ways through this problem area. Any learning unit developed from the area should concern itself with familiarizing students with major social problems and issues which should be explored by informed public opinion. The responsibilities of citizenship are generalized in a wider perspective at this point. As young people concern themselves about local and national issues and as they relate to the problems of carrying on government under constitutions and by selected representatives of the people, avenues to new units will be suggested. Several of the most obvious learning units which might become an outgrowth of a study of the problems of democratic government are housing, taxation, conservation of natural resources, and sharing in a world organization for peace.

12. **Problems of Community and Personal Health.** How can we achieve and maintain healthful living for ourselves and all others in the community? Include such problems as: (a) Ascertaining my present health status; (b) Understanding the problems and the importance of personal and community nutrition; (c) Understanding the facts about sexual development; (d) Cooperating with various community agencies in maintaining healthful living conditions; (e) Improving personal attractiveness and physical fitness by practicing healthful living; (f) Studying causes of accidents and removing these causes in homes and community, if possible; (g) Considering the social and economic aspects of personal and com-

munity health implied in health insurance, hospitalization, "socialized" medicine; (h) Providing and maintaining family health; (i) Understanding the problems of world health—the wider community; (f) Considering the present day causes of wide spread mental illness; (k) Understanding the importance of community and home life in development of mental health; (l) Considering the significance of recent findings in the field of psychosomatic medicine; (m) Clarifying the role of the federal government in making such protective devices as the Salk vaccine and fluoridation of water available to all.

Problems of community and personal health ranked high in the literature concerning problem areas reviewed by the writers—third in a list of fifty-two titles. The curriculum workers asked to give suggestions on the tentative formulation of problem areas overwhelmingly approved this area as appropriate for the core program. Several remarked that it was particularly helpful since students could immediately tackle concrete problems encountered here. The writers have found no study of adolescent needs which completely disregards problems in this area of living. In Doane's study of the needs of youth, when students were asked to choose the areas or "courses" they would like most to consider in school, *Health* ranked third, surpassed in percentage of choices only by *Vocational Choice* and *Getting Along with People*.[27] Doane's study showed that "How to keep well" would prove a more satisfactory focal point for instruction than would a topic such as "Glands and Their Functions." Alberty's study shows that youth develop concerns about maintaining personal health and promoting healthful living by providing for the protective and maintenance phases of health, providing for proper recreation and optimal physical and organic development, developing a zeal for promoting health in the wider community, and providing for adequate emotional and mental development in relation to personal health.[28] In Van Til's consumer education study, students ranked "Making the Most of the Health You Have" fifth out of a possible six fields chosen from a list of twenty-eight fields in which they would like most to take "courses." Van Til found it was not "normality" that troubled students. It was "how health affects your appearance

[27] Doane, *op. cit.*, pp. 79-80.
[28] Alberty, *op. cit.*, p. 20.

and your earnings." "What foods we need and how to get them" was of great interest.[29]

The continuous use of the problem-solving approach in such an area as health presents opportunity for growth in democratic values. These values can be developed through comparisons of the scientific method and various unscientific ways of reaching health conclusions. If pertinent concerns of adolescents such as nutrition, personal attractiveness, and earning capacity are related to health, this could be a significant opportunity for pupils to re-examine some of their basic values. The present major trends in health policies can be used to help youth generalize beyond their own experiences to a social concern about healthful living for all people. For instance, the current issues of internationalism, interdependence, growth of government regulation, and growth of technology, as they affect health in the home, community, and the world, might be used as points of discussion. Social concern might well be emphasized in this area as boys and girls study social diseases and their effect upon the general welfare. The maturity level of the group indicates the degree of readiness for such a discussion.

Cooperative planning may go even further than teacher-pupil, pupil-pupil, and teacher-teacher planning in this area. Various community groups might come into the planning of learning activities as students address themselves to community health problems. Such an activity might stem from an immediate problem such as an epidemic, rodent control, sanitary conditions in slum areas, or sources of milk supply and the like. Here there are concrete jobs to be done. There is a rich variety of resources in this area which might be drawn upon, i.e., movies, film strips and slides, doctors, nurses, public health officials, a wide variety of reading material and posters, as well as the conditions of the community itself. The subject matter of biology, physiology, psychology, economics, home economics, and sociology has a direct bearing upon many of these problems in their interrelated aspects. No one of these areas should presume to deal adequately with, for instance, the social and economic aspects of personal and community health implied in health insurance, hos-

[29] Van Til, *op. cit.*, p. 79.

pitalization, or "socialized" medicine. Further, continuity in the learning process may be provided in this area as students consider developments and their implications in the area of mental health.

Developments in this problem area might lead into such special interest areas as natural sciences, health and physical education, home economics, and economics and sociology. Leads are provided here for learning experiences developed from such problem areas as *Family Living, Use of Leisure, Economic Relationships in a Democracy, Social Relationships, Self-Understanding,* and others.

Keeping healthy, then, is a genuine adolescent concern of a personal-social nature.

13. **Problems of Economic Relationships in a Democracy.** How can we become more intelligent consumers? How does the pattern of our economic life relate to the ideal of democratic economic participation of all? Include such problems as: (a) How can I know that I am getting my money's worth? (b) Government protection of the consumer; (c) Problems of banking, investment, etc.; (d) Duties and responsibilities of labor and management in production and management; (e) Various economic systems and implications of each for producing and distributing goods in a democracy; (f) The Marshall Plan and its implications for world security; (g) The place of credit in the economic system; (h) Recognizing cause and effect relationships in spending, saving and employment; (i) Changing pattern of family spending in the American economy; (j) Recognizing the family's stake in the general economic policy; (k) Understanding the changing pattern of government spending in American economy and its effect on group and individual welfare; (l) Understanding the whys and hows of the American system of taxation; (m) Recognizing the relationship between economic and social status; (n) Having experiences in choosing and buying goods and being responsible for money and its use; (o) Recognizing the trend toward economic interdependence; (p) Noting the trend toward concentration of wealth and monopoly controls and effects on individual and group welfare.

Symonds found on inspection of rankings in his study concerning the problems and interests of adolescents that, on the average, students found money to be their most serious problem area. Comments such as "Money—everyone has to give thought to it" were numerous.[30] The Commission on Secondary School Curriculum in its category

[30] Symonds, *op. cit.,* p. 513.

"Economic Relationships" included the need for wise selection of goods and services and the need for effective action in solving basic economic problems as concerns of youth.[31] Alberty's study, as those already mentioned, included as adolescent concerns an understanding of and participating in the solution of basic economic problems, capital and labor, government control, conflicting economic systems, unemployment, standards of living, and the like.[32] This latter interpretation seems to put the problems of adolescents in a wider perspective, i.e., a personal-social relationship. This problem area is built upon this concept.

As to value formation, implications for democracy, and devlopment of skill in the problem-solving technique, this problem area abounds in opportunity. The approach to the area may be intimate, personal problems or problems prominent in the news, e.g., aid to Europe, conditions in Britain under a Socialist government, the high cost of living. An important aspect of consumer education is choice-making. A technological age makes consumer consciousness inevitable. As youth are guided in applying criteria in choice-making, there is opportunity to help them build a philosophy of life which may determine choices throughout life as well as providing immediate guidance in buying specific articles. Further emphasis can be given through this area to democratic values in a learning unit developed around the duties and responsibilities of labor and management in production and distribution. The principle to be applied here is the progressive widening of the areas of mutually shared interests. High school students should be helped to recognize the power of values in various economic policies. These powerful trends of our time need intellectualization: collective action by groups such as labor and management, a growing concentration of economic power in a few corporations, and increasing centralization of power in the national government. Men hold economic philosophies rather than economic theories, and this is particularly true of adolescents who grasp adult slogans without questioning them. Problems of the latter nature would be more meaningful, perhaps, in the later years of the secondary school.

[31] *Science and General Education, op. cit.,* pp. 235-291
[32] Alberty, *op. cit.,* pp. 20-21.

Since problems of production, distribution, and consumption arise in respect to any kind of goods and services which a group is considering, many meaningful direct experiences can be planned in relation to the community. For instance, price and quality of similar goods in different types of stores might be compared. Certain items might be tested in the laboratory and related to the requirements of the Pure Food and Drug Laws. Business men might be interviewed concerning the economic problems of the community. Some insight can be gained into how the work of the community is carried on, through reading, observation, field trips, and interviews. Such a study has direct implications for developing civic competence through an awareness of social concerns which arise from working conditions. Guidance becomes functional again as students study how to spend their money wisely, and begin to consider how the changing pattern of government spending has affected their own allowances and the expenditures of their families.

Cutting across subject matter lines is brought about in this problem area as students draw upon economics, sociology, home economics, English, mathematics, and other areas to solve their problems. Pointers to other learning experiences in problem areas such as *Family Living, Social Relationships, Intercultural Relations* and *Achieving World Peace* are suggested.

14. **Problems of Achieving World Peace in the Atomic Age.** What are the contributions we can make toward world peace? How does atomic energy affect our living today? Include such problems as: (a) Exploring the causes of cultural conflict, e.g., economic, political, social; (b) Widening the areas of mutual concern and interests in the immediate and wider group; (c) Understanding the bases of world peace; (d) Basing emotionalized attitudes on sound, intellectual grounds; (e) Sharing effectively in a world organization such as United Nations; (f) Studying how education of the individual as a unique, dynamic, flexibly experiencing person contributes toward improving the situation; (g) Exploring present and probable future uses of atomic energy; (h) Considering how the benefits of atomic energy might be made available to all our people; (i) Considering problems produced by the liberation of atomic energy, e.g., philosophical, psychological, technological; (j) Studying the structure and function of organizations dealing with problems created or accentuated by atomic energy, e.g., United States Atomic Energy Commission, United Nations, and proposals for control of atomic energy for world security—differences

between United States and Russia at this point; (k) Widening horizons to include "One World" by gaining functional knowledge of how people live in other geographical areas, e.g., emphasizing both cultural differences and similarities—arts and crafts, religion, family life, means of livelihood, food, and their life values.

Any learning unit developed from this problem area will presumably evolve out of a value problem. The question is: "What kind of world do we want?" The value problem arises over and over again as students are guided in reconstructing their beliefs from an "America First" attitude to economic stability, social justice, and political equality for all people. The Commission on Human Relations points to adolescent concern over the ways people dominate and hurt each other. Included in this category is concerns[33] over the frailties of justice and of group domination in nationalism and war. The basic problem of personal security with younger adolescents in this area should be gradually widened to the problem of maintaining and improving civilization.

A concept of "One World" may be developed through emphasizing the similarities as well as the cultural differences of the people of the world. Many worthwhile direct and vicarious experiences can be planned by students and teachers in this area. These might include personal contacts with people from foreign countries, a rich variety of reading materials, film strips, television, and movies. Some groups have found field trips to the U.N. a most revealing experience. The arts and crafts, the family life, and the religion of these people might be explored through using the resources of the special-interest areas and the community. The values of cooperative planning can be generalized to include "One World" at this point. Emphasis upon planning how all people might share in the benefits of atomic energy would seem to be a positive approach to problems produced by nuclear fission. Studying the functions and current proposals of organizations such as the Atomic Energy Commission, NATO, and United Nations and the implications of these proposals for the economic, social, and political welfare of all people points toward intelligent world citizenship. This problem area has possibilities for

---

[33] See Giles, McCutchen, and Zechiel, *op. cit.*, pp. 317-318.

extending the interests of individual students into the physical sciences, mathematics, related arts, e.g., arts and crafts, industrial arts, home economics, and foreign languages. The problems encountered in learning units developed from this area of living must be explored by drawing upon these subjects and others.

The problems of achieving unity while providing for diversity might first be approached from the level of human relationships in the core class. It must, however, go further—to the family, the community, the nation, the world.

15. **Problems of Intercultural Relations.** What are the factors in living democratically with many diverse social groups? What is our individual and group responsibility in becoming aware of and helping to decrease intercultural tensions? Include such problems as: (a) Understanding the relationship of various groups in the environment to development of intercultural attitudes, e.g., various types of homes, churches, schools, and other community groups; (b) Understanding the effects in the immediate and wider community of bias, prejudice, and discrimination against minority groups; (c) Building an increasingly mature understanding of what democracy means, historically and ethically; (d) Learning increasingly to use the method of conferring—the method of basing group action on group discussion and decision; (e) Coming to understand the international aspect of inter-group prejudices and discriminations; (f) Understanding and appreciating the composite character of American population and its consequent advantage to our civilization; (g) Acting on the basis of thinking rather than on habit or pure impulse; (h) Studying various historic causes and their supporting rationalizations of group prejudices; (i) Building the habit of acting on the best that we have found, of living up to the highest insight that we can gain through searching; (j) Studying the problems of race and the evidences against racism; (k) Developing an awareness of intercultural tensions arising in the immediate community, e.g., race, religion, nationality; (l) Developing a feeling of personal responsibility for solving these problems through individual effort and by cooperating with community agencies; (m) Contributing toward individual growth by continual widening of areas of mutual concern among various groups; (n) Understanding the bases of world conflict; (o) Noting the conflicts in the school-community situation; (p) Breaking down these conflicts through studying the "facts" in each situation, and by cooperative dealing with common problems and interests.

There are very definite implications for this problem area which might be drawn from several presented previously. For instance, in

Problems of Achieving World Peace, Problems of Communication, Problems of Social Relationships, Problems of Using and Conserving Natural Resources, and in others, there should be emphases upon intercultural relations. Such a relatedness in the core program is both planned for and appropriate. Continuity in the learning process is thus achieved. Careful planning between teachers and pupils can avoid repetitious emphases of the same aspects of problems and avoid oversights in emphases. The maturity level, needs, problems, and interests of a particular group would influence greatly the choice of the learning unit.

The Commission on Human Relations points to the concern of adolescents over status of race or minority groups, differences in the mores within the same community, being a member of a rural group, and feelings of inferiority. These are concerns of both majority and minority groups.[34] This is one of the ways the adolescent seeks to establish himself in society. Direct experiences can be used admirably to deal with such problems in the immediate environment —school, home, and community. Undoubtedly there are different races, religions, and nationalities present in any community. Insight into the meaning of democracy can be gained through an exploration of the economic, social, and political status of various cultural groups represented in the community. As adolescents analyze the sources of their beliefs they can be guided to see that many of them are not grounded in fact, but in bigotry, hear-say, and gossip.

The value of cooperative planning among all groups to raise the standard of living is a point which might be raised with youth. There are opportunities here to demonstrate how people from different groups might come together to work on a common project initiated by a core group, e.g., community recreation, a nursery school for children of working mothers, or raising funds for a more adequate community library. There is ample opportunity afforded in such a project to generalize the concept of cooperative planning to a wider perspective—the nation, and the world. The building of common concerns is one issue in outlawing war.

The problem-solving technique can be further developed in the

[34] See Giles, McCutchen, and Zechiel, *op. cit.,* p. 319.

more mature adolescent as he examines the bases of intercultural conflict. There are wide resources available on this subject to extend thinking—movies, reading materials, film strips, and the like. Current legislative action concerning civil rights and fair employment practices can be considered by students. Such action may have meaning for better intercultural relations. Youth can express their views on legislation by writing their representatives urging legislation serving the welfare of the majority of the people. This could be done if real insight into the problems is evidenced by youth. Civic competence is not a "gift." It is learned.

This problem area suggests the extension of individual interests into such areas as political science, history, sociology, anthropology, home economics, foreign languages, and others. Learning units developed from the broad scope of this problem area might lead to further experiences in such areas of living as *Achieving World Peace, Communication, School Living,* and *Democratic Government.*

Chapter IV sets forth the procedures used by two schools to establish a *problem area* structure for a core program. Both schools had access to the study described in this chapter. They also used other such studies published.[35] Both used other procedures for arriving at a *problem area* structure which were adapted to the needs of the particular situation.

SELECTED BIBLIOGRAPHY

Adolescent Needs

Caswell, Hollis L., et. al., *The American High School.* Eighth Yearbook of the John Dewey Society. New York, Harper & Brothers, 1947. Chapter V.

Education For All American Youth—A Further Look. Washington, D. C., Educational Policies Commission, 1952.

Fostering Mental Health in Our Schools. 1950 Yearbook of the Association for Supervision and Curriculum Development. Washington, D. C., National Education Association, 1950. Chapters VI and VII.

Growing Up in An Anxious Age. 1952 Yearbook of the Association for Supervision and Curriculum Development, Washington, D. C., National Education Association, 1952.

[35] *Op. cit.,* footnote p. 5.

Helping Teachers Understand Children. Commission on Teacher Education. Washington, D. C., American Council on Education, 1945.

How Children Develop. A Report of the Faculty of the University School. Columbus, The Ohio State University, 1946.

Science in General Education. Committee on the Function of Science in General Education. Progressive Education Association. D. Appleton-Century Company, Inc., 1938. Chapters I-IV inclusive.

Problem Area Studies

Alberty, Harold, *Reorganizing the High School Curriculum.* New York, The Macmillan Company, 1953 (Revised), Chapter VI.

Bostwick, Prudence and Chandos Reid, *A Functional High School Program.* New York, Hinds, Hayden and Eldridge, Inc., 1947.

Lurry, Lucile L., "The Contribution of Home Economics to Selected Problem Areas in the Core Curriculum of the Secondary School." Unpublished Doctoral Dissertation, Columbus, Ohio, The Ohio State University, 1949.

Van Til, William, "A Social Living Curriculum for Post-War Secondary Education." Unpublished Doctoral Dissertation, Columbus, Ohio, The Ohio State University, 1946.

Instruments To Determine Common Needs

Minnesota Personality Scale. Grade 11-16; separate forms for men and women. John G. Darley and Walter J. McNamara; Psychological Corporation, 522 Fifth Avenue, New York 18, New York.

Mooney Problem Check List. Revised Edition, New York, The Psychological Corporation, 522 Fifth Avenue, 1950. (Four forms: High School, Junior High School, College, Adult.)

Ohio Social Acceptance Scale. Bureau of Educational Research, Ohio State University, Columbus, Ohio.

Pond's Student Interest Inquiry. Department of Public Instruction, Harrisburg, Pennsylvania.

SRA Youth Inventory (228 S. Wabash Avenue), Chicago, Science Research Associates.

Social Intelligence Test: George Washington University Series. Grades 9-16 and adults; 1 form; F. M. Moss, T. Hunt, and K. T. Omwake; Center for Psychological Service, George Washington University, Washington 6, D. C.

IV

MAKING A
PROBLEM AREA STUDY

The task of making a problem area study might be further clarified if the accounts of how this was done in two schools were presented. These schools are located in a large county school system surrounding the District of Columbia. One school has a pupil population of 459 and is located in the semi-rural area of the county. The other school has an enrollment of over 1200 and is situated in the metropolitan area. Both faculties were afforded consultant services from the central office staff and pertinent literature was made available to each. In the smaller situation described, the principal cleared the way for the study to be undertaken and the guidance counselor provided the key leadership. In the larger situation the principal gave substantial leadership to the problem area study.

DISCOVERING NEEDS OF PUPILS[1]

For several years the staff of the Fairmont Heights High School (grades seven to twelve inclusive) has been engaged in the problem of curriculum development. In order to get an understanding of the problem facing this group in its efforts to define the needs of its pupils one must know something of the school, its pupils, and teachers. The boys and girls of this school come from many varied backgrounds. Many of these children have had very difficult experiences and have the inarticulated feeling that life is a day to day affair that does not make much sense but is to be lived in terms of rather immediate-felt needs and desires. Some of these children come from isolated rural communities and have to be trans-

[1] Submitted by G. James Gholson, Principal, Fairmont Heights Junior-Senior High School, Prince George's County, Maryland.

91

ported to school by bus, while others live in walking distance in nearby urban centers adjacent to the District of Columbia.

Prior to the opening of this school in September, 1950, many of the pupils had gone to smaller schools in the county, and a rather large number had attended school in the District of Columbia. Many of the teachers coming into the new school had taught in other situations in the county and some had come from teaching positions in other states, while others were just out of college with no previous teaching experiences.

The staff decided very early in its deliberation that this school should have real meaning for the pupils in its care and that the task was to help "life make sense" for these boys and girls. It would be foolish to say that the early gropings of this staff were on a highly organized action research basis. Instead the staff decided to use the best of its thinking plus insights and understandings culled from the literature concerning the growth and development of boy and girls in promoting a functional school program. If teen-agers are to grow and function well in their present world and aid in the reconstruction of a better world in which to live, the teachers realized that they must be developing clearer understandings of the pressing issues and tensions of our present day society and a keener understanding and appreciation of the variations and likenesses of adolescents as they interact with their physical and social environment.

Fortunately many of the teachers in this situation had gone through several years of the Child Study Program as initiated by the University of Maryland. In this study the teachers had gradually deepened their understanding of causes that underlie behavior of individuals and had increased their skill in identifying behavior characteristics.

It might be well to state here three guiding principles upon which the faculty agreed at the outset of its working together:

A. Every human being has worth and dignity and significance as a personality.

B. The scientific method of thinking is a basic tool in the solution of problems.

C. Reciprocal individual and group responsibility for promoting common concerns is a necessity in an evolving democratic society.

Constantly evaluating the on-going process of the school against the above criteria has helped the staff to be more conscious of its role in helping pupils to become significant members of a democratic society.

The staff had agreed on a tentative statement of philosophy which embodied: (1) The purpose of education; (2) the nature of the democratic society; (3) the nature of the learning process, and (4) the nature of the individual.

During the years, 1950-51 and 1951-52, the teachers were challenged through their grade level groups to develop creative learning experiences in terms of the needs of their pupils as a basis for the development of the scope in all areas selected. Emphasis was placed upon the problem-solving approach. At this time the junior high school was organized upon a core framework and the senior high school used the subject-centered organization. In this procedure the faculty, through the grade level groups, was encouraged to:

1. Gather information concerning Prince George's County including such matters as characteristics of the population, socio-economic conditions, county history and geographical conditions.

2. Gather information concerning the student body through achievement scores, personality tests, check lists, observation, quesionnaires, and conferences.

3. Make an analysis of needs of adolescents as revealed in the literature such as Educational Policies Commission's, "Imperative Needs of Youth," Prudence Bostwick and Chandos Reid's, *A Functional High School Program*, Robert J. Havighurst, *Developmental Tasks and Education*, Ohio State University School's, *How Children Develop*, The American Council on Education's, *Helping Teachers Understand Children*, Harold Alberty's *Reorganizing the High School Curriculum* and Lucile L. Lurry's "The Contribution of Home Economics to Selected Problem Areas in the Core Curriculum of the Secondary School."

From an analysis of these studies the faculty felt that its boys and girls had problems in these broad areas of living: *The Values of Living, Living in a Scientific World, Communication in Contemporary Living, Family Living, School Living and Living in a Democratic Society.* It is important to note that learning units from these areas were developed in both the general education and the special-interest areas.

The faculty during 1950-51 and '52 developed resource guides in each of these areas of living. These guides were intended to help teachers:

1. Guide adolescents in developing greater control of their activities through use of the problem-solving approach.
2. Identify in relation to the six problem areas: (a) Conflicts, issues, tensions, (b) possible activities, (c) suggested resources and (d) probable outcomes.

Teachers were urged to keep a record of their pre-planning and the teaching-learning experiences developed with the pupils. These were reported to the grade level group of teachers for criticism. The faculty developed the following criteria for evaluating these experiences:

1. Is it a "real" problem for these boys and girls?
2. Is the development in accord with the philosophy of our school?
3. Does it make provision for pupil-teacher planning?
4. Has there been a change in behavior of the boys and girls?
5. Do the conclusions suggest "next" steps?

In the latter part of the 1951-52 school year the faculty felt that readiness had been developed for extending the core program into the senior high school. In order to do this they took another look at the over-all framework to see if there were gaps in the kinds of experiences being developed. During this study an attempt was made to differentiate the roles of general education and special-interest area education in a total school program. The following criteria were proposed for the selection of problem areas to be used as the basic curricular structure of the core program grades seven through twelve:

A problem area should:

1. Be a problem pertaining to common needs and interests of boys and girls in this culture.
2. Cut across subject matter lines.
3. Provide opportunity for direct and vicarious experiences.
4. Have available resource materials.
5. Provide for skills which will lead toward growth in tolerance, language arts, creativeness, written and oral expressions, critical thinking, self-direction, cooperativeness, and aesthetic values.
6. Provide leads to other problems.
7. Provide opportunity for use of problem-solving techniques.
8. Provide opportunity for generalizations beyond the experiences of the group.
9. Provide a balance of over-all relationships between felt needs and the demands of society.
10. Provide opportunity for cooperative planning.

Using the criteria developed the faculty revised its list of problem areas as follows:

1. Problems of School Living
2. Problems of Personal and Community Health
3. Problems of Intercultural Relations
4. Problems of Economic Relationships
5. Problems of Self Understanding
6. Problems of World Peace
7. Problems of Conservation of Natural Resources
8. Problems of Home and Family Living

9. Problems of Finding Values by Which We Live
10. Problems of Democratic Government
11. Problems of Communication in a Contemporary World
12. Problems of Vocations and Employment

These problem areas were pegged at each grade level—in order that a learning unit might be drawn from each, once in the junior high school and once in the senior high school. As the areas were pegged, attention was given to such specifics as drop-out rates, period of assuming family responsibility, and the need for making a vocational choice. At the present time (1955-56) learning units must be drawn from the following areas at the designated grade level:

Seventh Grade:
Problems of School Living
Problems of Personal and Community Health with emphasis on personal health
Problems of Intercultural Relations
Problems of Economic Relationships

Eighth Grade:
Problems of School Living
Problems of Self Understanding
Problems of World Peace
Problems of Conservation of Natural Resources
Problems of Home and Family Living

Ninth Grade:
Problems of School Living
Problems of Finding Values by Which We Live
Problems of Democratic Government (processes and development)
Problems of Communication in a Contemporary World
Problems of Vocations and Employment

Tenth Grade:
Problems of School Living
Problems of Personal and Community Health (emphasis on Community Health)
Problems of Intercultural Relations
Problems of Vocations and Employment

Eleventh Grade:
Problems of School Living
Problems of Self Understanding
Problems of Democratic Government

Problems of Conservation of Natural Resources
Problems of Community in a Contemporary World
Problems of Home and Family Living

Twelfth Grade:
Problems of School Living
Problems of Finding Values by Which We Live
Problems of Achieving World Peace
Problems of Economic Relationships

This school plans to use the results of the present problem area study for a period of two years. During this time data will be collected through classroom experiences, follow-up studies of graduates and conferences with parents, pupils, and teachers to determine validity. The results of such studies will suggest our next steps.

A PROBLEM AREA STUDY FOR CORE CURRICULUM DEVELOPMENT[2]

As a part of a program to develop a tenth grade core program, the Gwynn Park Junior-Senior High School of Brandywine, Maryland, made a study of the needs, interests, and problems of a particular student group. Since a well-defined core program based upon adolescent needs was already in effect in this school in grades seven, eight, and nine, the purpose of the study was to identify evolving needs and interests in order that continuous exploration and attack might be made upon common problems of immediate concern to the boys and girls of the group.

A committee composed of the guidance counselor, a ninth grade core teacher, and a teacher interested in teaching in the proposed tenth grade core program, developed a plan for a systematic survey and analysis of what this group of boys and girls considered important problems to them. It was decided to use two formal instruments of the inventory type, *Inquiry on Student Needs*[3] and the *Mooney Problem Check List,*[4] and to supplement these with a *free choice listing* by the students of the problems which they considered of vital interest.

The tests were administered by the counselor with the assistance of the ninth grade core teacher. The purpose of the survey was explained to the pupils who used assigned numbers rather than names to further the

---

[2] Submitted by Josephine Kelly, former guidance counsellor, Gwynn Park Junior-Senior High School, Prince George's County, Maryland.

[3] Pond, Frederick L., *Inquiry on Student Needs*. Department of Public Instruction, Harrisburg, Pennsylvania.

[4] Science Research Associates, Inc., 57 Grand Avenue, Chicago 10, Illinois.

assurance of confidential treatment of the individual check lists. Both of the problem inventories selected gave broad coverage of the nature and areas of adolescent problems and were easy to understand, administer, score, and interpret.

The *Inquiry on Student Needs* projected fifty question items in ten interest areas—Work, Health, Citizenship, Home, Thrift, Science, Appreciation, Leisure, Other People, and Language. Since it was simply a questionnaire for the study of expressed interests it had no basic difficult key or pattern of desirable responses for yielding scores for comparative (norms) analysis. In fact, for the purpose of determining which problems were sufficiently widespread to have implications for curriculum development, it was only necessary to make a simple tabulation and list items for each area in rank order of response frequency with per cent of total response (Table I, below).

Table 1

Tabulated Results of Inquiry on Student Needs

Items of Each Area in Rank Order of Response Frequency and Percentage

Work

Question	Response	Frequency	Per Cent
1. Do you feel the need for more information about jobs and professions?	yes	62	88.6
	no	5	7.1
	?	3	4.3
2. Do you know about local job opportunities, requirements, and pay?	no	45	63.4
	yes	20	28.2
	?	6	8.4
3. Would you like to have some part-time on-the-job work experience for which you would receive school credit?	yes	44	62.0
	?	18	25.3
	no	9	12.7
4. Do you know for what kind of work each of your school subjects can help to prepare you?	yes	40	56.3
	no	26	36.6
	?	5	7.1
5. Do you need, for your future life work, some course that your school does not have?	no	32	45.1
	?	20	28.2
	yes	19	26.7

Health

Question	Response	Frequency	Per Cent
1. Are you as happy as other people seem to be?	yes	62	87.3
	no	7	9.9
	?	2	2.8
2. Are you worried about your own growth or health?	no	53	74.6
	yes	18	25.4
	?	0	.0

Table 1—*Continued*

Health—Continued

Question	Response	Frequency	Per Cent
3. Can you apply first aid, and artificial respiration?	no	46	64.8
	yes	15	21.1
	?	10	14.1
4. Are you developing skill in any sport which you can follow after you leave school?	no	34	47.9
	yes	25	35.2
	?	12	16.9
5. Do you know how to select a well-balanced diet of carbohydrates, proteins, vitamins, etc?	yes	31	43.7
	no	27	38.0
	?	12	18.3

Citizenship

Question	Response	Frequency	Per Cent
1. Would you like to share with your classroom teachers in planning your school work?	yes	59	83.1
	?	8	11.3
	no	4	5.6
2. Do you feel at ease in talking or working with a person of another color, race, or creed?	yes	48	76.2
	no	10	15.9
	?	5	7.9
3. Have you seen a court or election officers when they are at work?	no	50	70.4
	yes	18	25.4
	?	3	4.2
4. Can you compare the freedoms of the American way of life with those of Communism or Socialism?	yes	42	59.2
	?	16	22.5
	no	13	18.3
5. Do you wish other students would like you better?	yes	39	54.9
	no	19	26.8
		13	18.3

Home

Question	Response	Frequency	Per Cent
1. Do you know how many marriages out of ten in the U.S. end in divorce?	no	64	90.2
	yes	4	5.6
	?	3	4.2
2. Do you feel that there is lack of understanding between you and your parents or brothers and sisters?	no	53	76.8
	yes	15	21.7
	?	1	1.5
3. Do you understand your own sexual growth and its effects on what you think, feel, and do?	yes	52	73.2
	?	12	16.9
	no	7	9.9
4. Can you read the meters—gas, water, electric—in your home?	no	44	62.0
	yes	25	35.2
	?	2	2.8

Table 1—*Continued*

Home—Continued

Question	Response	Frequency	Per Cent
5. Do you need to learn about making dates or choosing a mate or making a home?	no	42	59.2
	yes	19	26.7
	?	10	14.1

Thrift

Question	Response	Frequency	Per Cent
1. Do you know how to pick the best quality in clothes and food?	yes	52	73.2
	no	14	19.7
	?	5	7.1
2. Do you know where to find information on what and how to buy?	yes	48	67.6
	no	20	28.2
	?	3	4.2
3. Do you know how to invest money—buy stocks and bonds, etc.?	yes	37	52.1
	no	24	33.8
	?	10	14.1
4. Are you, yourself, ever asked to judge the success of your school work or personal development?	yes	33	46.5
	no	22	31.0
	?	16	22.5
5. Can you tell if what is said in advertising or politics is true?	no	35	49.3
	yes	26	36.6
	?	10	14.1

Science

Question	Response	Frequency	Per Cent
1. Do you feel that your work in science is part of your own life and problems?	yes	59	83.1
	no	10	14.1
	?	2	2.8
2. Do you know how many people are killed every day on highways and in accidents in the U.S.?	no	56	78.9
	yes	12	16.9
	?	3	4.2
3. Do you need to know how to work out practical problems, gathering facts and information, and drawing conclusions?	yes	37	52.2
	no	19	26.7
	?	15	21.1
4. Do you understand how motors, toasters, thermometers, etc. work?	yes	34	47.9
	no	32	45.0
	?	5	7.1
5. Do you understand people—what makes them think, feel, and act as they do?	yes	29	40.8
	no	22	31.0
	?	20	28.2

Table 1—*Continued*

Appreciation

Question	Response	Frequency	Per Cent
1. Is your school a beautiful place in which to live nad learn?	yes	58	81.7
	?	7	9.9
	no	6	8.4
2. Have you been on any trips to art museums or concerts or for nature study?	yes	57	80.3
	no	13	18.3
	?	1	1.4
3. Do you believe that you are learning to enjoy better art, music and literature?	yes	50	70.4
	no	12	16.9
	?	9	12.7
4. Do you know the names of adult groups in your community which promote literature, art, music, etc.?	no	48	67.6
	yes	16	22.5
	?	7	9.9
5. Do you read the excellent fiction and other literature which is about your school subjects?	no	33	46.5
	yes	26	36.6
	?	12	16.9

Leisure

Question	Response	Frequency	Per Cent
1. Do you feel that you are "left out of things" in school?	no	62	87.3
	yes	5	7.1
	?	4	5.6
2. Does your community provide enough places for wholesome recreation?	no	35	49.3
	yes	28	39.4
	?	8	11.3
3. Are you doing any work on what may be your life-time hobbies?	no	35	49.3
	yes	28	39.4
	?	8	11.3
4. Is your leisure time being spent as you hope your own children will spend their leisure time?	yes	34	47.9
	no	21	29.6
	?	16	22.5
5. Would you like to work on some community welfare activities (Red Cross, etc.) in your leisure time?	no	33	46.5
	yes	26	36.6
	?	12	16.9

Other People

Question	Response	Frequency	Per Cent
1. Do you prefer usually to be by yourself rather than with other students?	no	63	88.7
	yes	7	9.9
	?	1	1.4
2. Do you need to know about introducing people, courtesy, etc.?	yes	38	53.5
	no	26	36.6
	?	7	9.9

Table 1—*Continued*

Other People—Continued

Question	Response	Frequency	Per Cent
3. Do you know how to be a good committee chairman?	no	37	52.2
	?	18	25.3
	yes	16	22.5
4. Do you feel the need to learn more about getting along with other people?	yes	34	47.9
	no	31	43.7
	?	6	8.4
5. Do you wish that your teachers would like you better?	yes	32	45.0
	no	26	36.7
	?	13	18.3

Language

Question	Response	Frequency	Per Cent
1. Do you wish that you knew how to study better?	yes	52	73.3
	no	18	25.3
	?	1	1.4
2. Do you know how to use the card catalog, the Reader's Guide, etc., in the school library?	yes	50	70.4
	no	18	25.4
	?	3	4.2
3. Are you developing the habit of daily newspaper reading?	yes	42	59.2
	no	23	32.4
	?	6	8.4
4. Do you use good written and spoken English in all of your classes?	no	31	43.7
	yes	22	30.9
	?	18	25.4
5. Can you write a good letter or composition?	yes	28	39.4
	no	26	36.7
	?	17	23.9

A study of the tabulated results revealed significant response and interest in the following areas:

1. General information about jobs and professions.
2. Information about local job opportunities, requirements and pay.
3. On-the-job work experience correlated with school.
4. Development of better study habits.
5. Opportunity to see government in action.
6. Comparative information on Democracy, Communism, Socialism, etc.
7. Development of skill in critical thinking (the recognition of the truth in advertising or politics).
8. Development of ability to work and play with other people (introductions and courtesy; how to be a good committee chairman; the techniques of being liked by other students and teachers).

The *Mooney Problem Check List* was used next to verify and supplement the findings of the first questionnaire. This check list provided a broad coverage with 210 problem items divided into the seven major areas of Health and Physical Development; School; Home and Family; Money; Work; Future; Boy and Girl Relations; People in General; and, Self-centered Concerns.

Since the results of this questionnaire reflected only positive reactions— pupils were asked to underline just the problems which were of concern to them—it was possible to tabulate and organize the data in simple form to show rank order of response frequency, per cent of total response, and the mean and median response for each of the major areas.

Table II

Tabulated Results of Mooney Problem Check List

Data Organized by Areas and Total Response

Problem Area	Frequency Score	Per Cent	Mean	Median
School	508	23.8	6.8	4.2
Money, Work, Future	347	16.3	4.6	1.3
Self-centered Concerns	313	14.6	4.2	1.3
Health & Physical Develop.	284	13.3	3.8	1.2
Rel. to People in General	269	12.6	3.6	1.2
Boy & Girl Relations	244	11.4	3.2	1.2
Home & Family	172	8.0	2.3	1.9
ΣFS=	2137	100.0	2.8	23.5

The problem *items* emphasized under each of the five highest ranking areas of interest in this check list were as follows:

1. School
   a. Desire for better study habits
   b. Lack of interest in books
   c. Fear of failure
2. Money, Work, Future
   a. Interest in occupational information
   b. Need for more educational planning
   c. Interest in self-appraisal and career planning
3. Self-centered Concerns
4. Health and Physical Development
   a. Problems of adolescent emotional and physical adjustment to an adult world
5. Relationship to People in General
   a. Problems of adjustment to immediate group living
   b. Desire to understand conditions blocking world understanding and peace

For the third phase of the study, the ninth grade core teacher conducted the "free choice" survey, requesting all ninth graders to list three problems which they would like to explore the following year if the core curriculum were extended to the tenth grade.

In order of response frequency and in original wording the four highest choices were:

1. Different countries
2. How do countries get into wars? What countries have been at war most? Why?
3. Choosing an occupation
4. Famous people all over the world

The committee then analyzed and correlated the results of the two questionnaires and the "free choice" listing, and the teacher interested in teaching tenth grade core prepared a possible scope for the following problem areas which were finally determined:

1. In the Personal-Social Area
   a. School Living
   b. Personality Development
2. In the Social-Civic-Economic Area
   a. Employment and Vocations
   b. Achieving World Peace in the Atomic Age

Possible scope and learning activities in each of these problem areas were suggested by teachers, pupils and administrators. This work was presented to parents for their suggestions. The parents asked, after studying the data, that the problem area *Family Living* be added to the scope. The framework indicated below incorporates the ideas of all concerned. This provided the starting point for the cooperative development of resource guides.

It was felt that this study, which was inexpensive and simple to conduct, afforded a sound basis for the blocking out of problem areas with potentialities for meeting the common needs and extending the interests of these particular boys and girls.

1. Problems of School Living
   a. Problems:
      (1) Understanding the contributions of the teachers to school life.
      (2) Understanding the opportunities offered by the school and how these can best be used by students.
      (3) Study of the cost of free public education.
      (4) What are the purposes to be accomplished through school clubs and extra curricular activities?

       (5) How can we use a study hall more efficiently and effectively?
  b. Learning Activities:
       (1) Personal interview with members of the faculty on such topics as: What is my responsibility and place in the total school picture?
       (2) Individual students arrange for members of the faculty to speak to the class on topics to be an outgrowth of one of the above problems.
       (3) Show in graphic form the amount of taxes being spent on education, etc. in Maryland, Prince George's County, and other places.
       (4) Make a comparative study of other state systems of taxation, and show in graphic form how the taxes are spent.
       (5) Posters, drawings, cartoons to be made by students illustrating such topics as:
          (a) Methods of taxation present and past.
       (6) Study the constitutions of the different clubs and develop a chart showing aims and purposes.
       (7) Make a schedule of classes for an imaginary school.
2. Problems of Personality Development
  a. Problems:
       (1) Why is personal appearance a vital part of your personality?
       (2) What are my own personality characteristics?
       (3) How can I make and carry out plans for improving my personality?
       (4) What are some of the problems that I have, and where can I go to obtain help with my problems?
       (5) Gaining some insight into the problems of fear and insecurity.
       (6) What are the social skills necessary for a happier life, and how can I acquire them?
       (7) What causes people to develop anti-social tendencies?
       (8) Achieving increasingly mature relationships with the opposite sex.
  b. Learning Activities:
       (1) Panel discussions on such topics as:
          (a) Why is personal appearance a vital part of my personality?
          (b) What makes some individuals feel insecure?
       (2) Make a personality inventory sheet and use it to evaluate your personality.
       (3) Sociodramas showing desirable and undesirable personality traits.

    (4) Have parents, teachers, and pupils discuss in a panel those characteristics which they look for in a student and consider desirable.

    (5) Give inventory tests such as: Test on Manners.

    (6) Show movies, film strips, etc. on subject.

3. Problems of Employment and Vocations

   a. Problems:

     (1) Education and its relationship to the students' lifetime vocation.

     (2) What vocational opportunities are available in the immediate community now?

     (3) Choosing a vocation appropriate to the changing American and world scene.

     (4) What are the requirements for

       (a) College entrance?

       (b) Other occupations?

     (5) The problem of getting and keeping a job—what are the procedures in obtaining a job?

     (6) Problem of labor management relationships.

   b. Learning Activities:

     (1) Make a survey of different college entrance requirements.

     (2) Make a survey of the vocational opportunities in immediate community.

     (3) Make and write research paper on an occupation of interest to the pupil.

     (4) Spend day on the job.

     (5) Dramatize the selling of themselves, product.

     (6) Dramatize applying for a job—have outsiders come in and act as interviewer—students evaluate themselves and classmates.

4. Problems of achieving World Peace in the Atomic Age

   a. Problems:

     (1) Conflicting Ideologies

       (a) What are the different conflicting ideologies?

       (b) When, where, and by whom were these ideologies originated?

       (c) For what reason or reasons do people adopt these different ideologies?

       (d) What problems are created by the existence of different ideologies side by side?

     (2) The problem of peace in an atomic age

       (a) At what period in the growth of the world did man turn to the idea of a world federation of states?

   (b) Trace the growth of the international organization of states.
     (2.1) Wilson's Fourteen Points
     (2.2) League of Nations
     (2.3) United Nations
   (c) What are and have been the weaknesses and strengths of world organizations?
   (d) What are the goals and objectives of the United States and her allies in respect to military preparedness?
   (e) What is the destructive potentiality of the hydrogen bomb?
   (f) What are the benefits to be derived from atomic energy?
   (g) Civil defense and its vital place in the world today.
  b. Learning Activities:
   (1) Organize and draw up a Civil Defense plan for the school.
   (2) Prepare a wall mural which shows the destructive powers of the hydrogen bomb—to be outgrowth of reading.
   (3) Show in graphic form the benefits of atomic energy and the need for it.
   (4) Develop charts showing the League of nations and United Nations.
   (5) Make a chart showing differences and similarities among different ideologies of the world.
   (6) Write a research paper on one of the prevailing ideologies in today's world.
   (7) Show films such as:
    The 400,000,000, Brandon Films, Inc.
    1600 Broadway, New York 19.
 5. Problems of Family Living
  a. Problems:
   (1) How can we become more intelligent consumers?
   (2) What are the characteristics of the democratic home?
   (3) Should everybody share in the maintenance aspects of family living?
   (4) Solving of family conflicts.
   (5) Planning in family living as to the use of resources such as money, time, energy.
   (6) The effect of technological development on home life in our society.
   (7) What makes a "house" a "home"?
  b. Learning Activities:

(1) Dramatize a typical democratic home.
(2) Set up a typical family situation and have group (family) budget money for the month.
(3) Make chart showing number of women employed today as compared to twenty-five years ago, and kinds of occupations they hold.
(4) Make a chart showing inventions which add to leisure time of family.
(5) Set up family problems and have groups solve problems; make note of methods used.
(6) Write a one act play showing typical American family and methods used to solve their family problems.

Since the basic philosophy of the existing core program of this school was that the core should concern itself with problems which are significant in the lives of adolescents in our society, the results of the problem area study were accepted by the school and made the basis of a plan for extending the core curriculum into the tenth grade.

Such a proposal did not entail drastic reorganization or parental skepticism in the case of the Gwynn Park Junior-Senior High School. The climate of the community had been entirely receptive to the idea of the core program at the junior high school level. However, in the interest of good home and school relationships, the Curriculum Development Committee planned a Parents' Night to present the proposed curriculum revision. The planning committees provided for the joint participation of parents, teachers, and pupils and the presentation took the form of a panel discussion followed by a social hour. With parents, teachers, and pupils enthusiastic about the program, it moved forward.

V

DEVELOPING RESOURCES FOR USE IN THE CORE PROGRAM

Dealing with large, comprehensive problem areas which cut across conventional subject-field lines creates a problem of resources. No single source can deal adequately with the wide range of problems of youth—how to care for personal belongings, how to use leisure time wisely, how to use the library, how to write a business letter, how to discover personal aptitudes and abilities, how to punctuate creative writing, how to dress appropriately within the limits of the family budget—to name a few. The teacher no longer can depend primarily on the textbook, but needs a vast reservoir of materials. The development of resource guides[1] has brought this problem under control. These are intended for teacher use in the preplanning which must preface teacher-pupil planning in the classroom. Resource guides do not prescribe the exact content or procedures but serve to identify the basic problems and issues that have a bearing on an area of living and to give security to the teacher by suggesting a wide variety of activities, evaluative techniques, and teaching materials.

In the preceding chapter, suggestions for developing the content of the core (broad problem areas in which youth usually have problems) were presented. The purpose of this chapter is twofold: first, to suggest a technique which a group of teachers might find helpful as they work together on developing resource guides for use in the core; second, to clarify this technique by presenting an illustrative resource guide.

[1] As used here resource guide is synonymous with resource unit.

108

Developing a Resource Guide

Let us suppose that a group of teachers is interested in developing a resource guide dealing with an area such as *Intercultural Relations*. What are the steps that such a group might take?

It would be advantageous, of course, to have represented in the group all the subject fields that have a contribution to make to the solution of problems of intercultural relations. This would certainly include teachers of social studies, science, language arts, music, physical education, mathematics, and the arts. In addition to utilizing the total resources of the school—persons and materials—the group, no doubt, would make every effort to draw on community resources as it seeks to isolate the problems and issues and the resources for dealing with them. In short, these teachers would marshal all of the available resources of the school and community as they work together on developing a guide that would suggest potentially rich experiences for pupils.

Many teachers and administrators underestimate the amount of time and energy which must be expended in order to build a resource guide. As a consequence, they may become frustrated when their goal is not readily achieved. The group may decide to accept a resource guide worked out by some other group or to put together fragments taken from several sources. The examination of suggestions included in various units undoubtedly is a vital step in building a resource guide, but it is fallacious to assume that resource guides worked out for one situation are adequate for another. Such shortcuts also eliminate the values derived from working together on a common problem.

The way in which the group proceeds will depend upon the specific situation. In some schools it may be desirable to work as a total group. In others, the most workable plan might be to assign specific jobs to small groups and individuals. Regardless of the way the group is organized for the development of a resource guide, however, there seem to be these steps involved: (1) formulating scope and objectives; (2) constructing possible activities; (3) developing evaluative techniques; (4) compiling sources of teaching materials. It is assumed, of course, that a sense of direction for such development is provided by the basic philosophy developed by the faculty of the school.

Formulating Scope and Objectives. Formulating scope and objectives is the initial step in the building of a resource guide. As a preliminary step the group should make a survey of the literature bearing on the problem area, call in resource people, and the like, in order to gain an over-all view of the area—the problems and issues involved. After the group has made a careful survey, a plan for formulating the scope and objectives needs to be worked out.

One way to define the scope is to organize the problems and issues that have a bearing on the problem area under appropriate categories. For example, problems and issues related to *Intercultural Relations* can be grouped in terms of three levels: Community, National, International. Another way to define the scope is to organize the possible learning experiences around the three phases of a learning unit—initiatory, developmental, and culminating. In neither case are these categories mutually exclusive for complex human problems do not lend themselves to neat compartmentalization. They serve, however, as centers for organizing the learning experiences.

Some teachers may wish to write out in considerable detail the issues and problems under the various categories. Others may be satisfied with a brief statement that "sets the stage" for the development of the rest of the guide. In any case, regardless of the amount of detail a group sees fit to include, a clear statement of the scope of the problem area must be made.

Specific statements of the basic values, the attitudes, skills, appreciations, and understandings to which the problem area is expected to contribute should be made. For example, if it is expected to contribute to an examination of beliefs and attitudes that influence intercultural relations, to an understanding of the composite character of the American population, and to an appreciation for the contributions of all cultures to the welfare of mankind, these should be stated clearly. This step requires particular attention for it is basic to the construction of possible student activities and the development of evaluative techniques.

Constructing Possible Activities. After reaching basic agreements
as to the general nature of the area, scope, and objectives, the group
is in a position to construct activities in which students might engage
as they come to grips with the problems in a particular area of living.
These activities should be constructed in relationship to the scope
and objectives and in terms of a set of criteria. The group would
naturally set up its own guide lines for the construction of activities.
The following set of criteria, however, might serve to give direction
to the efforts of the group. Core activities should:

1. **Have potentialities for developing and promoting values basic to
democratic living.** Activities should promote personal characteristics
essential to democratic living, such as social sensitivity, tolerance, cooperativeness, the disposition and ability to use reflective thinking in the
solution of problems, creativeness, self-direction, and esthetic appreciation.
Activities that encourage group work should be emphasized, since it is
through the group process that students learn the meaning of the shared
roles of leadership, the responsibilities inherent in freedom, the necessity
for critical thinking in the solution of problems, and the need for
continuous evaluation both of the products of group action and of the
processes employed.

2. **Deal with significant problems and issues that have a bearing on
a problem area without regard to subject-field boundaries.** Activities
should be directed toward solving students' problems, meeting their needs,
and extending their interest in a given problem area without regard to
the organization or content of any one subject-field. Activities that serve
merely as "busy work" or as "lesson-learning assignments" are relatively
fruitless and should be avoided.

3. **Be sufficiently diversified to provide for individual differences among
students.** To provide for the fulfillment of the highest potentialities of
each student, activities should include a wide variety of learning experiences such as dramatizing, experimenting, taking field trips, displaying,
reporting, seeing films and filmstrips, interviewing, drawing, painting,
constructing, discussing, and reading and writing. The number of activities available should be large enough to enable the teacher to provide for
individual differences among students.

4. **Suggest sufficient direction for action.** To be of maximum value
to the teacher, activities should be so stated as to imply a possible plan
for carrying them out. For example, proposing a field trip to a museum
is of little value unless accompanied by suggestions as to what students
might observe during their visit and what they might do as a follow-up

in terms of their learning unit. Activities, however, should not be so detailed that they eliminate or stifle teacher-pupil planning or pupil creative planning.

5. **Provide the kinds of experiences that are likely to contribute to the pupils' all-round development.** Since the physical, mental, social, and emotional aspects of behavior are inseparable and function as a unit, activities should provide for all phases of development. For example, an adequate treatment of race relations would include its biological, psychological, and social aspects.

6. **Be comprehensive rather than fragmentary in character.** Since learning takes place most effectively in terms of wholes rather than fragments, emphasis should be placed upon significant comprehensive activities rather than upon piecemeal activities which students must somehow fit together. "Comprehensive" means that a number of activities related to a particular problem or issue are grouped under an appropriate heading. For example, activities that relate to the community level in the problem area *Intercultural Relations* may be grouped under such headings as: Racial Problems, Religious Problems, Ethnic Problems, Socio-Economic Problems.

7. **Provide experiences appropriate for the various phases of a learning unit.** Learning units involve three interrelated phases—initiatory, developmental, and culminating. A list of possible activities should include those centering around defining and developing the problem, investigating the problem, presenting the findings and evaluating the results.[2]

Developing Evaluative Techniques. In developing a resource guide, some suggestions as to possible evaluative techniques should be included. These, necessarily, would be rather general in nature. Techniques appropriate for a particular situation will suggest themselves to teacher and pupils as they work and plan together in the classroom.

Some teachers may wish to develop a special section on evaluative activities to be used at the conclusion of the guide. Others may feel

[2] Adapted from the criteria set up cooperatively by Elsie J. Stalzer (Alberty), "Contributions of Mathematics to a Proposal for Reorganizing General Education in Secondary Schools on the Basis of a Core Program." Unpublished Doctoral Dissertation, Columbus, Ohio, The Ohio State University, 1952, William Jennings, "Contributions of Business Education to Selected Problem Areas of General Education in the Secondary School." Unpublished Doctoral Dissertation, Columbus, Ohio, The Ohio State University, 1952; and Monir Kamel Mikhail, "Contributions of Science to Selected Problem Areas Proposed for a Program of General Education in the Secondary School." Unpublished Doctoral Dissertation, Columbus, Ohio, The Ohio State University,

that the objectives and activities already worked out are sufficiently suggestive of specific evaluative techniques and that no further attention—other than a brief discussion of general techniques—need be given to this phase of the guide. However, regardless of the amount of time to be spent in dealing with this phase of the guide, there should be ample opportunity to explore and reach some agreements on the general procedure involved in developing evaluative techniques. One way to reach such agreements is to devise several evaluative techniques which *might* be useful in determining whether the objectives of the problem area have been achieved.

The general procedure in developing evaluation techniques involves formulating and defining objectives, suggesting situations in which the achievement of the objectives can be demonstrated, and selecting promising evaluation techniques. The group has already developed a set of objectives for the resource guide. The next step is to define each of the objectives.

In defining the objectives, the group should attempt to clarify the meaning of the objective by describing the kinds of behavior they had in mind when this objective was formulated. This step is essential because the behaviors implied by a list of objectives are not always clear. For example, in a resource guide on *Intercultural Relations*, an objective such as "practicing wholesome, friendly, mutually respectful human relationships in everyday living," may mean different things to different people. Only if there is a clear description of the behaviors expected can there be agreement on what is to be evaluated. In the case of the example, some student's observable behavior might be described as follows: accepts the contributions of all members of the class regardless of racial, religious, national, or socio-economic background; associates with and is friendly toward individuals of different groups; refrains from using names such as "nigger," "wop," or "hunky"; recognizes and combats prejudice.

The next step is to identify situations in which students have an opportunity to display these types of behavior. When the objectives are clearly defined this step is not difficult. For example, one behavior pattern described above was "associates with and is friendly toward individuals of different groups." Students have opportunity to exhibit this behavior in connection with unit activities which require that they work in committees, participate in class discussions, respond to sociometric surveys, and the like. Teachers must be alert to other situations which provide the student with an opportunity to display the desired behaviors. Such situations as walking through the halls, eating lunch with other students, forming casual groups on the playground, and participating in athletics and social clubs are rich sources of evidence of the student's growth toward the achievement of the objectives. This step suggests a wider range of situations which might be used in evaluation than has commonly been recognized. Evaluative situations need not and should not be limited to those of the paper and pencil variety. Any situation in which students have an opportunity to exhibit the expected behavior is appropriate.

Finally, techniques for evaluating the changes that take place in student behavior must be worked out. In the case of the example, some techniques which the group might consider are: the observation of students as they work in groups; the analysis of tape-recorded class discussions; the use of published tests concerned with human relations; anecdotal records of student growth in developing understandings and appreciations basic to the unit; informal conferences with students to discuss specific phases of the problem; reports from parents and others of the degree to which students have developed as a result of the unit study. These techniques illustrate the variety which might suggest themselves to teacher and students as they define their goals. The techniques which might be included in a resource guide would necessarily be more general. These general techniques would probably include both informal value-analysis techniques and formal procedures for testing the outcomes of the unit.

Compiling Sources of Teaching Materials. As teachers survey and analyze the problem, and construct appropriate activities and evaluative techniques, they should build lists of resources for student and teacher use. These lists should include books, pamphlets, and periodicals, films and filmstrips, recordings, free and inexpensive materials, community resources and resource people, maps and charts, and the like. Where possible, the cost of these teaching materials and their sources should be included.

PROBLEMS OF EDUCATION IN AMERICAN DEMOCRACY:[3]
AN ILLUSTRATIVE RESOURCE GUIDE

As never before, the American public seems deeply concerned about its school system. In the vast literature on education, there is more discontent than complacency, more blame than praise, and there is an uneasy feeling that the schools have somehow failed to do their job. Educational controversies on aims and direction, and content and method exist throughout our educational system.

The schools are a vital force in strengthening and furthering the democratic ideals. Educators and the public should assume the responsibility for examining and evaluating the educational programs and procedures of the schools. Such critical examination calls for an enlightened citizenry with an understanding of the implications of the educational problems which confront the individual, community, state, and nation and the processes through which intelligent action may enhance the common welfare.

This resource guide is designed to help students become increasingly aware of the problems confronting education at all levels.

Objectives   To help students:

1. Explore educational opportunities in the school and community and know how to make best use of them
2. Appreciate the values of education to both the individual and society
3. Evaluate the effectiveness of the school in meeting their needs as well as those of the community
4. Develop an insight into the relationship of education to the standard of living in a community
5. Gain an understanding of the impact of education on such social institutions as the home, church, and government
6. Study the organizations and functions of the local, state and federal governmental agencies controlling school systems
7. Realize the responsibilities of governmental units toward providing equality of educational opportunity for all American youth
8. Understand the influence of pressure groups on education
9. Examine current criticisms of education and develop constructive measures for eliminating the causes of dissatisfaction

---

[3] The statement of objectives, scope, and activities while drawing heavily upon, is a revision of the cooperative research of Stalzer (Alberty), Jennings, and Mikhail. (See *Ibid.*) The selections dealing with evaluation, bibliography, and teaching aids are additions to the original study.

10. Understand the role of education in perpetuating and re-creating democratic ideals
11. Trace the development of education in the United States
12. Compare the educational systems of various countries
13. Understand the role of education in promoting international understanding

Scope Studying problems of education at the:
   I. Personal-school level
  II. Community level
 III. State and national levels
  IV. World-wide level

Activities

I. *Studying Problems of Education at the Personal-School Level*
   A. School Plant
      1. Set up criteria for evaluating the physical plant of the school and suggest possible improvements.
      2. Make a map of school buildings and grounds. Locate laboratories, shops, libraries, core rooms, gymnasium, lunch room, offices, school store, and football and baseball fields. Make copies available to new students.
      3. Take pictures or make sketches of several school buildings in the community. What changes are in evidence in the newer buildings? Discuss.
      4. Plan a model school building. Make a display of the drawings or models constructed by various members of the class.
   B. Student and Staff Relations
      1. Set up role-playing situations which illustrate the "do's and don'ts" of good school citizenship.
      2. Discuss the responsibilities of school citizenship. Plan an assembly program to share the thinking of your class with the rest of the school.
      3. Invite students who will be new in the school in the coming year to participate in some social activity. Help them become acquainted with other students and with the various aspects of school living.
      4. Make a moving picture or filmstrip of the life of the school, emphasizing opportunities for participation in social activities.
      5. Give a puppet show or a musical production built around the life of the school.
      6. Make a "Who's Who" booklet of members of the staff and distribute to new students.

7. For a period of time act as assistants to various teachers in the school. Help with such items as attendance, records, scheduling, individual teaching, visual aids, and source material.

8. Plan a social event for students and staff members.

C. Curricular Offerings

1. Make a student handbook. Include such points as a description of the core and electives programs, resources and services available to students, school rules and regulations, requirements for graduation, the grading system, school organizations and activities, and school songs and traditions.

2. See the filmstrip *A Core Curriculum Class in Action* or the film *We Plan Together*. As a follow-up discuss problems basic to effective work in core periods: On what basis should a learning unit be chosen? How can the block of time be used most effectively? How can progress be evaluated?

3. Invite teachers from the various special interest areas to discuss the general nature of these areas and their possible contributions to vocational and avocational pursuits. To what extent does the school provide for the various special interests?

4. Invite your principal to lead a discussion on the philosophy and purposes of the school.

5. List the curricular offerings of your school and compare them with other schools of the same size; larger schools; smaller schools.

6. Discuss the choices an individual has to make as he plans his particular program of studies. How can a person plan his own program in terms of his own needs and interests?

7. Invite your principal or a member of the board of education to talk about the history of your school—when it was started, who could attend, what courses were offered, and how it has changed.

8. Form a panel of teachers and students to lead a discussion on the educational problems and needs of your high school. Make suggestions as to how your class can take responsibility for improving the school.

9. Write a paper on "What I Hope to Get out of High School."

10. Survey the types of activities in which students like to participate. To what extent does the school provide for these activities? Make recommendations for introducing or eliminating activities and submit them to the student council.

II. *Studying Problems of Education at the Community Level*
  A. School-Community Relations
      1. Have a round-table discussion on desirable home-school relations and the techniques a school can use to help laymen understand the school program. Which of these techniques are being used by the school? How effective are they?
      2. Plan a community survey to find out what laymen like best about the school, what things they think could be improved, what the school should do that it is not now doing. Share these findings with members of the school staff.
      3. See the films *And So They Live* and *Children Must Learn*. As a follow-up, form a panel of parents, teachers, and students to discuss how the school can improve community living.
      4. Prepare a handbook describing the school program. Make copies available to parents and others interested in the school program.
      5. Plan a "Parents' Day" on which parents have an opportunity to visit the school and participate in the various activities.
      6. Keep a record of the use made of school facilities by community groups. What facilities are available? What rules and regulations apply to the community use of these facilities?
      7. Plan a "Community Education Day." Outline a program including use of newspapers, radio and television, posters, and programs in all the schools.
  B. Community Organizations
      1. Make a survey of community educational services. Are community needs being met? Compare findings with available information on conditions in other communities. Make recommendations for improvement.
      2. List the organizations which serve youth in the community through a definitely organized program. What are their purposes and activities? To what extent is there an overlapping of functions? Evaluate the services in terms of their educational value.
      3. Secure data on the number of students who participate in leisure-time organizations such as the YMCA, YWCA, Boy Scouts, Girl Scouts, and Camp Fire Girls. Ask members of

these organizations to discuss the aims and activities of the organizations. What services do such organizations render to the school?

4. Interview the educational directors of several churches. What is the nature of the church program? What provisions are made for the various age levels? Is the leadership salaried or voluntary? What activities of a recreational and social nature does the church sponsor?

5. Make a directory of community organizations and activities. Include: addresses, telephone numbers and names of leaders; purposes; nature of the activities; and types of assistance they offer the schools.

C. Community Agencies

1. List the movies and television programs seen by members of the class during a given period of time. How did each influence the attitude and behavior of the students? To what extent are movies and television supplementing or counteracting the influence of the school, the home, and the church?

2. Measure in column inches the amount of space devoted to items on education in several newspapers. What items are given most space? least space? What is the attitude of these newspapers toward education in general? The local public schools in particular?

3. Invite a representative from one of the local newspapers to participate in a panel discussion on the topic, "The Role of the Press in Solving the Educational Problems of a Community."

4. Post a list of radio and television programs of educational significance on the bulletin board. How many students listen to these programs?

5. Check lists of most popular books and look at newsstands to get an idea of what outside influences may contribute to a person's education. Compare your findings with those of other members of the class.

D. Pressure Groups

1. Make a study of interest and pressure groups in the community. What is the nature of these groups? How do such groups exert pressure on the school?

2. Interview the principal or superintendent and secure information about some instances where the school was subject to external pressure. How did the school handle the problem?

E. Adult Education
    1. Invite the director of the adult education program to discuss the need for adult education and the importance of continuing one's education beyond "schooling."
    2. Plan visits to adult education agencies such as agricultural groups, government vocational classes, libraries, museums, and evening school. Describe and evaluate the activities of these agencies.
    3. See the film *Not by Books Alone*. As a follow-up discuss how the library can serve the citizens in a community. Evaluate the library in your community.
    4. Use role playing to contrast the attitude toward adult education of people fifty years ago and today.

F. Community College
    1. Visit a community college in the vicinity and collect information on its enrollment, student population, staff, financial support, and curriculum.
    2. Invite a member of the staff of a community college to discuss the objectives and functions of the college.
    3. Make a chart showing the growth of the community college during the period 1930 to the present. What factors have contributed to this growth?

G. Special Education
    1. Make a study of the special education programs and services available to meet the needs of the exceptional child in the community. How many children are involved? Are the necessary resources available for their care and treatment? What provisions are made for their education?
    2. Visit a special class or school. Ask the teacher to explain such features as: medical care and therapy; admission and withdrawal; housing and equipment; special guidance for children and parents.
    3. See the film *That the Deaf May Speak*. As a follow-up, discuss the problems faced by children who are born deaf and how the school can help them to lead a normal life.
    4. Have several class members spend a day with handicapped students. Try to find out some of the problems they face and how they attempt to solve them. Findings might be presented by means of sketches, stories, or oral reports.
    5. See the film *Institutional Training*. Discuss some of the problems associated with educating the mentally deficient.
    6. Have a round-table discussion on the importance of special

education. Summarize the discussion by making a series of sketches or cartoons.

H. Support and Control

1. Interview the superintendent of schools relative to the organization, cost, and management of schools of the district.

2. Visit the offices of the board of education and obtain information concerning its membership, organization, and functions.

3. Invite a member of the board of education to talk about plans for attacking educational problems in the community; for example, the teacher shortage or lack of building facilities.

4. Attend a meeting of the board of education. Report your observations to the class.

5. Dramatize educational problems in the community; for example, portray two taxpayers arguing for and against the increase in the mill levy for public-school support.

6. Make a report on how education is financed in the community. What are the chief sources of revenue for the support of public education?

7. Make charts and graphs showing the cost of public education in your school district. Compare these figures with those for several other districts. How do you account for any differences?

8. Illustrate by means of a graph how the school tax dollar is spent.

I. Drop Outs

1. Make a study of the drop-out problem. At what age and grade do most students drop out? What are the chief reasons given by drop outs for leaving school? Suggest changes that might encourage students to remain in school.

2. See the film *Problems of Pupil Adjustment, Part I—The Drop Out*. Make a concrete proposal for meeting the problem of "drop outs" and compare it with the program stressed in the film *Problems of Pupil Adjustment, Part II—The Stay In*.

3. Interview several students who have dropped out of school and list their reasons for doing so. Compare your findings with those of other members of the class.

4. Find out the number of youth of school age in the community. Compare this figure with the number of youth attending school. What are the implications? Explain.

III. *Studying Problems of Education at the State and National Levels*

    A. State Support and Control

        1. Make a chart showing the organization and functions of the State Department of Education.

        2. Discuss the selection and responsibilities of the various state school officials.

        3. Write to the offices of the Secretaries of State for information concerning legislation affecting schools. What are the laws in the various states relative to instruction in the United States Constitution, history, ideals, and patriotism, the use of the flag in public schools, and observance of special days? Summarize the findings on a chart.

        4. Make a chart describing the types of school districts found in your state.

        5. See the film *Design of American Education*. As a follow-up make a chart showing the organizational structure of American education.

        6. Compare state standards for minimum educational programs. Consider such points as: qualifications of teachers, supervisors, and administrative officers; teacher salaries; curriculum requirements; compulsory school attendance.

        7. Make a study of the present sources of school revenue in your state. What changes, if any, would you suggest in these sources?

    B. Inequalities

        1. On a map of the United States show the expenditure per pupil of each state for education. Where does your state rank? What factors may account for this?

        2. Collect evidence concerning educational inequalities in: rural and urban schools; small and large schools; accredited and non-accredited schools; private and public schools. Discuss the causes of the differences and their significance in a democracy.

        3. Discuss the decision of the United States Supreme Court regarding school segregation. What are some of the problems involved in desegregation? What progress has been made toward the solution of these problems?

        4. Write a short story showing the consequences of educational inequalities.

        5. Review such books as George S. Counts, *Selective Character of American Education*; Howard M. Bell, *Youth Tell Their Story*; August B. Hollingshead, *Elmtown's Youth*;

W. L. Warner and others, *Who Shall Be Educated?* and
give reports to the class.

6. Make a pictograph showing the percentage of children in
the United States that enter the first grade, the seventh
grade, the ninth grade, and that graduate. What does this
indicate about American education?

7. Outline a plan on the local, state, and national levels for
providing a greater measure of educational opportunity.

8. Investigate and report to the class various proposals for
reform in the area of school finance. Is there a trend in
any one direction?

9. Discuss: Should the federal government help the states
meet current costs of school operation?

C. Historical Development

1. Prepare reports on education in: the Colonial period; the
early national period; the period 1865-1890; the period
1890 to the present.

2. Compare the modern secondary school with the Latin
grammar school by means of skits or short plays. The comparison might emphasize such points as purposes, curriculum, and method.

3. Report on the influence on education of the following: the
church; the scientific movement; the changing social order;
legislation; national committees and organizations; educational leaders.

4. Have a panel discussion on "Evidences of America's Faith
in Education." Include such examples as compulsory education laws and compulsory attendance laws.

5. Construct a "time and event" line showing people and
events that have contributed to the development of American education.

6. Make a series of models or sketches showing the changes
in the physical plant of schools from Colonial days to the
present.

7. Make a collection of songs commonly sung in schools from
Colonial days to the present. Present a musical program
of these songs for the rest of the school.

8. Make a mural depicting the crucial issues in American
education in various historical periods.

9. Present a pageant depicting the growth and development
of public education in America.

D. Education and Democracy

1. Have a panel discussion on the role of the citizen in solving

problems of public concern in a democracy and in an autocracy. What are the implications for education?

2. Evaluate your own learning experiences in terms of their contribution to skills for democratic living. Compare your evaluations with those of other members of the class.

3. List experiences which you think your own school might provide to help you participate effectively in a democratic society.

4. Invite teachers and parents to participate in a round-table discussion on "How Schools May Further Democracy."

E. Conflicting Philosophies

1. Visit some schools that are termed "progressive" and some that are termed "traditional" and compare their curricula and practices.

2. Invite several parents to participate in a discussion on "What Boys and Girls Should Achieve in High School."

3. Make a survey of the literature to determine the major criticisms of present-day education. These might be depicted in cartoon form.

4. Make a scrapbook or bulletin board display of current information (articles, pamphlets, photographs, and cartoons) concerning issues in American education, criticisms of education and related matters.

5. Write to the Association for Supervision and Curriculum Development, 1201 Sixteenth St., N.W., Washington 6, D. C., for an "Information Kit Concerning Destructive Criticism of Public Education." ($1.50)

6. Discuss issues such as the following:
   a. Should secondary education be made available for all youth or for a limited group?
   b. Should persons who are not loyal to democratic principles be employed in the schools?
   c. Should controversial issues be dealt with in the high schools?
   d. Is the high school, as now organized, meeting the needs of youth, or should there be a basic reorganization?

7. Dramatize modern educational problems. Use such situations as: A family discusses the value of present-day teaching methods; youth accuses public education of inadequate preparation to meet the demands of social living.

8. Examine critically the following beliefs:

    a. Every high school graduate will become an intelligent voter.

    b. A city school does more for its students than a rural school.

    c. There are too many "frills" in modern education.

    d. Anyone can obtain an education in the United States.

9. Collect cartoons, short stories, poems, and songs concerned with school life. Discuss the concept of education each reflects.

F. Improving Education

    1. Investigate and report on the work of various organizations and institutions which have promoted public education; for example, the National Education Association, the Ford Foundation, the W. K. Kellogg Foundation, and the Progressive Education Association.

    2. Write to the U. S. Office of Education for information about its organization and functions.

    3. Write brief biographies of several individuals who have made outstanding contributions to American education; for example, John Dewey, Horace Mann, Booker T. Washington.

    4. Summarize and report to the class recent research in the field of education.

    5. Investigate recent proposals for reorganizing secondary education. These might be summarized on a chart.

    6. Make a study of the causes and effects of the teacher shortage. What attempts are being made to alleviate the situation?

    7. Make a graph comparing the amount of money spent for education each year with that spent for alcohol, cosmetics, and tobacco. How do you account for the results?

    8. List the bills concerned with public education that have been before Congress within the past ten or fifteen years.

    9. Invite your principal or superintendent to lead a discussion on "Issues and Trends in American Education."

    10. Make a study of teaching as a career. For helpful materials write to the Future Teachers of America, 1201 Sixteenth St., N.W., Washington 6, D. C.

    11. See the films *Fight for Better Schools, Teacher's Crisis,* and *Sixth Chair.* What are some of the major problems in education? Discuss the dangers of public complacency toward education.

IV. *Studying Problems of Education at the World-Wide Level*

    A. Education in Other Countries

        1. Invite a foreign student or a foreign person living in the community to speak about the educational system of his country.

        2. Exchange letters with students in other countries. The whole class or the school might correspond and exchange school work with a class or a school in another country. Write to the International Junior Red Cross, 6 rue de Berri, Paris 8, France, for a list of names and addresses.

        3. Invite members of the community to tell the class about their visits to schools in other countries.

        4. Examine recent attempts of nations to insure a type of teaching compatible with their ideologies. See Zeimer, *Education for Death* (Nazi Germany prior to World War II) and Counts, *I Want to Be Like Stalin*.

        5. See such films as *Schools to the South* and *The Three A's*. As a follow-up, compare the educational systems of various countries. Consider such points as organization and administration, curriculum, support and control, bases for admission, materials and techniques.

        6. Present scenes from *The King and I* for an assembly program.

    B. UNESCO

        1. Make a chart showing the organization of UNESCO. Discuss its purposes, membership, and program.

        2. See the filmstrip *Story of UNESCO*. Discuss how students and others may participate in the work of UNESCO.

        3. Discuss the handicaps under which UNESCO operates. Formulate a plan for making it more effective.

        4. Have a panel discussion on the role of education in bringing about better human relations among the peoples of the world.

    C. Help for Undeveloped Countries

        1. Indicate on a world map the percentage of illiteracy in various countries of the world. In what countries does the problem seem most acute? How do you account for this?

        2. Report on efforts in various countries to eradicate illiteracy.

        3. See the film *That All May Learn* and discuss its implications for the education of peoples all over the world.

        4. Have a panel discussion on "The Development of Tech-

nical 'Know How' in the Undeveloped Countries of the World."

5. Initiate a school-wide drive to collect books and materials to be sent to schools in undeveloped countries.

D. Educational Exchange

1. Make a graph showing the number of foreign students in the United States during the last twenty-year period. What trend is apparent? What factors have contributed to this state of affairs?

2. Illustrate graphically the number of Americans studying in foreign countries during the last twenty-year period. Is the number increasing or decreasing? What are the implications for world understanding?

3. Invite an exchange teacher or student to describe the educational system of his country.

4. Report on the provisions of the Fulbright Act. What procedures have been developed for its administration? What are its difficulties and limitations?

5. Evaluate the Fulbright program as a tool for promoting international understanding.

Evaluation

Most teachers are familiar with the conventional types of evaluation (true-false, matching, and completion tests, and the like). There are times when testing for facts and using instruments of this type are helpful to both the students and the teacher. For example, it might be advantageous to test, at the beginning of a learning unit concerned with problems of American education, to see how much the students know about the subject, and then again at the conclusion. Such tests are often helpful in providing information for future planning.

One of the most useful evaluative techniques is observation. Informal observation of student attitudes and reactions, associations with others, participation in class discussions and activities, self-initiated projects, and the like, yield a wealth of evidence of growth on the part of students. Other general techniques which teachers might use in evaluating student progress include: anecdotal records of student growth in developing the understandings, skills, and appreciations basic to the learning unit; student self-analyses and work samples; reports from parents, teachers, and others of the degree to which the student has developed as a result of the unit study: sociometric surveys.

The evaluative techniques described below are illustrative of those which teachers and students might use to secure evidence of progress toward the goals of a learning unit on education.

Informal Value Analysis Techniques

1. Analysis of Writing

    Students reveal many of their values in their writing. Papers may be analyzed for statements and phrases which indicate the ideas of which a student approves or disapproves. Such analyses help students to look critically at their own values in terms of their consequences. An analysis might reveal, for example, that a student places a very high value on a college education. He needs to examine what characterizes a well-educated person and to explore other educational opportunities in the community.

2. Role-playing

    Role-playing is an effective technique for helping students gain insights into their own values and those of others by enacting various roles. The following situations drawn from the list of activities presented in this resource guide are suggestive:

    a. Set up situations which illustrate the "do's and don'ts" of good school citizenship. (Student and Staff Relations)
    b. Two taxpayers argue for and against the increase in the mill levy for public school support. (Support and Control)
    c. A family discusses criticisms of modern education. (Conflicting Philosophies)

3. Generalizations

    After some work on a learning unit on education, students might be asked to write a number of generalizations which express their beliefs. Such statements are indicative of the students' values and may be analyzed for inconsistencies. An example of a series of generalizations written by a student follows:

    a. All boys and girls should have an equal opportunity for education.
    b. The federal government should not help the states meet the cost of education.
    c. Anyone can obtain an education in the United States.

These generalizations express conflicting values and indicate that the student is confused in his thinking.

4. Reactions to Situations

    Set up hypothetical problem situations that involve choice between alternative values and ask members of the class to react to them. Following is an illustration:

Barton Junior High School was overcrowded, and the Elm City Schools wanted a new junior high school building. A bond issue was proposed by the board of education, and a special election was scheduled. A small group opposed the property tax, but the majority in opposition consisted of those who argued that the Barton School would not be overcrowded if the Negro students attending the school were sent across town to Edison Junior High School which had a very heavy concentration of Negro students anyway. What course of action should the school board take and why?

5. Reactions to Books, Pamphlets, Articles, and Films

This is another informal technique for securing evidence concerning the students' insight into problems of education. Articles such as "Quackery in the Public Schools," *Atlantic Monthly* (March, 1950); "An Open Letter to Teachers," *Harper's* (July, 1952); and the materials in the "Information Kit Concerning Destructive Criticisms of Education" might be useful in this connection. Reactions to films such as *Children Must Learn* and *As Our Boyhood Is* would give further evidence. Books such as *Were We Guinea Pigs?*, *Education for Death*, *I Want to Be Like Stalin*, and *Our Children Are Cheated* might be used.

Formal Instruments of Evaluation

1. *Beliefs about School Life* (Form 4.6). Evaluation in the Eight-Year Study, American Education Fellowship, Chicago, 1939. Consists of 118 statements, classified under the following areas of issues: school government, curriculum, grades and awards, school spirit, pupil-teacher relations, and group life.

2. *Test on Beliefs on Social Issues* (Form 4.21-4.31). Evaluation in the Eight-Year Study, American Education Fellowship, Chicago, 1939. Consists of 200 statements, classified under the following areas of issues: democracy, economic relations, labor and unemployment, race, nationalism, militarism.

3. *Cooperative Test on Recent Social and Scientific Developments.* Cooperative Test Service, New York, 1946-47. Consists of 116 multiple-choice items on social, economic, political, military, scientific, technical, and medical developments. Not a test of current events but rather of more fundamental developments and trends.

4. *Interpretation of Data Test* (Forms 2.51-2.52) Evaluation in the Eight-Year Study, American Education Fellowship, Chicago, 1939. Consists of ten exercises in which data are presented in one of a variety of ways—line graphs, bar graphs, pictographs, statistical tables, running paragraphs, and charts. Evaluates the student's ability to draw conclusions and to make interpretations of the new data presented to him.

5. *Nature of Proof Test* (Form 5.22). Evaluation in the Eight-Year Study, American Education Fellowship, Chicago, 1939. Consists of a series of described situations which presumably justify the conclusion stated at the close of each description. Measures the abilities connected with analyzing written arguments.

6. *Mooney Problem Check List*. The Psychological Corporation, New York, 1950. Consists of 330 troublesome problems which often face students in high school—problems of adjustment to school, curriculum and teaching procedure, health, money, social life, and the like.

BIBLIOGRAPHY AND TEACHING AIDS

Readings for Teachers

The following references are intended for the use of teachers. Many of them, however, might also be used by pupils.

Aikin, Wilford M., *The Story of the Eight-Year Study*. New York, Harper & Brothers, 1942. The story of a nationwide effort to improve secondary education through experimentation.

Alberty, Harold, *Reorganizing the High School Curriculum*. New York, The Macmillan Company, 1953. A comprehensive treatment of the urgency of rethinking the purposes and program of the high school. Emphasis upon analysis of the needs, problems, and interests of adolescents as basic for curriculum development.

————, and others, *Let's Look at the Attacks on the Schools*. (Mimeographed) Columbus, The Ohio State University, 1951. Identifies and evaluates ten basic criticisms of public education made by individual and organized groups of laymen and by professional educators.

Alexander, William M., and J. Galen Saylor, *Secondary Education; Basic Principles and Practices*. New York, Rinehart & Company, 1950. Basic reference on history, development, organization, and inequalities in education.

Allen, Hollis P., *The Federal Government and Education*. The Original and Complete Study of Education for the Hoover Commission Task Force on Public Welfare. New York, McGraw-Hill Book Company, 1950. See in particular Chapters 3, 5, 10, and 14. Title is self-explanatory.

American Council on Education, *The Relation of Religion to Public Education*. Washington, D. C., The Council, 1947. A discussion of problems involved and a statement of principles for practice.

Bell, Bernard I., *Crisis in Education; A Challenge to American Complacency*. New York, McGraw-Hill Book Company, 1949. Points out fault he sees in American education. Proposes a complete reorganization regarding age limits, teachers' preparation, subjects taught, and reorganization of the educational system.

Bell, Howard M., *Youth Tell Their Story*. Washington, D. C., American Council on Education, 1938. A study of the conditions and attitudes of Maryland young people between the ages of 16 and 24. Shows need for equalization of educational opportunity, employment, guidance, economic security, vocational training, etc.

Biennial Survey of Education in the United States, 1944-46. Washington, D. C.: U. S. Government Printing Office, 1949. Chapter V, "Statistics on Public High Schools, 1945-46." Detailed information concerning the status of public high schools.

Bogue, Jesse Parker, *The Community College*. New York, McGraw-Hill Book Company, 1950. Chapters 3 and 4. Sets forth the basic functions of the community-junior-college. Presents historical overview of its development and future trends in upward extension.

Caswell, Hollis L., et. al., *The American High School*. John Dewey Society, Eighth Yearbook. New York, Harper & Brothers, 1946. Explains the need for a future program in general education, providing for vocational education and the preparation of teachers for a new type of high school.

Brubacher, J. S. (editor), *The Public School and Spiritual Values*. New York, McGraw-Hill Book Co., 1944. Deals with non-sectarian approach to religious teaching and an attempt to ascertain what is common to the various denominations.

Cook, Lloyd A., and Elaine F. Cook, *A Sociological Approach to Education*. New York, McGraw-Hill Book Company, 1950. Stresses the relationship of school and the community with particular reference to the community influences affecting youth.

Counts, George S., *The Selective Character of American Secondary Education*. Chicago, The University of Chicago Press, 1932. Presents data collected from four American cities concerning social status of children and their persistence in high school.

————, and N. Lodge (Translators), *I Want to Be Like Stalin*, by B. P. Yesipov and N. K. Goncharov. New York, John Day Company, 1947. Translations of portions of a Russian teacher-training manual describing the organization, practices, and purposes of Russian education.

Cubberley, Ellwood P., *Public Education in the United States*. Boston, Houghton Mifflin Company, 1934. Traces the development and presents problems included in extending education.

————, *State School Administration*. Boston, Houghton Mifflin Company, 1927. Chapter 6. Traces development of the district, town, or township and county systems. Gives background and development of federal support and aid.

Dewey, John, *Democracy and Education; An Introduction to the Philosophy of Education.* New York, The Macmillan Company, 1916. Discusses the ideas implied in a democratic society and applies them to the problems of education.

Dillon, Harold J., *Early School Leavers; A Major Educational Problem.* New York, National Child Labor Committee, 1949. A study of dropouts and their reasons for leaving school.

Edmonson, J. G., Joseph Roemer, and Francis L. Bacon, *The Administration of the Modern Secondary School.* New York, The Macmillan Company, 1948. Chapter 27, "The Extension of Secondary Education; The Junior College." Title is self-explanatory.

Educational Policies Commission, *Education for All American Youth.* —*A Further Look.* Washington, D. C., National Education Association, 1952. Describes ideal rural and urban schools as they might be developed in the next few years. Essential orientation is that of the life-centered, community school.

Edwards, Newton, and Herman Richey, *The School in the American Social Order.* Boston, Houghton Mifflin Company, 1947. A history of American education, showing how social, economic, and political factors have influenced educational policies and practices.

Encyclopedia of Educational Research. New York, The Macmillan Company, 1950. Pages 1152-1200 present a digest of the general development, organization, curriculum, and administration of secondary education.

Everett, Samuel (editor), *The Community School.* New York, D. Appleton-Century Company, 1938. Presents the philosophy of community education, the program and principles of nine community schools, a survey of additional community programs, and an analysis of the programs in terms of basic issues.

Fine, Benjamin, *Our Children Are Cheated.* New York, Henry Holt and Company, 1947. Discussion of the breakdown of American education—the teacher shortage, lowered morale, inadequate equipment.

The Forty-Eight State School Systems. The Council of State Governments. Chicago, The Council, 1949. A study of the organization, administration, and financing of public elementary and secondary education.

Fuess, C. M., and E. S. Basford (editors), *Unseen Harvests.* New York, The Macmillan Company, 1947. Selections on education from ancient to modern writers.

Gaumnitz, Walter H., and Grace S. Wright, *Broadening the Services of Small High Schools.* Washington, D. C., U. S. Office of Education, Bulletin 1948, No. 9. Title is self-explanatory.

Good, Harry G., *A History of Western Education.* New York, The Macmillan Company, 1947. A general history of Western education from Greek times to the present, describing the growth of schools and educational thought as part of the general history of society.

Gruhn, William, and Harl C. Douglass, *Modern Junior High School.* New York, The Ronald Press Company, 1956. Surveys the history, philosophy, and functions of the junior high school; discusses present practices and trends; describes new programs and procedures.

Hollingshead, August B., *Elmtown's Youth; The Impact of Social Classes on Adolescents.* New York, John Wiley and Sons, Inc., 1949. Concerns a typical mid-western town and the impact of social status on its youth in the school and community.

Hullfish, H. Gordon, *Keeping Our Schools Free.* Public Affairs Pamphlet, No. 199. New York, Public Affairs Committee, 1953. Concerned with sources of danger to academic freedom. Proposes five basic safeguards to protect teachers against unjust treatment.

Knight, Edgar W., and Clifton B. Hall, *Readings in American Educational History.* New York, Appleton-Century-Crofts, 1950. Contains information about early legislation, educational plans proposed by national committees and educational leaders, and arguments for and against federal aid to education. (Compilation of materials.)

Leonard, J. Paul, *Developing the Secondary School Curriculum.* New York, Rinehart & Company, 1953. Chapters 1, 2, and 6, Historical development of secondary education.

National Association of Secondary School Principals, *Planning for American Youth; An Educational Program for Youth of Secondary School Age.* Washington, D. C., The Association, 1944. A summary of *Education for All American Youth.*

National Education Association, *The Facts on Federal Aid for Schools.* Washington, D. C., The Association, September, 1950. Title is self-explanatory.

Newcomer, Mabel, *An Index of the Taxpaying Ability of State and Local Governments.* New York, Bureau of Publications, Teachers College, Columbia University, 1935. Title is self-explanatory.

Olsen, Edward G., *School and Community.* New York, Prentice-Hall, Inc., 1945. Examines the underlying philosophy of community education, investigates ten vital ways to relate school instruction with community life, considers problems involved, and summarizes basic principles of action.

Quattlebaum, Charles A., *Federal Aid to Elementary and Secondary Education.* (Mimeographed) Chicago, Public Administration Service, 1948. An analytic study of the issue, its background and relevant legislative proposals, with a compilation of arguments pro and con, statistical data, and digests of pertinent reports and surveys.

Rugg, Harold, *Foundations for American Education*. Yonkers, New York, World Book Company, 1947. Shows what education can learn from psychology, sociology, ethics, and esthetics. Ranges over social-cultural scene of past sixty years.

Russell, John Dale, and Associates, *Vocational Education*. Prepared for the Advisory Committee on Education, Staff Study No. 8. Washington, D. C., U. S. Government Printing Office, 1938. Chapters 7, 8, and 9. Contains texts of Smith-Hughes and George-Dean Acts.

Thayer, V. T., *American Education Under Fire*. New York, Harper & Brothers, 1944. Deals with certain crucial issues that confront the citizen as well as the professional educator. Concludes with a broad outline of the task of the modern school.

UNESCO Literature; A Bibliography. Paris, UNESCO Publication 216, 1948.

Warner, W. Lloyd, and others, *Who Shall Be Educated? The Challenge of Unequal Opportunities*. New York, Harper & Brothers, 1944. Describes how our schools, functioning in a society with basic inequalities, facilitate the rise of a few from lower to higher levels but continue to serve the social system by keeping down many who try for higher places in our social structure.

———, and others, *Democracy in Jonesville; A Study in Quality and Inequality*. New York, Harper & Brothers, 1949. The typical American town—its social structure, politics, high school, ethnic groups, beliefs, values, and conflicting social logics.

Were We Guinea Pigs? Class of 1938, University High School, The Ohio State University. New York, Henry Holt and Company, Inc., 1938. An account of life in a "progressive" school. The experiences of the first class to graduate from University High School.

Work Conference on Life Adjustment Education, *Why Do Boys and Girls Drop Out of School and What Can We Do About It?* Report of Representatives of School Systems in Cities of More Than 200,000 Population. Washington, D. C., U. S. Office of Education, Circular No. 269, 1950. Title is self-explanatory.

Zeimer, Gregor, *Education for Death*. London, Oxford University Press, 1941. The making of the Nazi—education in Germany prior to World War II.

Readings for Pupils

Books and Pamphlets

Adams, A. Elwood, and Edward E. Walker, *Living in the City*. New York, McGraw-Hill Book Company, 1949. Chapter 7. A brief discussion of public and privately supported education and the role of non-school agencies in education.

Arnold, Joseph I., *Challenges to American Youth.* Evanston, Illinois: Row Peterson and Company, 1949. The Fifth Challenge: The school. Focuses on the problems of providing education to insure an intelligent citizenship in a complex society.

Bennett, Margaret E., and Harold C. Hand, *School and Life.* New York, McGraw-Hill Book Company, 1938. Problems typically encountered by students in their first years of high school.

Bossing, Nelson L., and Robert R. Martin, *Youth Faces Its Problems.* Units 25, 26, 27. Chicago, Laidlaw Brothers, 1950. Discusses the importance of education, some problems encountered in getting an education, some of the problems of society in providing an education.

Capen, Louise I., *Being A Citizen.* New York, American Book Company, 1950. Chapter 6. Emphasizes the importance of education, knowing the educational opportunities offered by the school.

Cummings, Howard, and Everett B. Sackett, *Our Schools.* New York, Harper & Brothers, 1939. A history of American education and contributions of other lands to American education.

Eastburn, Lacey A., et al., *Planning Your Life for School and Society.* New York, Charles Scribner's Sons, 1939. Unit 2. A study of high school organization and the adjustment to group life it requires.

Education. The Building America Series. Association for Supervision and Curriculum Development, Vol. 13, No. 3 (March, 1948).

*Erdman, Loula, *Fair Is the Morning.* New York, Longmans, Green, and Company, Inc., 1945. The story of a teacher in a rural school.

*————, *Separate Star,* New York, Longmans, Green, and Company, Inc., 1944. The story of a girl's first year of teaching.

Gavian, Ruth, and others, *Our Changing Social Order.* Boston, D. C. Heath and Company, 1947. Chapters 31, 32. Discusses opportunities for education and education in better ways of living.

Greenan, John T., *Everyday Problems of American Democracy.* Boston, Houghton Mifflin, 1948. Chapter 11. Discusses federal support of education.

*Harper, Martha B., *Winter Wedding.* New York, Longmans, Green, and Company, Inc., 1950. A love story of the years following the Civil War involving a teacher in a one-room school.

*Hilton, James, *Good-bye Mr. Chips.* Boston, Little, Brown and Company, 1934. The story of an English schoolmaster and of his associations with three generations of schoolboys.

Krug, Edward, and I. James Quillen, *Citizens Now.* Chicago, Scott,

* Fiction.

Foresman and Company, 1952. Unit I. Shows how the family and school take care of certain needs. Emphasizes educational opportunities and planning for the future.

————, and ————, *Living in Our Communities*. Chicago, Scott, Foresman and Company, 1946. Chapter 5. Shows how the home, church, school, motion pictures, newspaper, radio, clubs, museums, libraries and individuals all help the community meet its need for education. A brief overview of the history of American education.

Life Adjustment Booklets. Chicago, Science Research Associates. In this series of 48-page booklets are many which relate to problems of education. Some of the appropriate booklets are:

Bennett, Margaret E., *High School Handbook*. Information to help young people adjust to high school.

Lindquist, E. F., and others, *What Good Is High School?* The part that high schools play in equipping students with "tools" for everyday living.

Schloerb, Lester J., *School Subjects and Jobs*. How school courses can help students prepare for future careers.

Taylor, Florence, *Why Stay in School?* Illustrations of the value of completing high school, and what happens to students who drop out.

Warner, W. Lloyd, and Robert J. Havinghurst, *Should You Go to College?* A discussion of the pros and cons to consider in making this decision.

McGregor, A. Laura, and Harold L. Holbrook, *Our Junior High School*. Boston, Allyn and Bacon, 1940. Interprets the junior high school. Designed to help students understand the relation of its aims and purposes to their individual lives.

*McLelland, Isabel C., *Hi! Teacher*. New York, Henry Holt and Company, Inc., 1952. The story of Alison Gray (beginning teacher) and her teaching experience in Cow Creek.

*Ormston, Mary, *Forty Faces*. New York, Doubleday, Doran, and Company, Inc., 1940. Story of Jean who goes to a teachers college and her experiences in student teaching.

*Rosenheim, Lucile G., *Kathy the New Teacher*. New York, Julian Messner, Inc., 1949. A romance that tells of Kathy's first year of teaching.

Magazine Articles

American

"How Good Are Your Schools?" September, 1951.

"Religion and Our Schools," May, 1952.

Atlantic

* Fiction.

"Are Our Public Schools Doing Their Job?" February, 1949.
"Act of Faith," June, 1950.
"Essentials of Education," January, 1952.
"For a Faster Schooling," April, 1952.
"Do American Schools Educate?" February, 1953.
"Who Wants Progressive Education?" April, 1953.
"How Dangerous Is John Dewey?" May, 1953.

Harper's
"What Should Colleges Teach Women?" November, 1949.
"Why the Private School," August, 1951.
"A Bonanza for Education," March, 1952.
"An Open Letter to Teachers," July, 1952.

Life
"For Better Schools," January 30, 1950.
"U. S. Schools," October 16, 1950 (Whole issue).
"A Big Public Institution," December 14, 1953.

The Nation
"Attempt to Pass Bill Providing Federal Aid to Schools," March 18, 1950.
"Battle for Free Schools," (A series of eight articles), October 27-December 15, 1951.
"Progressive Education Condemned," January 26, 1952.
"Right to Teach," July 12, 1952.
"Teacher as Rebel: His War for Freedom," May 16, 1953.

New Republic
"State of the Union; Adequate Education," January 16, 1950.
"Aid to Education Bills," February 20, 1950.
"American Education and American Life," March 20, 1950.
"Schools without Teachers," April 10, 1950.
"Freedom to Learn," March 23, 1953.
"Why We Have Poor Teachers," September 14, 1953.
"Do We Have Poor Teachers?" October 19, 1953.

The New York Times Magazine
"Are Your Girls Getting Boys' Education?" May 14, 1950.
"Education Is the Teacher's Job," June 3, 1951.
"Challenge to the Critics of the Schools," September 23, 1951.
"Fault Is Not the Teacher's," November 18, 1951.
"Job of the Teacher in Days of Crisis," December 14, 1952.
"Danger in What We Don't Know," March 22, 1953.

Saturday Evening Post
"New Education Could Do with Some Geography," January 21, 1950.
"Strong Local Support for Schools Is Way to Escape Federal Aid," January 28, 1950.

"I'll Stick Up for the Schools," April 15, 1950.

"How to Study Abroad for Free—Fulbright Scholarships," April 4, 1953.

Saturday Review of Literature

"Our Dangerous Juvenility: Review of *Crisis in Education*," April April 30, 1949.

"Lynching for Education: Review of *This Happened in Pasadena and American Education under Fire*," May 19, 1951.

"Public School Crisis: Review of Reports on Six Communities," September 8, 1951.

"Textbook Problem: Symposium," April 19, 1952.

"Mind and Merriment: Review of *What Is Progressive Education?*" September 13, 1952.

"Changing Attitudes: Why and How—Slogans in Education," September 12, 1953.

"Quackery in the Public Schools: A Review," September 12, 1953.

Scholastic

"College Scholarships: Should the Government Provide Them for Deserving High School Students?" May 17, 1950.

"Planks in a Program of Education for Freedom," October 11, 1950.

"Opportunities for Education in America," March 14, 1951.

"You're in High School Now," May 2, 1951.

"Student Flood Taxes All Schools," October 10, 1951.

"Our American Schools," November 7, 1951 (whole issue).

"Controversial Issues in Schools," September 24, 1952.

Vital Speeches

"Education, Our First Line of Defense," March 15, 1941.

"Fundamental Education; A Basis for International Understanding," December 15, 1950.

"How Well Are Our Schools Doing the Job?" March 1, 1952.

"Communism and Education," January 1, 1953.

"Need for New Directions in Education," April 1, 1953.

"Are the Public Schools Irreligious?" April 15, 1953.

"Educating Ourselves for Peace and Freedom," June 1, 1953.

"Noblest Profession of Them All," October 15, 1953.

"Some Educational Imperatives," October 15, 1953.

Films and Filmstrips

And So They Live	New York University
25 min sd	New York, New York
$95 rent $6	1940

Depicts the tragic poverty of the land in a rural southern community, the lack of proper diet, housing, and sanitation, the need for better adaptation of the school program to the problems of the community.

As Our Boyhood Is	Brandon Films, Inc.
18 min sd	New York, New York
$50 rent $4	1946

An account of the best in education for Negroes in rural areas with enough indication of the worst, to show that while progress has been made, there is much work to be done.

Assignment for Tomorrow	National Education Association
30 min sd	Washington, D. C.
	1945

Documentary Film—the place and importance of the teacher in American life.

A Better Tomorrow	United World Films, Inc.
24 min sd	Castle Films
$30.84 free-loan	Hollywood, California
	1945

Shows activities of children in New York City Public Schools, particularly in three progressive high schools.

Children Must Learn	New York University Film Library
13 min sd	New York, New York
$75 rent $5	1945

Illustrates the unsatisfactory relationship between education and the local necessities of life which characterize American education in many parts of this country.

A Core Curriculum Class in Action	Wayne University
46 fr si with text	Detroit, Michigan
$3	1950

Follows a typical ninth grade core class from its first class meeting through various teacher-pupil-planned activities and the final evaluation of the work done.

Design of American Education	McGraw-Hill Book Company
16 min sd	New York, New York
$80	1952

The organizational structure of American public education.

Earning Money While Going to *School* 10 min sd $50 color $100	Coronet Films Chicago, Illinois 1950

Serves as a guide for students considering part-time work while in school.

Fight for Better Schools 20 min sd $55	March of Time Forum Films New York, New York 1950

Story of the nation-wide interest in better public schools, showing the importance of an active and informed citizenry in reaching this goal.

Grass Roots Ambassadors 30 min sd color free-loan	Allis-Chalmers Mfg. Co. Milwaukee, Wisconsin 1952

A film on the International Youth Exchange pictured working in Europe and the United States.

High School: Your Challenge 12 min sd $62.50 color $125	Coronet Films Chicago, Illinois 1951

Explains in simple terms why a high-school education is essential in today's world.

Homework: Working on Your Own 19 min sd $50 color, $100	Coronet Films Chicago, Illinois 1953

Shows three areas in which homework skills are necessary—handling problems of a place and time to study; scheduling and arranging projects according to materials needed for study; and developing the habit of studying "on your own."

Horace Mann 19 min sd $85 rent $4.50	Encyclopedia Britannica Films, Inc. Wilmette, Illinois 1951

Portrays important episodes in the life of the "father of the common schools."

Hungry Minds 11 min sd $25 rent $1.50	Brandon Films, Inc. New York, New York 1945

Documentary report of intellectual starvation in countries scourged by Nazi occupation.

Institutional Training	University of Minnesota Audio-
15 min si	Visual Education Service
$36 rent $1.20	Minneapolis, Minn.
	1939

Depicts the activities of the School for the Feebleminded at Faribault, Minnesota.

Not By Books Alone	Social Documentary Films
22 min sd	College Park, Maryland
color $100	1945

How one library serves the citizens of its community in education, enrichment, and recreation, making better homes, earning a living, and intelligent citizenship.

One Tenth of Our Nation	International Film Bureau
26 min sd	Chicago, Illinois
$75 rent $4.50	1940

Gives an authentic picture of the education of Negro children in the rural South, from one-room shacks to high schools and colleges.

Pop Rings the Bell	National School Service Institute
20 min sd	Chicago, Illinois
$60	1944

Shows how technological developments resulting from the war and the approach of the air-age are making, and will increasingly make, new demands upon the schools of the nation.

Problem of Pupil Adjustment,	McGraw-Hill Book Company
Part I—The Drop Out	New York, New York
20 min sd	1950
$95	

Shows the characteristics of the high school program which led Steve Martin to leave school as soon as the law permitted.

Problem of Pupil Adjustment,	McGraw-Hill Book Company
Part II—The Stay In	New York, New York
19 min sd	1950
$95	

Shows what can be done to meet the problems of drop outs when individual pupil needs are met in a school program that stresses learning in terms of adjustment to actual everyday living.

Santa Fe Indian School   Harmon Foundation
15 min si part color   New York, New York
$70   rent $3   1946

Shows purpose and activities of this government school.

School Activities and You   Coronet Films
11 min sd   Chicago, Illinois
$50   color $100   1951

A high-school girl learns the importance of choosing activities for their values by considering what she can learn, what her interests are, how much time she can give, and how to arrange a well-balanced program.

Schoolhouse in the Red   Encyclopedia Britannica Films, Inc.
42 min sd color   Wilmette, Illinois
$194.75   rent $5   1948

Deals with the sociological and psychological factors involved when small communities face up to the problem of joining their school districts with a larger unit.

Schools March On   March of Time Forum Films
18 min sd   New York, New York
$55   1951

Shows what happened in one mid-western county when outmoded one-room schools were eliminated by reorganization and consolidation resulting in larger, well-equipped and well-staffed schools.

Schools to the South   Castle Films
15 min sd   San Francisco, California
$19.96   1943

Portrays the schools of Latin America and the trends in education in these countries.

Secure the Blessings   National Education Association
30 min sd   Washington, D. C.
$55   1951

Dramatizes the role of the public school in a democracy.

Sixth Chair   National School Service Institute
18 min sd   Chicago, Illinois
$75   free-loan   1949

Highlights such problems in education as building construction and modernization, class size, more teachers, up-to-date educational tools, and portrays the dangers of the public's complacency toward education.

Story of UNESCO
46 fr si with text
$6.50

Nestor Productions, Inc.
Los Angeles, California
1948

Explains the ideals and concepts of UNESCO and opens the door to participation by students and others in its work.

The Teacher
13 min sd
$70   rent $3.50

Encyclopedia Britannica Films, Inc.
Wilmette, Illinois
1951

The story of a middle-aged fourth-grade teacher is used to explain the role of the teacher in the community, her professional and personal life, and her contribution to the furthering of education.

Teacher's Crisis
17 min sd
$55

March of Time Forum Films
New York, New York
1947

An objective portrayal of the present educational scene. Visits to America's classrooms and school board meetings reveal many discontented and ill-qualified teachers on the one hand and many disinterested communities on the other.

That All May Learn
19 min sd
rent $2.50

United Nations Film Division
New York, New York
1949

The story of a Mexican farmer and his family who are exploited because they cannot read or write. Stresses the need for education of all peoples all over the world.

That the Deaf May Speak
42 min sd color
free-loan

Ideal Pictures Corp.
Chicago, Illinois

Traces the progress of the pupils from nursery school through junior high at the Lexington School for the Deaf in New York City. Indicates the problems faced by children who are born deaf and the program of the school to help them to lead a normal life.

This Is My School
12 min sd color
free-loan

Cherry Lawn School
Darien, Connecticut
1947

A student's story of what a school has meant to him, written, photographed, and produced by two students.

The Three A's   British International Film Service
20 min sd   London, England
rent $2.50   1948

Age, ability, aptitude—the three A's. Shows how the modern British school coordinates classroom studies with practical experience, so that the children learn to apply their knowledge to the demands of every-day life.

This Is Their Story   Film Program Services
20 min sd   New York, New York
$49.50   rent $3   1950

Shows what young people are doing throughout the world to restore education and culture.

We Plan Together   Teachers College, Columbia University
20 min sd   New York, New York
$75   1948

Shows an eleventh grade core class cooperatively planning and working over a period of several months.

What Greater Gift   National Education Association
28 min sd   Washington, D. C.
$75   color $170   1953

A high school girl, contemplating teaching as a career, sees classroom scenes which show what teaching is like today, and learns of the professional preparation, understandings and skills essential to good teaching.

Wilson Dam School   Tennessee Valley Authority
20 min sd   Knoxville, Tennessee
free-loan   1942

Shows a "progressive" school in action.

SELECTED BIBLIOGRAPHY

Developing Resources for Use in the Core

Alberty, Harold, "The Construction and Use of Resource Units in the Social Studies Area," *University of Pennsylvania Bulletin*, III, 201-209 (June 30, 1948).

————, *Reorganizing the High-School Curriculum.* New York, The Macmillan Company, 1953 (Revised), Chapters 14 and 15.

Faunce, Roland, and Nelson Bossing, *Developing the Core Curriculum.* New York, Prentice-Hall, Inc., 1951. Chapter 7.

Jennings, William E., "Contributions of Business Education to Selected Problem Areas of General Education in the Secondary School," Unpublished Doctoral Dissertation, Columbus, Ohio, The Ohio State University, 1952.

Klohr, Paul R., "Resource Unit in Curriculum Reorganization," *Bulletin of the National Association of Secondary-School Principals,* **XXXIV,** 74-77 (May, 1950).

Mikhail, Monir Kamel, "Contributions of Science to Selected Problem Areas Proposed for a Program of General Education in the Secondary School," Unpublished Doctoral Dissertation, Columbus, Ohio, The Ohio State University, 1952.

Mudd, Dorothy, *A Core Program Grows.* Bel Air, Maryland, Board of Education of Harford County, 1949, Chapter 3.

Stalzer (Alberty), Elsie J., "Contributions of Mathematics to a Proposal for Reorganizing General Education in Secondary Schools on the Basis of a Core Program," Unpublished Doctoral Dissertation, Columbus, Ohio, The Ohio State University, 1952.

Toops, Myrtle, *Working in the Core Program in the Burris Laboratory School.* Muncie, Indiana, Ball State Teachers College, 1955, Chapter VI.

Resource Guides

Alberty, Harold, *Reorganizing the High-School Curriculum.* New York, The Macmillan Company (Revised). 1953, Chapter 15.

————, and others, *Helping Teen Agers Explore Values.* Columbus, Ohio, The Ohio State University Press, 1956.

Fairmont Heights High School Resource Guides. Upper Marlboro, Maryland, Board of Education of Prince George's County, 1953. (A series of resource guides for grades 7-12 inclusive.)

Garrett County Resource Units. Garrett County, Maryland, Board of Education, 1950. (A series of resource units for grades 7, 8 and 9.)

Hand, Harold, *Living in the Atomic Age.* A Resource Unit for Teachers in Secondary Schools. University of Illinois Bulletin XLIV, No. 23. Bureau of Educational Research Bulletin No. 57. Urbana, Illinois, The University of Illinois, December, 1948.

Jennings, William E., "Contributions of Business Education to Selected Problem Areas of General Education in the Secondary

School," Unpublished Doctoral Dissertation, Columbus, Ohio, The Ohio State University, 1952.

Lurry, Lucile L., and others, *Problems of Family Living*. Tallahassee, Florida, State Department of Education, 1951.

Mikhail, Monir Kamel, "Contributions of Science to Selected Problem Areas Proposed for a Program of General Education in the Secondary School," Unpublished Doctoral Dissertation, Columbus, Ohio, The Ohio State University, 1952.

Prince George's County Resource Guides. Upper Marlboro, Maryland, Borad of Education of Prince George's County, 1953. (A series of resource guides for grades 7, 8, and 9.)

Problems of Communication. A Resource Guide for Use in Junior and Senior High School Core Classes. Faculty Study Group of The University School, Columbus, Ohio, The Ohio State University, 1956.

Stalzer (Alberty), Elsie J., "Contributions of Mathematics to a Proposal for Reorganizing General Education in Secondary Schools on the Basis of a Core Program," Unpublished Doctoral Dissertation, Columbus Ohio, The Ohio State University, 1952.

Toops, Myrtle Dewey, *Problems of Growing Up*. Muncie, Indiana, Child Development Service, Ball State Teachers College, 1948.

Worcester County Resource Units. Snow Hill, Maryland, Board of Education of Worcester County, 1952. (A series of resource units for grades 7, 8, and 9.)

VI

THE CORE PROGRAM IN
ACTION IN THE CLASSROOM

One of the most frequent questions asked by core teachers is how to get from a resource guide to a learning unit. Basic to this question is an understanding of the fundamental differences between a resource guide and a learning unit. In the first place, a resource guide is not a learning unit, but rather it is a useful tool in the preplanning which must preface teacher-pupil planning in the classroom. A learning unit is developed cooperatively in the classroom by teacher and pupils in terms of the particular needs, problems, and interests of the group. It is usually drawn from possibilities suggested by a resource guide, but no single learning unit is expected "to cover" the scope of a resource guide. The scope of a resource guide is such that it provides materials for several learning units; the suggestions it contains apply at several grade levels; and there is no organization for day-to-day use in the classroom.

The original question might be rephrased: How can a resource guide be utilized in planning, developing, and evaluating a learning unit? In order to answer this question it is necessary to consider: the kind of preplanning a teacher does when he is committed to teacher-pupil planning in the classroom; and, how the teacher plans, develops, and evaluates a learning unit cooperatively with pupils.

The Preplanning of Learning Activities

Pupil-teacher planning is in no way a replacement of the teacher's preplanning of learning activities. The cooperative development of

147

learning activities at any level requires considerably more preplanning on the part of the teacher than a text-book centered, teacher-directed program. More important than the amount of preplanning to be done is the *how* and *what kind* of preplanning a teacher must do in order to prepare for teacher-pupil planning in the classroom.

In the discussion which follows, the steps which a teacher would probably include in his preplanning will be described.

A Continuing Study of the Pupils in the Class. The teacher's knowledge of the individual needs, problems, and interests of the pupils in the class is essential to cooperative planning in the classroom. There are many resources which the teacher might utilize in learning about the pupils with whom he is to work.

School records and reports are a rich source of information about individual pupils. A careful perusal of the school files will yield a wealth of information on the student's health (physical and mental), academic record, home background, personality development, achievement on standardized tests, and the like. Copies of reports written to parents, records of parent conferences, and special recommendations by the pupil's previous teachers are usually on file also.

Files of material are often passed on from one core teacher to another. These may include sample student papers, descriptions of core experiences, and special class projects carried on in the core block of time, pupil and teacher evaluations of core activities and special projects, notations concerning reading interests and difficulties, brief statements concerning individual and group strengths and weaknesses, and recommendations for future action.

As a part of the continuing study of the learner in the classroom, the teacher will no doubt utilize such techniques as anecdotal records, sociograms and other sociometric devices, problem checklists, and interest inventories. Informal conferences with the pupil, his classmates, parents and teachers, guidance counselor, and the school doctor or nurse give further insight into the individual pupil— his particular needs, problems, and interests.

A Study of the Broad Problem Area. In order to help pupils identify and work toward the solution of the problems of concern to them, the teacher must have a thorough understanding of what is involved in the problem area, possible outcomes, and how these might be achieved. The teacher is one of the best resources available to pupils and as such must be prepared to help them make wise choices as they cooperatively develop the learning unit in the classroom. This does not mean that the teacher should have all of the "answers" at his disposal or that he should formulate the problems to be dealt with and the method of attack so that pupils have no part in decision-making. It *does* mean that he should make a critical study of the problem area so that he will become aware of possibilities within the area.

A well-developed resource guide gives security to the teacher as he carries out this step in the preplanning of learning activities. It defines the scope and objectives and identifies the major problems and issues within the area. Suggested activities and evaluative techniques provide a storehouse of suggestions upon which the teacher may draw. Selected references listed in the bibliography help the teacher locate and become familiar with the literature pertaining to the problem area.

An Investigation of Resources. A third step in the preplanning of learning activities involves locating resources available in the school and community. This step is particularly important since a learning unit cannot be successfully developed without adequate available resources.

A well-equipped library offers books on many levels of interest and reading difficulty, and the librarian usually can provide bibliographies and reading lists suitable for various individuals in the class. Library resources, however, are not limited to books. They include magazines and newspapers, pamphlets and clippings, government publications and graphic materials such as pictures, posters and charts, and book jackets and maps. In arranging materials for effective use, some librarians have organized the materials for core classes in terms of the school's stated problem areas. The librarian should, of course, have a copy of each resource guide developed for use in the school.

Other core teachers and teachers in other departments within the school usually have files of material that would be helpful in the preplanning of learning activities. Parents often take an active part in exploring and suggesting community resources. These suggestions are then incorporated in the file on community resources which suggests a variety of trips, speakers, consultants, and the like. In some schools these materials are pooled in some central place, usually the library; in others, they are filed in various places throughout the building.

Audio-visual aids usually include slides, filmstrips, motion pictures, radio, television, records, and tape recordings. These should be checked as to availability and scheduling.

The resource guide should be invaluable as the teacher seeks to become familiar with these and other resources in the school and community. The section on teaching materials includes a list of available books and pamphlets for pupil and teacher use, magazine articles, community resources, films, and filmstrips, records, and tape recordings. The section on activities contains many suggestions or implications for using various school and community resources.

In some schools the teacher may be able to preplan with other staff members at grade-staff meetings called for this purpose. In others he may have to seek out individual teachers. In any event, working with other teachers is a very important part of preplanning. It cannot be done in a vacuum; it necessitates the utilization of all available resources in relation to a problem area or a learning unit.

Pupil-Teacher Planning

Several descriptions of core classes in action are presented in order to shed some light on how teachers plan cooperatively with pupils. These are accounts of actual situations.

WHAT ARE THE MAJOR PROBLEMS FACING AMERICAN EDUCATION TODAY?[1]

The group consisted of twenty-three tenth grade boys and girls, eight of whom were new to the school that year. These pupils were preparing to

[1] This is an account of a learning unit developed in The Ohio State University School. The core teacher was Elsie J. Alberty.

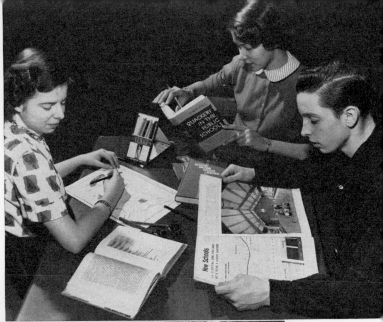

A tenth grade core group investigates current
criticisms of public education. (Upper)

A panel summarizes a comparison of conventional and
progressive methods in secondary education. (Lower)

Courtesy of Public Schools, Prince George's County, Maryland

Working Together to Develop a Core Program

Administrators, teachers, pupils, and parents work together on the development of resource guides in the core program. (Upper)

An art teacher helps a core teacher perfect his techniques in paper sculpture during a workshop for core teachers. (Lower)

Individual guidance is a paramount concern in the core program.

Courtesy of The Ohio State University
School, Department of Photography,
The Ohio State University, Columbus, Ohio

Courtesy of the Public Schools, Prince George's County, Md.
Photographer—Thomas Southall

Pupils plan effective ways to present their findings related to the existing county tax base and the support of public education.

Pupils in an eleventh grade core class learn to use the projector.

Pupils in this group have a wide range of vocational interests—social wor medicine, teaching, law enforcement, photography—yet core is required of *a*

develop a learning unit drawn from the area "Problems of Education in American Democracy."

Located on the campus of a large state university, the school does not serve any particular geographical area. Many of the pupils were first introduced to the core program and teacher-pupil planning on entering the school. Those who had attended the school for a period of years had become well acquainted with the program; consequently, for many of the new pupils, the transition from their previous school experiences to those provided in the school was disconcerting.

Several pupils did not participate in group discussions and forfeited their opportunity to share in the making of decisions which affected them. One or two others who had not experienced teacher-pupil planning looked upon this as an excuse to do nothing. After a short period, however, the pupils new to the school had adjusted well and were accepted by the rest of the group. References to "old and new" pupils were decreasing.

The teacher had participated in the development of a resource guide dealing with problems of education (See pp. 115-144.) and had the advantage of being well acquainted with the problem area and with resources for dealing with problems in this area. Staff members representing various fields—mathematics, history, language arts, related arts, science, home arts, and physical education—as well as other core teachers were consulted. The librarian was alerted and a collection of books and materials related to the area was placed on a special shelf in the library.

Preliminary Planning. The teacher opened the initial session by making some general comments relative to the problem area from which the learning unit was to be drawn. She followed this up with some comments on how the group had worked together as they had developed the previous learning unit. Several members of the group referred to their notes and supplied the recommendations for future action that the group had set down at the completion of the unit. After a general discussion, it was generally agreed that the group needed to focus special attention on: keeping discussions moving and to the point; encouraging everyone to participate in the activities of the class; meeting deadlines; and making effective use of the block of time. Next, the group talked over the general approach to be used in selecting the unit. The first step was to construct some guide lines for selecting the learning unit. After considerable discussion, the group set up the following criteria:

The core unit:

1. Should be broad enough to interest the whole group (taking into account as much as possible the interests of any minority group).
2. Should be important to us now as well as in the future.
3. Should not be a mere repetition of any previous unit.

4. Should be one in which adequate resources are available.
5. Should deal with "modern" problems.
6. Should have opportunities for trips and speakers. (This criterion was discussed at some length. It was finally agreed that a learning unit would not be chosen because it offered many opportunities for trips and speakers, but that trips, speakers, and other resources would be utilized wherever they might contribute to the study of the learning unit.)

After the criteria were agreed upon, there was a general discussion of problems that the group might investigate. Several of the problems suggested were: What is progressive education? Why is our school program different from that of other schools in Columbus? How is education in the United States different from that in other countries? With these possibilities in mind, the class agreed that the next several core periods should be set aside for exploring other possibilities and that each individual should formulate a list of problems to submit to the class.

Everyone in the class had an opportunity to explore the resources available in the library. These consisted of books, pamphlets, and current periodicals, newspapers and clippings, and charts and pictures. Several pupils and the teacher brought materials from home, and these were used to start a classroom library. The group agreed to ask the librarian for additional materials for the classroom library when the learning unit was more clearly defined. Four pupils explored possibilities by interviewing teachers and parents concerning the major problems of education in the United States. In all, the group spent about seven days on this phase of the planning.

Selecting the Learning Unit.   The members of the group suggested the following problems as appropriate for group study:

1. Should religion be taught in the schools?
2. What causes prejudice in schools?
3. How does the school program of today differ from that of 50 or 100 years ago?
4. How can you spread progressive education?
5. Why do kids quit school?
6. What courses should be required?
7. Should social activities (clubs, dances, etc.) be mixed with education?
8. How many progressive schools are there in the United States?
9. Should scholarships be provided for those who cannot go to college? On what basis should they be awarded?
10. How should you prepare for college?
11. How are handicapped people educated?
12. What are some criticisms of education? Why is it being criticized?

13. Is there a way to teach retarded children?
14. How does University School compare with North High School?
15. Why doesn't everyone have an equal opportunity for education?
16. How can a school building contribute to better education?
17. Why are sports given such an important place in some schools?
18. Should schools teach sex?
19. What are the advantages, if any, in going to a trade or professional school instead of college?
20. Why aren't there more progressive schools in the United States?
21. Do children in progressive schools learn the fundamentals?
22. Is it necessary to study psychology to be successful in working with people—to be a teacher, for example?

Each person who suggested a problem was given an opportunity to tell why he thought it appropriate and the possibilities he saw. A number of the suggested problems concerned progressive education. One pupil suggested that the learning unit be built around these problems. This suggestion was met with considerable enthusiasm on the part of the class. Another pupil suggested that a unit on the development of education in the United States included the problems concerned with progressive education and would more nearly meet the criteria.

After considerable discussion of these and other suggestions, the group agreed upon this organization:

What Are the Major Problems Facing American Education Today?

1. How has public education developed in America?
2. What types of programs are found in high schools today? (How does our school compare with other schools in Columbus?)
3. What is progressive education?
4. What are some criticisms of present-day education?
5. How is education financed?
6. Why do boys and girls drop out of school?
7. How can a school building contribute to an educational program? (This was added to the list several days after the unit was organized. Three boys expressed a keen interest in the problem and volunteered to investigate it.)

There was no formal statement of class goals, but it was generally agreed that the group wished to develop an understanding of the problems facing American education and how the group might contribute to their solution.

Developing the Learning Unit.   The group as a whole assumed responsibility for studying problem (1)—the history and development of American education. This was done by using several common references, viewing films, and through group discussion. With the help of the teacher, the group formulated the following list of questions:

1. How were the first schools in America supported?
2. What were some of the first laws in America relating to education?
3. How does the modern high school compare with schools in the various periods of our history? (Purpose, curriculum, method of teaching.)
4. What were some of the crucial issues in education in the various periods of our history?
5. Who are some of the people that have contributed to the development of American education?

These questions served as a guide for study and gave some direction to group discussions. Responsibility for dealing with the remaining six problems was assumed by small groups organized on the basis of interest. Individuals were encouraged to work on problems of special concern to them.

Several weeks were spent in planning ways to secure information, delegating responsibilities to different members of the groups, working in the classroom and in the school library, interviewing people who might shed some light on the problem, taking trips to other schools, and viewing pertinent films and filmstrips. The members of the class frequently came together for discussion and sharing of information. Several progress reports were made by each of the small groups. After approximately three weeks of study, the small groups presented their findings to the rest of the class. In presenting their material, the groups utilized panel discussions, guest speakers, role playing, films, charts and graphs, scrapbooks, and photographs.

The group making a study of the kinds of programs found in high schools today spent most of their time studying the University School program and how it compares with the programs of other high schools in and around Columbus. They began their presentation by asking the class to respond to the following questions:

How Well Do You Know Our School?

Who's Who?
  Can you name the following?

Director	Secretaries
Librarian	Nurse
Teachers	Doctor
Custodians	Chairman of the Parent Council

What?
   Can you give a general description of the school program?
   Can you describe the core program?
   Can you describe the electives program?
   What resources are available in the library?
   What health services are available to you?
   What are some of the social activities?
   How is the school program different from that of public schools? Like that of public schools?

When and Why?
   When was the school built?
   Who were some of the people who helped start the school?
   What is the relation of the school to the rest of the university?
   What are the functions of the school?

How many?
   What is the total enrollment?
   How many are enrolled at each grade level?
   What percentage of those who enter the first grade graduate?
   Who may enroll in the school?
   What is the average number of students in a class?
   How many teachers are there? Other employees?
   What is the enrollment in the city of Columbus? By Groups: elementary, junior high, senior high? How many teachers in Columbus?

These questions gave direction to the panel discussion which followed. At the conclusion of their presentation, the members of the panel made available to the class some descriptive materials they had obtained from two high schools in the vicinity as well as materials describing our own school program. As a follow-up of their report, the director of the school was invited to discuss the purposes of University School and the major characteristics of its program. The school librarian was asked to describe the early years of the school.

In leading a panel discussion on the reasons why boys and girls drop out of school, the group responsible presented data from several sources—studies reported in the literature, interviews with five students who recently had dropped out of high school, an interview with a high-school guidance counselor. This group also showed two films related to the problem: *Problem of Pupil Adjustment, Part I—The Drop Out; Part II—The Stay In.*

The group which made a study of criticisms of present-day education interviewed parents and teachers in addition to consulting resources available in the library. They presented their findings by means of a dramatic sketch in which they cast themselves as members of a family that had just heard a radio commentator attack modern education. Father, Mother, Grandpa, Brother (high-school age), Sister (elementary-school age) discussed present-day education.

On the day before they were to report, the group making a study of progressive education asked the members of the class to write a paper on "What I Hope to Get out of High School." The papers were analyzed and a list of the items most often mentioned was placed on the bulletin board. After some comments about the various meanings attached to the term progressive education, the group showed two films to the class— *Broader Concept of Method, Part I, Developing Pupil Interest; Part II, Teacher and Pupils Planning and Working Together.*

As a follow-up, the group helped the class contrast the characteristics of so-called "progressive" and "traditional" schools. They followed this with a panel discussion on which school—"progressive" or "traditional"— is better able to help boys and girls achieve what they hope to get out of a high-school education.

The three boys who volunteered to investigate how a school building can contribute to an educational program compiled a large scrapbook of materials showing the latest developments in school building design. They also mounted a number of photographs of school buildings in this area. They concluded their presentation with a discussion of possible improvements in our own school building.

Several graphs and charts were developed by the group studying how education is financed. These included a chart showing the sources of revenue for education in this state, a graph showing the expenditure per pupil of each state for education, and a graph comparing the expenditures for education and other selected items such as alcoholic beverages and tobacco. The group had become quite interested in inequalities in education and pointed much of the discussion toward this problem. Following the showing of the films *As Our Boyhood Is* and *And So They Live*, the group concluded their discussion of inequalities with a brief summary of the controversy over federal aid to education.

At the conclusion of the presentations, the class responded to a test which consisted of questions submitted by the six small groups and the teacher. These questions served as a basis for a final discussion on the problems defined for study.

During the course of the unit study, the group had a number of visitors, several of whom made a real contribution to the work of the class. A college student from Mexico sat in on the class over a period of approximately three weeks. During this time the members of the class had an opportunity to learn about education in Mexico as well as the visitor's reaction to education in this country. This stimulated several pupils in the class to make brief individual studies of education in other countries such as England, Russia, and Nazi Germany. A member of the State Department of Education visited in the school for several days. When he visited the core class, the pupils described the problems they were investigating and asked him to tell them something about the state department and its functions. Two other visitors served as resource persons during the course of the unit. A high school boy and a junior high school girl who visited the class were asked to describe their school programs.

Evaluating the Learning Unit. Evaluation was a continuous process from the time the unit began until the succeeding unit was undertaken. During the course of the learning unit, the teacher had an opportunity to observe pupils in total group and small group situations. Evaluations of committee work and self-evaluations, followed up by informal conferences to discuss specific problems, yielded considerable information on the pupil's progress in working in group situations. Individual projects and research papers, logbooks and scrapbooks, and reading records were important sources of evaluative data. A paper and pencil test was developed cooperatively by the pupils and teacher. It was concerned with the history and development of American education and with the problems investigated by the six small groups. The test follows:

Unit Test

Education

1. The University School has more than 10,000 visitors each year. Assume that you have been asked to describe the program of the school to a group of these visitors. What would you tell them? What would you show them?

2. Assume that you are going to visit a school. If you wish to find out whether the school is "traditional" or "progressive," what are some of the specific things you would look for?

3. Discuss at least three criticisms of modern education. How would you answer these criticisms?

4. Discuss briefly five of the following:
    a. "released time"
    b. Eight-Year Study
    c. Core
    d. Massachusetts Law of 1647
    e. "progressive" education
    f. Academy
    g. Latin grammar school
    h. drop outs

5. Do one of the following:
   a. On a map of the United States show how the states compare in terms of expenditures per pupil for education. What factors may account for this? Where does Ohio rank? How would you account for this?
   b. Make a graph to represent the growth of enrollment in the secondary school at ten year intervals from 1890 to 1950. Discuss reasons for this growth and its social consequences.
   c. Are all of our states equally capable of supporting good schools? Support your answer with data presented graphically.
   d. Make a graph showing how the average annual earning of teachers compares with that of factory workers, lawyers, secretaries, and physicians. What do you make of this?
6. Do one of the following:
   a. Compare the modern secondary school with the Latin grammar school by means of written discussion (essay), charts, cartoons, or sketches. You probably should include such points as purposes, curriculum, teacher procedures.
   b. Describe the contribution of one of the following persons to American education: Horace Mann; Booker T. Washington; John Dewey; Thomas Jefferson.
   c. Describe the educational system of some country other than the United States.
7. Give a summary of and your comments on *at least three readings* concerned with education. (This information should be placed on the sheet titled "Record of Unit Reading.")

At the conclusion of the learning unit, each member of the class was asked to submit the list of generalizations he had made as a result of the unit study. These were then compiled and distributed to the whole class. After considerable discussion, this list of generalizations was agreed upon by the class:

1. Education is an important factor in our lives.
2. Much education takes place outside of school.
3. Our schools should reflect the ideals of democracy.
4. Every boy and girl should have an opportunity to get a high-school education.
5. The modern high school differs from the Latin grammar school and the academy in purpose, curriculum, and method.
6. Relatively few high schools have a core program; most school programs are organized in terms of separate subject-matter courses.
7. A school program should deal with problems of present-day living.

8. In the United States the organization and administration of schools is controlled by the states.
9. For the most part, the local government finances the public schools.
10. Not all local governments can support education to the same degree.
11. A school building should be designed in relation to the school program.
12. Changes in high-school programs have not kept up with changes in the high-school population.
13. The kind of education we have in America will determine the future of our country.

Finally, the class devoted two periods to an evaluation of the study. considerable attention was given to such points as the achievement of class goals, organization of the study, amount learned, group work and presentations, and class discussions. Following is a copy of the rating sheet which served as a take-off point for this discussion.

Evaluation of the Core Unit

1. Organization
   1. Exceptionally well-organized
   2. Well-organized
   3. Part well-, part poorly-organized
   4. Poorly-organized
   5. Indefinite and confusing
2. Content
   1. Interesting all the way through
   2. More often interesting than dull
   3. Half interesting, half dull
   4. More often dull than interesting
   5. Dull most of the way through
3. Amount learned from unit study
   1. Tremendous amount learned
   2. Much learned
   3. A moderate amount learned
   4. Little learned
   5. Practically nothing learned
4. Class discussion
   1. Moved exceptionally well
   2. Usually moved smoothly
   3. Sometimes went well, sometimes poorly

    4. Frequently "off-the-beam"
    5. "Bogged down" much of the time

5. Resource people
    1. Very helpful in the unit study
    2. Fairly helpful in the unit study
    3. Helped somewhat in the unit study
    4. Helped little in the unit study
    5. Were of no help in the unit study

6. Audio-visual aids
    1. Extremely well related to content of unit
    2. Pretty well tied in with unit material
    3. Helped somewhat in understanding unit material
    4. Had little relationship to unit material
    5. Seemed isolated and not related to unit

  7. Would you recommend the study of this unit to members of other core classes?
    1. Yes. Recommend it highly
    2. Yes. It is probably more worthwhile than some other units.
    3. Undecided
    4. No. It is probably not as worthwhile as some other units.
    5. Definitely no.

8. Overall rating of unit
    1. An outstanding unit
    2. A good unit
    3. An "all right" unit
    4. A poor unit
    5. A very poor unit

9. Other comments

The class recommended that committee responsibilities be more clearly defined, that there be more frequent progress reports and more opportunity to share results of individual research, and that the class continue to work toward more effective discussions. In general, the members of the class agreed that the learning unit was "good" and that they would recommend the study of this unit to members of other core classes.

Resources. A wide variety of resources was utilized by the members of the class as they made a study of the major problems facing American education. The bibliography which follows was developed by the pupils with the help of the school librarian and the core teacher. The reader will recognize this as a working list which accounts for the discrepancies in correct bibliographical form.

Books

Aikin, Wilford, *The Story of the Eight-Year Study.* New York, Harper & Brothers, 1942. The story of an exciting experiment in education, an experiment in which The University School participated. (Fairly easy reading.)

Alland, Alexander, and James Waterman Wise, *The Springfield Plan.* New York, The Viking Press, 1945. The story of how one American community set out on a city-wide project for democratic living. (Easy reading.)

Benedict, Agnes E., *Progress to Freedom.* New York, G. P. Putnam's Sons, 1942. The story of American education. (Fairly easy reading.)

Bossing, Nelson, and Robert Martin, *Youth Faces Its Problems.* New York, Laidlaw Brothers, 1950, Units 25, 26, and 27. Discusses the importance of education, some problems encountered in getting an education, and some of the problems of society in providing an education. (Easy reading.)

Brown, Spencer, *They See for Themselves.* New York, Harper & Brothers, 1945. Discusses experimental methods in education. (More difficult reading.)

Cary, Sturges F. (Ed.), *New Challenges to Our Schools.* New York, The H. W. Wilson Company, 1953. Describes what goes on in the public schools and what Americans think of their schools. (Fairly easy reading.)

Cuber, John F., and Robert A. Harper, *Problems of American Society.* New York, Henry Holt and Company, Inc., 1948, Chapter XV. A general discussion of education in America. (More difficult reading.)

Duggan, Stephen, *A Student's Textbook in the History of Education.* New York, D. Appleton-Century Company, 1936. (More difficult reading.)

Gavian, Ruth Wood, A. A. Gray, and Ernest R. Groves, *Our Changing Social Order.* Boston, D. C. Heath and Company, 1947. Chapters 31 and 32. Discusses opportunities for education and education in better ways of living. (More difficult reading.)

Gillin, John Lewis, and John Philip Gillin, *An Introduction to Sociology.* New York, The Macmillan Company, 1942 Chapter 17. Discusses formal and auxilary educational institutions. (More difficult reading.)

Greenan, John T., *Everyday Problems of American Democracy.* New York, Houghton Mifflin Company, 1948, Chapter XI. Discusses federal support of public education. (Easy reading.)

Landis, Paul H., *Our Changing Society.* New York, Ginn and Company,

1942, Chapter XIX. Discusses the school's task in a dynamic society. (Fairly easy reading.)

Mann, Erika, *School for Barbarians*. New York, Modern Age Books, 1938. Discusses education in Nazi Germany. (More difficult reading.)

Mead, Margaret, *Growing Up in New Guinea*. New York, W. Morrow and Company, 1930. A comparative study of education in New Guinea. (More difficult reading.)

Quinn, James A., and Arthur Repke, *Living in the Social World*. New York, J. B. Lippincott Company, 1948, Chapter XXIII. Discusses education as training for social living. (Fairly easy reading.)

Rienow, Robert, *American Problems Today*. Boston, D. C. Heath and Company, 1953, Chapter VI. Discusses federal aid to education. (Fairly easy reading.)

Slosson, Edwin E. *The American Spirit in Education*. New Haven, Yale University Press, 1921. A history of American education. (More difficult reading.)

Were We Guinea Pigs? Class of 1938, University High School, The Ohio State University. New York, D. C. Heath and Company, 1940. An account of life in a "progressive" school. (Easy reading.)

Ziemer, Gregor, *Education for Death*. London, Oxford University Press, 1941. The makings of the Nazi. (Fairly easy reading.)

Pamphlets and Mimeographed Materials

Alberty, Harold, and others, *Let's Look at the Attacks on the Schools*. Columbus, Ohio, The Ohio State University Press, 1952. Identifies ten criticisms of public education.

America's Free Schools. New York, Council for Democracy, 1941. Discusses urgent issues in education; for example, inequalities, academic freedom.

A Description of Curricular Experiences, The Upper School, The University School, The Ohio State University. Columbus, Ohio, The Ohio State University, 1952.

Education. The Building America Series, Association for Supervision and Curriculum Development. Washington, D. C., National Education Association, 1948.

Education and the People's Peace, Educational Policies Commission. Washington D. C., National Education Association, 1943. A proposal for systematic use of organized education to help establish and maintain peace.

The Federal Government and Education. Washington, D. C., U. S. Government Printing Office, 1955. A summary of the findings and proposals of the President's advisory committee on education.

Hullfish, H. Gordon, *Keeping Our Schools Free*. Public Affairs Pamphlet No. 199. New York, Public Affairs Committee, Inc., 1953. Discusses the nature and importance of academic freedom and proposes five basic safeguards to protect teachers against unjust treatment.

The Philosophy and Purposes of The University School. A Report of the Faculty of The Ohio State University School. Columbus, Ohio, 1938.

What Is Democracy? America's Schools Are Writing the Definition. Washington, D. C., U. S. Office of Education, 1949. Twenty articles on "Education for Freedom" reprinted from *The Christian Science Monitor*.

Fiction

Erdman, Loula Grace, *Fair Is The Morning*. New York, Longmans, Green, and Co., 1945. The story of a teacher in a rural town.

———, *Separate Star*. New York, Longmans, Green and Co., 1944. The story of Gail's first year of teaching.

Fisher, Dorothy Canfield, *Seasoned Timber*. New York, Harcourt Brace and Co., 1939. The story of a principal of a small-town academy who becomes involved in a township election.

Furman, Lucy, *The Quare Woman*. Boston, Little, Brown and Co., 1930. A story of the Kentucky mountains.

Harper, Mary Barnhart, *Winter Wedding*. New York, Longmans Green and Co., 1950. A love story involving a teacher in a one-room school.

Hilton, James, *Good-bye Mr. Chips*. New York, Little, Brown, and Co., 1934. The story of an English schoolmaster and of his associations with three generations of schoolboys.

McLelland, Isabel C., *Hi! Teacher*. New York, Henry Holt and Co., 1952. The story of Alison Gray and her teaching experience in Cow Creek.

Rosenheim, Lucile G., *Kathy the New Teacher*. New York, Julius Messner, Inc., 1949. A romance that tells of Kathie's first year of teaching.

Magazine Articles

American

Yauch, "How Good Are Your Schools?" September 1951. A yardstick to show whether your town is doing an up-to-date job.

Pope, "Religion and Our Schools." May 1952. A discussion of a red-hot controversy.

Harpers
   Woodring, "An Open Letter to Teachers." July 1952. A discussion of current criticisms of public education.
   Hill, "A Bonanza for Education." March 1952. A proposal for solving the financial crisis in education by a U. S. Senator.
Ladies Home Journal
   White, "When a Boy Quits School." January 1951. A discussion of the drop out.
Life
   "Education in the U. S." October 16, 1950 (Whole issue).
The Nation
   Mitchell, "Battle for Free Schools: Fever Spots in Education," October 27, 1951. Attacks on "progressive education."
   Watson, "Battle for Free Schools: Fear of the 'Thing' " November 3, 1951. What critics of "progressive education" fear.
   Burkhart, "Battle for Free Schools: Big Business and the Schools," November 10, 1951.
   Nathanson, "Battle for Free Schools: The Foot in the Door," November 17, 1951. Religion and public education.
   Bond and Puner, "Battle for Free Schools: Jim Crow in Education," November 24, 1951. Discrimination in public schools.
   McLaughlin, "Battle for Free Schools: Education is Not Expendable," December 1, 1951. Arguments for federal aid to education.
   Benne, "Battle for Free Schools: What's Wrong with Our Schools," December 8, 1951.
   Brameld, "Battle for Free Schools: Four-Point Agenda for Education," December 15, 1951.
   Brameld, "Time out for Faith—Opposing Views on Released Time." February 9, 1952.
The New Republic
   "The Trend to Education," January 19, 1953.
Platform
   "Is Federal Aid the Answer?" September, 1948.
   "The Teacher Shortage." March, 1947.
Popular Mechanics
   "Look What's Happened to the Little Red Schoolhouse." September, 1950. Discusses school architecture.
Senior Scholastic
   "Our American Schools." November 7, 1951 (Whole issue).
Saturday Evening Post
   Saul, "I'll Stick Up for the Schools." April 15, 1950. The president of the Philadelphia Board of Education defends the public schools against those who criticise their curriculum and teaching methods.

Films

The following films were viewed—either by the whole class or by one of the six small groups:

And So They Live.
> Depicts the poverty of the land in a rural southern community, the lack of proper diet, housing and sanitation, the need for better adaption of the school program to the problems of the community.

As Our Boyhood Is
> An account of the best in education for Negroes in rural areas with enough indication of the worst to show that while progress has been made, there is much work to be done.

Assignment for Tomorrow
> The place and importance of the teacher in American life.

Broader Concept of Method, Part I—Developing Pupil Interest
> Presents a frank picture of the conventional, teacher-dominated, lesson-hearing type of recitation, and shows effects of this method upon student attitudes and responses. The film then shows alternative techniques to achieve broader educational objectives. An atmosphere of freedom of discussion leads to a suggestion for a class project.

Broader Concept of Method II—
> Continues the development of the project initiated by the class in Part I.

Children Must Learn
> Illustrates the unsatisfactory relationship between education and the local necessities of life which characterize education in many parts of this country.

Fight for Better Schools
> Story of the nation-wide interest in better public schools, showing the importance of an active and informed citizenry in reaching this goal.

Problem of Pupil Adjustment, Part I—The Drop Out
> Shows what led a boy to leave school as soon as the law permitted.

Problem of Pupil Adjustment, Part II—The Stay In
> Shows what can be done to meet the problems of drop outs.

Resource Personnel

The following served as resource persons:
> The director of the school
> The school librarian

The principal of a Columbus high school
A high-school guidance counselor
A college student from Mexico
The teacher of boys' physical education in the school
Two high-school students who visited the class
A member of the State Department of Education

Other Activities. Many activities in addition to those concerned with the unit of study were carried out in the core block of time. These included class business meetings, discussions of "current events" and happenings around school, the planning of a class dance, announcements and administrative details, and individual and group conferences.

Time was provided in each week's schedule for free reading. Suggested book lists appropriate for various interest and reading levels were developed by the librarian, members of the class, and the teacher. Students were encouraged to keep a record of their reading, and periodic conferences were scheduled to discuss specific problems.

During the course of the learning unit, it became apparent that note-taking and outlining presented considerable difficulty for a number of pupils in the class. As a consequence, time was set aside in the schedule to work on these skills. Materials drawn from student logbooks and papers, as well as resources found in the library, proved very helpful.

Each student was responsible for completing two peices of creative writing during the course of the learning unit on education. Some of these were related to the work of the unit, but generally such was not the case. In several instances, students requested that they be permitted to use other media such as watercolors, oils, and chalk. In these cases it was suggested that they might submit one such piece of work and that the other be in writing. These were shared by the class and suggestions for improvement were made.

THE SEAS AROUND US[2]

The Basic Education program in the eighth grade of the Sarasota Junior High School in Sarasota, Florida, consists of a two and one-half hour block of time which takes the place of the general education subjects of language arts, social studies, and science. The curriculum in Basic Education classes is structured to the extent that the faculty has suggested nine broad problem areas appropriate for both seventh and eight grades. These areas, however, are merely guideposts and by means of teacher-

[2] Prepared by Jean V. Marani, Basic Education teacher, Sarasota Junior High School, Sarasota, Florida.

pupil planning, the actual pattern of the curriculum is determined. The problem areas around which the school's program evolves are the following:

1. Orientation and Adjustment to the School
2. Home and Family Living
3. Mental and Physical Health
4. Leisure and Recreation
5. Development and Conservation of Natural Resources
6. Transportation and Communication
7. World Understandings
8. Democratic Heritage
9. Science and Technology

Teacher-pupil planning is the heart of the school's program, and it serves to translate the larger areas into actual curricular experiences. The actual determination of specific learning units rests with the teacher and the pupils. Careful analysis is made by the teacher of the needs, problems, and interests of his group. Their background from previous years is considered as well as the requirements of their age and maturity. The problem areas themselves represent the thinking of the faculty as they analyzed the characteristics of adolescents, their developmental responsibilities both now and in the future, and the demands of our democratic society.

Planning the Unit. In keeping with the curriculum pattern of the school, the choice of a learning unit, to last from about the first of October to the first of December, was determined by the members of the eighth-grade Basic Education class and their teacher. In approaching this important task, many factors were considered and discussed for several days. The list of suggested problem areas for grades seven and eight was written on the board and the contribution of each one to the educational background of the pupils was considered. The pupils were encouraged to recall the major learning units which they had had during the past two years. This step seems very important to avoid repetition and the predominance of a subject area, such as science or social studies, in the experience of pupils. During the orientation period pupils were given opportunities to examine their strengths and weaknesses in skill subjects such as spelling, reading, and grammar. These points were discussed as pertinent to a sound choice of a unit. The academic program of the high school was also considered as it related to the learning experiences of eighth graders.

After several periods of general discussion, the class was ready to develop a set of criteria for guiding them in choosing a unit. The following criteria were adopted by the class:

1. Is the unit new and interesting?
2. Can you learn something of value for now and later?
3. Is good material available?
4. Does the unit provide many different ways to learn—trips, research, creative projects, etc.?
5. Is the unit on our level and yet challenging to us?
6. Can other teachers help?
7. Does the unit cover many subject areas?
8. Does the unit require a fair amount of time?

After discussing the importance of these criteria, the class felt ready to suggest possible units for study. These were based on the analysis of their recent experiences in the seventh grade, on the interest and problems they recognized, and on the scope of the curriculum as suggested in the problem areas. The units that were suggested ranged from "Wars of America," "Diplomacy of America," "Foreign Countries," to "The Seas Around Us." The choice was made, not by voting, but by discussing the various units in the light of the criteria; thus, a gradual elimination was possible. While the class was listing its suggestions, the teacher contacted other teachers who taught the group to ascertain ways in which they could help. This information was given to the pupils to help them determine their final choice. This portion of the planning took several days, but it is the essence of teacher-pupil planning and cannot be telescoped into a few minutes.

The choice of the unit on "The Seas Around Us" was an outgrowth of several factors. During September, the Red Tide problem beset the West Coast of Florida, and this provided motivation for discussing the seas. The onset of the hurricane season was instrumental in focusing attention on the power of the seas. Another influence was the teacher's comments on a similar unit observed at The Ohio State University School. Undoubtedly the novelty of this unit appealed to the pupils and had some bearing on their eagerness to pursue a similar unit. However, the pupils realized that they were not being forced into a decision. The unit seemed to meet the criteria most adequately and combined possible learnings units from two problem areas: Development and Conservation of Natural Resources, and Science and Technology.

The role of the teacher in the choosing stage is that of a guide and advisor. He must be prepared to help pupils judge topics in terms of criteria, and he must be prepared to lend the weight of his experience to this evaluation. The balance between coercion and guidance is precarious, and the spirit of teacher-pupil planning dissolves if pupils are asked to make a choice and discover that they were "tricked" into selecting the teacher's predetermined plan.

Once the unit had been chosen, the work of defining its scope began. One method of handling this consists of discussing scope in its broad sense and at the same time examining material pertinent to the topic. This was the procedure followed in this unit. Pupils formulated questions they wished answered during the study. These were given to a committee which put them in outline form, discarding the duplications. The outline was then brought before the class for final correction and approval. A mimeographed copy was given to each pupil. The questions which defined the broad scope of the unit follow:

I. The Nature of the Seas
   A. What forces made the seas?
   B. What makes the seas salty?
   C. What are the major wind and water currents of the seas and what causes them?
   D. What forces cause and control tides?
   E. What are the major oceans of the world, their size and location?
   F. Under what conditions does ice form in the seas?

II. Conditions under the Seas
   A. What is the contour of the floor?
      1. Where are the deepest points?
      2. How are the oceans charted?
   B. What causes volcanoes on the sea floor?
      1. What is an under-water earthquake?
      2. What causes tidal waves?
   C. What light conditions exist in the seas?

III. Life in the Seas
   A. What kinds of animals live in the seas?
      1. What kinds of fish and mammals live in the seas?
      2. What kinds of sharks are there?
      3. What animals are kings of the seas?
      4. What types of fish live in deep water?
      5. Upon what do fish feed?
      6. Does a whale spout water?
   B. What kinds of shells are found in the seas?
      1. What makes a shell?
      2. What animals live in shells?
   C. What plants live in the seas?
      1. What kinds of seaweed are there?
      2. What is the Sargossa Sea?
   D. What makes a coral reef?
   E. How do sea animals differ from land animals?

IV. Man and the Seas
   A. How do the seas affect weather and climate?
   B. How have the oceans been used in past wars?
   C. How does man use the life and minerals of the seas?
   D. What are the dangers of the seas?
   E. How are cables laid under the seas?
   F. What power is there in the seas?
   G. How have the seas provided transportation?
V. Local Conditions
   A. What causes the Red Tide?
   B. What is being done about beach erosion?

The teacher and the class also formulated a list of guiding principles or major objectives which set the tone of the unit. These were more a product of teacher-planning since pupil discernment of broad goals is limited; however, discussion made the goals acceptable as measuring marks in evaluating the progress of the class in the unit. The objectives were:

I.   To understand the geological development of the sea.
II. To understand the forces of wind, current, and tides.
III. To understand the interdependency of animal and plant life in the seas.
IV. To understand the adaptability of life to the environment of the seas.
V.   To understand the importance of the seas to man.
VI. To understand the influence of the seas on the life and history of man.
VII. To improve techniques of research.
VIII. To develop increased appreciation of literature through reading stories of the sea.
IX. To develop creativity of expression in word and picture.
X.   To see more clearly the beauty of the seas.
XI. To develop all phases of communicative skills to a higher degree.
XII. To develop improved skills in working cooperatively.

While the preliminary planning was being completed, several student committees developed the direction of the unit. For example, one committee collected books pertaining to the sea and placed them on a "reserve" shelf in the library; the librarian, the teacher, and other faculty members contributed to this collection. Another committee prepared a list of activities for the group. Several pupils suggested field trips and visual aids that might prove valuable. A textbook committee listed references in the science, history, and literature books that pertained to the unit. All these activities served to clarify group thinking as to ways of answering the questions posed by the class.

Throughout the course of the unit, committees performed such functions as: preparing bulletin board displays, writing letters to order research materials, planning trips, securing art supplies, and collecting materials. Each of these activities constitutes one more experience in building the skills of group planning and cooperative problem solving which forms the basis of the democratic way of life.

Developing the Unit. The basic plan of attack in studying "The Seas Around Us" consisted of research to answer the questions outlined by the class and learning activities to insure that concepts and factual information became a part of each pupil's background of knowledge. To achieve the former, the class divided itself into four major groups corresponding to the major divisions of the outline. It was decided that all pupils should work on Number V, Local Sea Conditions. Grouping was on the basis of interest since the amount of material available on each division seemed quite extensive. Each member of the committee was responsible for answering all the questions in his group. Approximately five weeks (with library periods of at least two hours each week) were allotted to gathering material; this indicates the extensiveness of the pupils' research. Many visited the public library. The room library provided much information, and magazines and other periodicals suggested leads and hints.

After weeks of preparation each committee gave its report. The plan called for each member to present his answers to each question unless it was repetitious. This method encouraged wide research and the presentation of many theories to the class. At the conclusion of each group report, questions were asked and any points not adequately covered were explored further (this happened in several cases). While listening to the reports, the students took very few notes. The class felt it would gain more from listening. To insure all pupils' having access to all the research, each committee prepared a complete written summary of their findings. The teacher and the committee spent several hours in "readying" each report for typing and mimeographing. Each pupil received a copy, and many favorable comments about this procedure were expressed.

Research alone does not constitute the extent of learning or problem solving in any unit. Many concepts discovered during the course of reading in the library were expanded into group learning activities. In addition, individual reports and projects served to deepen the concepts and ideas contained in the unit. The approach to learning in this unit consisted, then, of research by groups and by individuals, in reporting by groups and individuals, in both oral and written summaries, and in clarifications and explanations by the teacher. The weight of responsibility lies with the teacher in directing the unit, but the burden of transmitting information and learnings is shared by all in the class. Activities of a varied nature avoid the dullness of drill, and extensive learning results from this problem-solving approach.

TYPICAL WEEKLY SCHEDULE

12½ hours

Monday: Homeroom activities, current events, library research, spelling.

Tuesday Library research, discussion of progress and explanation for group learning activity, grammar and short drill, spelling.

Wednesday: Movie, free reading period, individual help, spelling.

Thursday: Project time, grammar, creative writing, spelling.

Friday: Free reading, discussion of unit problem, spelling, evaluation, planning for next week.

This schedule is flexible and is typical of the period of research on the unit. The planning and reporting weeks prolong these activities. The schedule is always written on the board and serves as a guide for everyone.

Teaching the Unit. In the material which follows, the various activities, techniques, and resources . . . were used which are listed. Unless otherwise indicated, all the material was of value in the learning process. The specific information is not exhaustive, but should provide a basis upon which a teacher might construct her own unit.

Activities. The following activities were developed through teacher-pupil planning. Not all the ideas were furnished by the pupils, for the teacher has the responsibility for insuring that the activities provide for individual differences and reflect the broad objectives of the unit.

1. The first major group activity consisted of identifying the bodies of water that constitute the "Seas Around Us." This immediately led to research as sources listed conflicting facts. Each pupil was given a map (from a ditto map prepared by a student) and with the aid of materials in the room, each ocean and sea was identified. Now we had a common background when speaking of the seas surrounding us.

2. A study of the major ocean currents and the prevailing wind currents followed, and again maps, globes, and atlases were used to locate information. Naturally much interest developed in the Gulf Stream due to its proximity to Florida. The teacher read several descriptions of the major currents, and pupils recorded pertinent information on their maps and in notebooks. Oral evaluation indicated that this group study was of unusual interest and certainly represented "new facts" to the entire group. A sample test over the material served to organize the material; later a test

was given over the factual material but in such a way that the information was used to solve reasoning problems.

3. A very fruitful group activity concerned the Gulf Stream. Pupils gathered information about the current from their regular research reading and supplemented it with material read by the teacher. This was combined into an outline on the board and the course of the current was carefully charted on student maps. After more oral discussion, each pupil wrote a theme on "The Cycle of the Gulf Stream." These themes were not graded but corrected and returned with comments. Pupils were given a period in class to rewrite them, and they filed both papers in their folders. This was a popular activity.

4. At this point research in the library reached a point at which more common background knowledge was needed. The seventh and eighth grade science books provided resource material. The entire class read and discussed references from both books. This activity helped direct research and provided information on an easy level for those with learning difficulties.

5. Questions concerning tides and waves was another group learning activity. Although tides had been studied in lower grades, the concept was not sharp, and the pupils profited by a review of the factors involved in this phenomenon. Several theories of tidal variations were introduced and diagrammed. Concepts of the size and types of waves were clarified by diagrams, pictures, and many descriptions read by the teacher. A factual test concluded this activity.

6. The teacher read many accounts of the sea to the pupils during the unit. The pupils were quick to bring to class stories and articles pertaining to the unit. The language used to describe the sea by such authors as Michener and Carson fascinated the pupils. This activity was very fruitful in stimulating reading.

7. Vocabulary building was an absolute necessity in the study of this unit and constituted an almost daily activity. As new words were encountered in reading and class discussion, they were written on the board and the pupils developed definitions. These written in the notebooks each pupil kept on the unit. Some of the most frequently used words were placed on a chart on the bulletin board. Learning to spell all the words was not required, but after working with them, correct spelling was facilitated.

8. During the early days of the unit, pupils often encountered the technical terms for the phyla of the animal kingdom. These broad classifications were discussed and a chart of the divisions placed on the bulletin board. By reference and use pupils acquired a knowledge of the divisions and examples of the animals in each classification.

9. Reading for pleasure as well as information constituted a major

goal of the unit. Through teacher-pupil planning the goal of reading at least one book on the sea was set for the entire class. To insure time for this, approximately one to one and a half hours each week were scheduled for reading. Various techniques were used to stimulate wide reading:

    a.   Informal book reporting—pupils related a few highlights from the book being read.

    b.   Excerpt reading by the teacher—this resulted in pupils reading such books as *Captains Courageous, Kon-Tiki, The Sea Around Us, Moby Dick* and many others.

    c.   Book lists—each pupil wrote the name of his book and his comments on a chart—this was posted in the room and carefully watched by pupils seeking a new book to read.

10.   Mobile construction was a new and intriguing experience for pupils. None of them had seen a mobile until the teacher demonstrated the building of a simple one. The idea blossomed and many chose a mobile as a creative project thus providing excellent articulation between the industrial arts and arts and crafts teachers. Research was required in building the mobiles since the examples of sea life used had to be accurate. A further development of this activity was the construction of Christmas mobiles for home and classroom decoration. The idea also spread to other rooms.

11.   Another activity was the reading of specific literature assignments. In addition to providing excellent stimulation for extensive reading, this assignment enabled pupils to improve their discriminatory abilities in judging literature. Many spirited discussions accompanied the reading periods, and pupils were encouraged to develop their ideas in essay form.

12.   Since a major objective of the unit was to discover the influence of the seas on history, specific reading assignments were given. In addition pupils constructed an outline of the "sea history" of America. Group construction of an outline offered a fine opportunity to develop a sense of logic as well as giving many pupils a chance to participate.

13.   Each pupil undertook one research project and one creative activity. When the pupil completed his individual project, he presented his efforts to the class in a brief report. The most frequently chosen projects were: a booklet of pictures and drawings of sea animals and plants; a map of the oceans showing the principal currents; a series of pictures of various types of sea life; reports on animals and plants in the sea. The making of shell collections and the construction of mobiles and other creative activities were also described to the class. A short evaluation was held at the conclusion of each report.

14.   A basic learning experience for all pupils occurred almost daily during discussion periods. At this time questions were raised and time was devoted to the mass of information brought by pupils (articles—even the

book *Fantasia* was utilized—clippings, and pictures). From these, many facets of the unit were discovered and integrated into the background of the pupils. There were numerous questions from pupils during the study, and the learning which occurred during these interchanges was gratifying.

15.   The final week of the unit was devoted to summary and evaluation. The techniques used are described below.

Summarizing Activities.   Several projects were carried on by groups of pupils at this stage of the unit. This procedure was followed to provide more adequately for individual differences and to allow pupils to have a choice in planning several varied activities. These projects served not only as summarizing activities but as evaluative techniques, for they indicated pupil understanding of the scope of the unit. The whole class participated in the planning of these projects.

1.   A bulletin board display at the entrance to the library was the responsibility of seven pupils. They chose to display individual projects. The planning of the position of each article and picture was time-consuming, but the finished display demonstrated to them, to the class, and to the school the variety of experiences pupils had had in the unit. This project was undertaken several weeks before the conclusion of the unit.

2.   Back-to-school-night, sponsored by the PTA, provided a summarizing activity for pupils. A committee functioned to select examples of the work of the class to display for parents. Since we had not concluded the unit, the material was incomplete, but it served to illustrate the types of learning being carried on. Needless to say, the mobiles engendered much parental comment.

3.   Several pupils made a mural in which they illustrated the variety of plant and animal life in the sea. They used the material in *Life* ("Creatures of the Sea," November 30, 1953) as a guide. A rough outline of the mural was made on newsprint and then transferred to brown wrapping paper; poster paint was then applied. The mural now decorates the wall in the classroom and will be used in a county-wide school exhibition. The arts and crafts teacher cooperated with us in this activity.

4.   One large group of pupils chose to compile a scrapbook on the salt-water world for their activity. They sorted all the individual reports of their classmates and selected many to be put in the book. In addition they chose pictures (original and from magazines) to decorate the pages. The finished product represented a good summary of what the class learned about sea life.

5.   A remaining group designed a huge map of the world to show the prevailing ocean currents as well as the depth of the sea. They scaled the map to fit into a nine-foot square of oak tag and drew the continents to scale (the mathematics teacher helped here). The currents were red (warm

water) and blue (cold water) arrows and pointed in the direction of movement. The continental shelf and other variations in depth were shown by gradations in color. Various points were marked with numbers according to the depth. This map is now framed and hangs in the room.

Evaluation. The concept of evaluation which is being developed in our school is individualistic in nature. Each child is encouraged to set goals for himself and to demonstrate self-direction in reaching these goals. Evaluation is viewed as a continuous process involving constant examination of progress in terms of the goals that have been selected and a readjustment of procedures in the light of these evaluations. Evaluation is attempted in every phase of the study of a unit, not just in periodic tests. However, examinations are not neglected, but their use is predicated on their value as tools in judging total progress toward the major objectives. Some evaluative techniques used in the unit are described below.

1. At the beginning of the unit each pupil was asked to write a paragraph on the topic: "What I Know about the Seas." This same activity was assigned at the conclusion of the unit. Pupils were able to see in a very graphic manner the extent of their learning. This was in no sense a test, and pupils understood the comparative values of the two papers before they undertook the writing. No grade was given on either paper, though comments were made concerning expression and thought content.

2. At frequent intervals during the unit, pupils were asked to write short evaluations of the various techniques used in class or on procedures used in problem solving. This was an attempt to determine pupil understanding of the purposes of learning techniques, for oral participation in evaluation is always limited to the more vocal pupils. This does not negate the place of oral evaluation but supplements it.

3. Much evaluation occurred informally when pupils and teacher examined problems of finding information and carrying through projects. Pupils need to be helped in developing self-direction, but they must be given latitude to demonstrate it. The lengthened general education period affords much time for the individual conferences which characterize evaluation at its best.

4. Periodic tests covering areas of learning in the unit were used. Following (pp. 177 and 178) are two examples.

5. The periodic reporting period came after five weeks of unit study had elapsed. It frequently happens that the end of a reporting period does not coincide with the termination of a unit, but evaluation of progress can still be included on a report card. During class, each pupil had an individual conference with the teacher concerning his progress in the basic education subjects of language arts, science, and the social studies. The folders of pupils, observations by the teacher, and the pupil's self-evalu-

ation formed the basis for determining the grade (letter grades are used in the school) each was to receive.

6.   During the last week of the unit, each pupil prepared a summary of all his activities and projects undertaken during the unit. He included a brief description of each item, the grade he had received, and any comment by the teacher. This record sheet was used by the pupil and the teacher in a conference to determine his over-all grade on the unit and to help in writing a short statement of his accomplishments to accompany the next report card. The pupils liked this procedure because "it helps me to see where I am and what I've done."

Items in the record were: sources of information used, the approximate time spent in research and on projects and activities, themes and topics of a written nature, summaries of field trips, tests, committee reports, books read, literature grade, summary activity, and miscellaneous comments by the pupil.

7.   After much discussion and debate, the class evolved the following plan for a final evaluation of their work in the unit. Part A was a series of questions which they could answer using the mimeographed summary of committee reports, the information in their notebooks, data from the summary projects, and special reports they had made. They wished to be graded on content and expression. Part B was a traditional-type objective test covering the more important factual data which they had handled; they did request that the questions require "thinking, not just all memory." In preparation for this twin-barreled activity, the class spent several days in reviewing the material in their committee reports and in a final clarification of any foggy details. Both Part A and Part B were teacher-constructed due to the nearness of Christmas vacation.

Ocean Currents and Winds

Answer each question to the best of your ability. Write enough so that a person who did not understand much about the topic would not be confused.

1.   Explain the effects of the following currents on the climate of the lands they pass: (a) Gulf Stream, (b) Humboldt, (c) Benguela, (d) Labrador.
2.   How do the "Roaring Forties" get their name? Where are they located?
3.   Describe the location and source of the West Wind Drift.
4.   Why are the fogs dense in the vicinity of the Aleutians and the Grand Banks?
5.   How are the Grand Banks constantly being built up?

6. Why is the water saltier at the Equator than at the Poles?
7. Give three reasons why the Gulf Stream and the Japanese currents are twins.
8. What direction do winds and currents move south of the Equator? North of the Equator?
9. What is the difference between Trade Winds and the West Winds?
10. What basic causes influence the wind and currents to move in the direction you stated in question eight?
11. Give the approximate dimensions and speed of the Gulf Stream at (a) the Florida Straits, and (b) Cape Hatteras?
12. How did the cycle of the Gulf Stream help the Spanish in their conquest and settlement of the Americas?
13. On the back of your paper draw a rough sketch of the Gulf Stream and give the names of its various currents.
14. Why are the icebergs of the North Atlantic more of a menace than those of the Antarctic region?

Tides and Waves

1. Draw and label a diagram of a typical wave.
2. What forces cause the tides in the Bay of Fundy to be so tremendous?
3. Draw a diagram illustrating the fact that we have two high tides and two low tides at opposite points on the globe at the same time. Write a brief description of this phenomenon.
4. Define "fetch," "bore," and "tidal wave."

Final Examination

Part A. Answer the following questions using your notes. Be brief but include enough material to "clinch" your point.
1. Discuss the influence or effect of the following on man:

    (a) salinity of sea water   (d) waves
    (b) currents   (e) plankton
    (c) tides   (f) tidal waves

2. Explain the truth or falsity of the following:
    (a) Sharks will always attack you.
    (b) The ocean floor is flat.
    (c) Fish always eat plants.
    (d) The Sargasso Sea is a true sea.
    (e) A whale spouts water.

(*f*) All water is either salt or fresh.
(*g*) Deep sea fish are giants and are vicious.
(*h*) Sea plants are not true plants.
(*i*) Sea and land animals differ.
(*j*) The whale is king of the sea.
(*k*) Shells are dead.

3. How are the ocean depths measured?
4. Explain the theories of the creation of the (a) oceans, and (b) coral reefs.
5. Name the true oceans.
6. Give three reasons why the continental shelf is abundant in life.
7. Name three products from sharks.
8. Why are deep sea fish carnivorous?
9. Why do most corals grow between Brazil and Cape Hatteras?
10. How are shells formed?
11. List three reasons why deep-sea fish are so small.
12. Give three ways sea and land animals differ.
13. List three factors limiting divers.
14. Describe the contour of the sea bottom.

Part B. Underline the word(s) which best complete the statement.

1. The lowest form of life in the animal kingdom: (a) chordata; (b) fish; (c) algae; (d) protozoa.
2. A sloshing back and forth of the water in an ocean or sea basin is: (a) isolation; (b) gravitation; (c) oscillation; (d) bore.
3. To live, plants must have: (a) oxygen; (b) light; (c) soil (d) fertilizer.
4. The layer of material at the ocean bottom is: (a) sand; (b) debris; (c) ooze; (d) fish bones.
5. When water freezes it: (a) contracts; (b) expands; (c) turns to ice; (d) turns blue.
6. The deepest point in the sea is: (a) Caymen Trench; (b) Guam; (c) Japanese Trench; (d) North Pole.
7. Light penetrates to about: (a) 500 ft.; (b) one mile; (c) 500 fathoms; (d) 10,000 ft.
8. The color of the deep sea is: (a) blue; (b) aqua; (c) green; (d) black.
9. Plankton colors water: (a) green; (b) murky; (c) blue; (d) silver.
10. Cold water is found at the bottom of the ocean because: (a) it is frozen; (b) it is denser than warm water; (c) it is saltier.
11. The green coloring in seaweed is: (a) lime; (b) algae; (c) chlorophyll; (d) sap.
12. The main chemical composing shells is: (a) polyps; (b) sodium; (c) lime carbonate; (d) coral.

13. The largest mammal is: (a) squid; (b) whale shark; (c) blue whale; (d) elephant.

14. The largest fish is: (a) squid; (b) whale shark; (c) tuna; (d) marlin.

15. The largest invertebrate is: (a) giant clam; (b) squid; (c) giant kelp seaweed; (d) Portuguese-man-of-war.

16. The animal building coral is: (a) clam; (b) plankton; (c) polyp; (d) protozoa.

17. Seaweed is most nearly: (a) vine; (b) animal; (c) plant; (d) plankton.

18. The family of shells, clams, squid, etc. is: (a) protozoa; (b) porifera; (c) echinodermate; (d) mollusca.

19. The family to which all vertebrates belong is: (a) man; (b) mammals; (c) chordata; (d) fish.

20. A ring-shaped coral reef is: (a) barrier reef; (b) island; (c) lagoon; (d) atoll.

21. Winds blowing from east to west are: (a) Roaring Forties; (b) west wind; (c) Trades; (d) West Wind Drift.

22. The simplest form of plant life is: (a) protozoa; (b) eel grass; (c) algae; (d) plankton.

23. The pasturage of the sea is: (a) eel grass; (b) seaweeds; (c) plankton; (d) detriti.

24. The fastest ocean current is: (a) Japanese; (b) Humboldt; (c) Gulf; (d) California.

25. The eating of both plants and animals is: (a) carnivorous; (b) herbivorous; (c) omnivorous.

Vocabulary of the Unit. During the course of the unit, many new words were encountered. The majority were learned by repetition in the readings and by hearing, but many words needed explanation and study to become clarified for the pupils. The words were not taught as definitions to be memorized but as tools necessary to the understanding of the resource material.

continental shelf	vertebrate	tides	atoll	sound
sea erosion	carnivorous	crest	ooze	nocturnal
chlorophyll	herbivorous	diurnal	drift	protozoa
oceanology	omnivorous	reef	current	porifera
invertebrate	oscillation	algae	doldrums	bore
mollusca	chordata	trades	gulf	bay
salinity	mammals	fetch	sea	ocean
polyps	trough	plankton	shoal	chitin

Films and Filmstrips. The following films and filmstrips were obtained from the county film library and were thus available when they could best be utilized.

1. *Beach and Sea Animals.* This film is quite elementary but pupils used it as a resource for their special reports. Black and white, 10 minutes, sound.
2. *Volcanoes in Action.* Helps pupils understand the phenomenon of volcanic action as a theory for the creation of the seas. Black and white, 10 minutes, sound.
3. *What Makes Rain.* Helpful in explaining the relation of the water cycle to the seas. Black and white, 10 minutes, sound.
4. *Shellfish of the Seashore.* This filmstrip proved valuable in illustrating the habits of starfish, clams, etc.

Due to the location of Sarasota and the familiarity of pupils with the sea and the life therein, the need for movies was not as great as it would be in other sections of the country.

Field Trips. The entire class visited the Nautilus, a shell shop in Sarasota, Florida. There they saw numerous shell products, examples of marine life, specimens of rare and unusual shells, and the entire process of readying a shell for sale. Purposes of the trip were listed and discussed by the class before going. Most pupils took notes. The owner showed her shop to the students and answered their many questions concerning this relatively new business. On returning, a letter of thanks was written. Oral evaluations were held, and then each pupil wrote his individual impressions of the trip using the theme title of "Observations at the Nautilus." The owner was shown these papers and used pupil comments in preparing for future field trips. This was a very profitable excursion.

Since a basic objective of the unit was a greater appreciation of the beauty of the seas, a trip was planned to the John and Mabel Ringling Museum of Art in Sarasota. One of the librarians helped the class plan the trip by outlining the pictures and statues she intended to show them. All exhibits pertained to the general theme of marine life. A highlight of the trip was the showing of the color film, "Feeding Habits of Marine Animals." The material presented in the film was extremely timely. Much of the modern art depicted marine life, and the pupils preferred these paintings to the more established works. Again oral evaluation preceded the writing of a theme on the general topic of "Observations at the Museum." A letter of thanks was written to the guide. This trip was a rich experience for all. (It might be mentioned that the assignment of the theme summarizing the field trips was very flexible and pupils took complete advantage of the latitude to write their individual impressions and comments.)

Textbook Assignments. We cannot conclude that subject matter and textbooks are eliminated from the classroom scene, merely because a unit of work cuts across the conventional subject-field organization. Rather we must conclude that subject matter and textbooks are used with great frequency in problem-solving situations and are used with purpose and intent. Pupils do not resolve problems or questions in a vacuum; much research provides them with the answers to their queries. Therefore, the references listed below are not to be considered as dogmatic assignment to be memorized, but as sources of information to help pupils in finding data applicable to their questions. In the case of the references in literature and social studies books, the intent was to guide pupils toward a realization of the major objectives.

Science

Smith, Victor, et al., *Enjoying Science*. New York: J. B. Lippincott Company, 1946, pp. 57-60, 63-64, 118-119, 290-292, 453-454, 463-467, 479-485, 540. (This is an eighth grade text.)

———. *Exploring Science*. New York: J. B. Lippincott Company, 1946, pp. 108, 132-133, 161-162, 295-296. (This is a seventh grade text.)

Powers, Samuel, Ralph. *Exploring Our World*. New York: Ginn and Company, 1940, pp. 55-68, 80-81, 138, 142-145, 364-372. (This is a seventh grade text.)

These references refer to such topics as how fish swim, adaption of life to the sea, under water volcanoes, tides, currents, wind, water cycle, etc.

Social Studies

Hartman, Gertrude. *America, Land of Freedom*. Boston: D. C. Heath and Company, 1946. In compiling an outline of America's seafaring history pupils read the following page references:
Early Atlantic explorations: 5-16; St. Augustine: 26; Verrazano and Jacques Cartier: 28; John Cabot: 35; Armada: 40-42; Roanoke: 43 and 45; Jamestown: 46-51; Whaling industry 85-86; Shipbuilding in New England: 85, 89, 580; slave trade: 121; Navigation Acts: 120-140; War of 1812: 237-241; travel to California: 339-340; Clipper ships: 338, 450-451; Atlantic Cable: 464-466; Ocean ships: 449-451; "Maine": 546; Panama Canal: 548-49; Submarine warfare: 559-561.

MERICAN FAMILY FORUM

REDERICK SASSCER HIGH

Tommy Seers Student

Betty Rey Student

Bob Nott Student

Ruth J. S. Youll Moderator

Ethel MacGarner Student

Mrs G. Fredine Parent

Courtesy of The Ohio State University School, Department of Photography, The Ohio State University, Columbus, Ohio

Courtesy of the Public Schools, Prince George's County, Maryland Photographer—Thomas Southall

eachers plan together in an on-going core program. (Upper)

n identifying problems of common concern this group gathered data from its eers, a family relations expert, a parent and the school's principal. (Lower)

Courtesy of the Public Schools, Prince George's County, Marylan
Photographer— Thomas Southa

Courtesy of Florida State Universit
Demonstration School, Tallahassee, Floric

These groups are working together on various aspects of their common proble
—How our concepts of Democracy has evolved. (Upper)

Exploring common problems calls for cutting-across conventional subject-fie
lines. These pupils used subject matter from biology, home economics, a
language-arts and mathematics in a *learning unit* from the problem area, Sel
Understanding. (Lower)

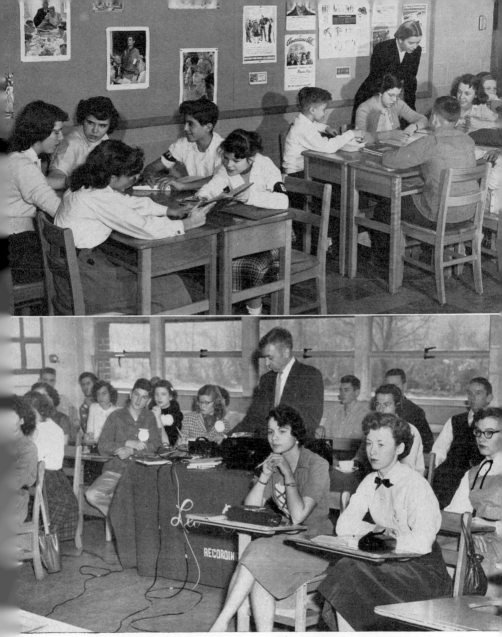

Courtesy of the Public Schools, Prince George's County, Maryland
Photographer—Thomas Southall

...he teacher provides guidance to small groups working on the improvement of
...eir reading skills in a free reading period in the core program. (Upper)

...n eleventh grade core class listen to a play-back of a recording made by their
...oup in an evaluation session. (Lower)

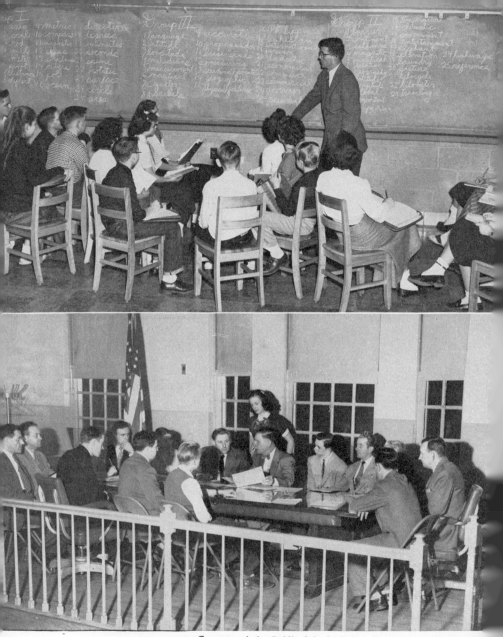

Courtesy of the Public Schools, Prince George's County, Maryla[
Photographer— Thomas South[

A seventh grade core teacher works with three spelling groups on graded wo[
lists related to their unit "How People Live in Korea." (Upper)

Pupils in the core program use the community as a resource in exploring pro[
lems. These pupils are at work with their teachers and civic leaders pooli[
their ideas for a country-wide clean-up campaign. (Lower)

English

From the errors noted in pupil papers the entire class entered upon a study of the agreement of subject and verbs. This involved work with hidden subjects, person and number, and tenses.

Literature

Ross, Jacob. *Adventures for Reading: Book II.* New York: Harcourt, Brace and Company, 1947.
  "Spot Landing," aircraft carriers, 3-12.
  "The Inchcape Rock," poem, 19-20.
  "Old Ironsides," poem, 63-64.
  "A visit from the Sea," poem, 121-122.
  "A Nautical Extravaganza," poem, 295-296.
  "Daniel Webster and the Sea Serpent," fantasy, 2, 96, 308.
  "Forty Singing Seamen," poem, 308-310.
Eberhart, Wilfred, et al., *Reading Literature: Book II.* Evanston, Illinois: Row, Peterson Company, 1950.
  "How Old Stormalong Captured Mocha Dick," 52-64.
  "Skipper Ireson's Ride," poem, 76-79.
  "Sea Tramps," poem, 231.
  "Clipper Ships," poem, 246-247.
Broening, Angela, et al., *Best-Liked Literature: Book II.* New York: Ginn and Company, 1947.
  "The New Stokes," 153-154.
  "Swimming Song," poem, 299.
  "On the Beach," poem, 300-301.
  "The Adventures of Baron Munchousen," fantasy, 455-457.
  "Island Sentinels on Guard," Pacific, 481-491.
Neville, Mark. *Exploring New Fields.* New York: Rand, McNally and Company, 1942.
  "Under the Sea," 71-76.
  "The Wreck of the Hesperus," poem, 281-285.
  "Sea Fever," poem, 289-290.
  "Comments on Fishing," 493-495.
  "Anecdotes of Whaling Days," 513-517.
Starbuck, Edwin Diller, *Action Speaks.* Yonkers-on-Hudson, New York: World Book Company, 1936.
  "A Modern Buccaneer," 188-243.
  "Captain Scott," 60-293.

Activities

1. Select a poem that you liked particularly well and write a paragraph telling why.
2. Write a good one-paragraph summary of any story in this group.
3. Select the stories or poems which you think added to your knowledge of the sea—tell why in a few sentences.

It might be mentioned at this point that since our school is located in a tourist town, we constantly meet the problem of pupils entering during a unit. Their orientation consists of a review of what is being done by the entire class, a session with the handbook for new pupils which the basic education class has written, assistance and explanation by the teacher, and the assignment of all textbook reading the class has done. Then pupils are encouraged to undertake several projects concerning the unit. Through these procedures pupils soon feel a part of the school and adjust to the classroom situation in short order.

Bibliography.   The references which follow compose the resources used by pupils and the teacher in this unit. The annotations indicate their usefulness. The references were largely those in the school library though some were secured from the public library and home libraries. Pupils, the teacher, and the librarian assisted in finding the books and putting them on a "reserve" shelf in the library. Some of the material was kept in the classroom. No attempt has been made to list the references and resources to be found in encyclopedias, biology books, nature books, and other standard reference sources found in any library. However, the abundance of material on this topic is staggering.

Books

Axelrod, Herbert T. *Tropical Fish as a Hobby.* New York: McGraw-Hill Book Company, 1952. Excellent reference; much information about the habits of these strange fish.

Beaty, John Y. *The Ocean Book.* Chicago, Illinois: Beckley-Cardy Company, 1946. Easily written story of a trip along the coast of the United States—basic reference for slow students.

Beebe, William. *Exploring with Beebe.* New York: G. P. Putnam's Sons, 1932, pp. 23-155. Beebe gives excellent descriptions of life on the surface of the sea and a beautiful account of his diving exploits.

————. *The Arcturus Adventure.* New York: G. P. Putnam's Sons, 1926. Excellent colored pictures of strange sea life; also good description of the Humboldt rip current, underwater volcanoes, and related topics.

Breland, Osmond P. *Animal Facts and Fallacies.* New York: Harper & Brothers, 1948. pp. 131-168. Interesting facts; fine for slower students.

Brindze, Ruth. *The Gulf Stream.* New York: The Vanguard Press, 1945. Easy reading; gives an arresting account of this famous current, its history, and its importance.

Carson, Rachel L. *The Sea Around Us.* New York: Oxford University Press, 1951. A beautifully written account of the seas—a bit difficult for students, though the sections on wind, waves, and currents are fine for better students. Excellent resource for teacher—can be read to students. This was a basic reference.

Chapin, Henry, Smith, F. G. Walton. *The Ocean River.* New York: Charles Scribner's Sons, 1952. Excellent reference on the Atlantic Ocean; good background for teachers though better students can read it profitably.

Colman, John S. *The Sea and Its Mysteries.* New York: W. W. Norton and Company, Inc., 1950. A rather difficult book though it provides outstanding background information for teacher. Superior students can use it also. Survey of the seas from beginning to present.

Cousteau, Captain J. Y. *The Silent World.* New York: Harper & Brothers, 1950. An exciting account of the development of aqualung diving in France with new and interesting data on undersea life. Boys will like this—adult, though readable by any student of junior-high age.

De Laubenfels, M. W. *Pageant of Life Science.* New York: Prentice-Hall, Inc., 1949. Excellent source of drawings of animal and plant life in the sea—a basic biological text though useful throughout the unit.

Douglas, John Scott. *The Story of the Oceans.* New York: Dodd, Mead, and Company, 1952. Excellent reference for currents, life in the seas, and conditions under the surface. Primarily for teacher, though good students can use it.

Hausman, Leon A. *A Beginner's Guide to Fresh-Water Life.* New York: G. P. Putnam's Sons, 1950. Contains selected references to little-known fresh water life.

Huntington, Harriet E. *Let's Go to the Seashore.* New York: Doubleday and Company, Inc., 1941. Excellent pictures; easy text though brief.

Michener, James. *Return to Paradise.* Chapter I on the coral atoll. A beautiful description of the birth of an atoll and of the life found on it—perfect to read to a class.

Reed, W. Maxwell, Bronson, Wilfred S. *The Sea for Sam.* New York: Harcourt, Brace and Company, 1935. A comprehensive source book for students and teacher covering every phase of the unit. It is scientifically accurate and very readable. Could be a basic reference for this unit.

Robertson, Gladys, and Bevans, Michael. *Strange Sea Life.* New York: Henry Holt and Company, Inc., 1950. Accurate and readable account of sea animals and plants—good basic reference.

Walsh, Mary and Carter, Helene. *Water, Water Everywhere.* New York: Abingdon-Cokesbury Press, 1953, pp. 32-48. Simple discussions of currents, ocean depths, etc.

Burgess, Thornton W. *The Burgess Seashore Book for Children.* Boston: Little, Brown, and Company, 1948. The title is misleading; the book gives good factual data about many sea plants and animals told in story form.

Hylander, Clarence J. *Sea and Shore.* New York: The Macmillan Company, 1950. Traces the development of life in the sea—good reading for junior high.

Magazines

Barnett, Lincoln. "The Earth is Born," *Life,* XXXIV (December 8, 1952). Good for origins of the seas.

————. "The Miracle of the Sea," *Life,* XXXV (February 9, 1953). Outstanding, readable, and challenging.

————. "The Pageant of Life," *Life,* XXXV (September 7, 1953), pp. 54-74. Excellent information and pictures especially of early life in the seas.

————. "Age of Mammals," *Life,* XXXV (October 19, 1953), pp. 90-109. Brief references involving sea mammals.

————. "Creatures of the Sea," *Life,* XXXV (November 30, 1953), pp. 78-100. Outstanding reference, should require this as reading for the unit; pictures and text very challenging and interesting.

Beebe, William. "Depths of the Sea," *National Geographic,* January, 1932. Specialized reference.

————. "Wanderer under the Sea," *National Geographic,* December, 1932. Underwater explorations—reference.

————. "Half Mile Down," *National Geographic,* December, 1934. Explorations in the bathysphere.

"The Great Barrier Reef," *The New Yorker,* August 15, 1953, pp. 31-. A very vivid account of the reef and its growth, though a little hard to read.

Colton, F. Barrows. "Our Global Ocean, Last and Vast Frontier," *National Geographic,* January, 1945. Good material on charting and measuring the seas.

Cousteau, Jacques-Yves. "Fish Men Explore a New World Underseas," *National Geographic* CII (October, 1952), pp. 431-472. Fascinating account with pictures of aqualung explorations—boys eager to read this.

Ewing, Maurice. "New Discoveries in the Mid-Atlantic Range," *National Geographic*, XCVI (November, 1949), pp. 611-640. Good information and pictures about the depths of the Atlantic and the mysterious underwater ranges.

Moore, Hilary, Philips, Craig, and Hutton, Jacqueline. "Strange Babies of the Sea," *National Geographic*, CII (July, 1952), pp. 41-56. Excellent story with pictures though material is a bit technical—students can use it.

Platt, Rutherford. "Shells Take over Your Horizons," *National Geographic*, XCVI (July, 1949), pp. 33-84. A fine article with excellent pictures of most shells—students can use this.

Smith, Walton, F. G. "River of Life," *Nassau*, IV (Mid-season, 1952), p. 41. A very good but simple description of the Gulf Stream.

Zahl, Paul. "Man-ofWar Attacks Bikini," *National Geographic*, CI (February, 1952), pp. 185-212. Story and pictures of strange sea life—good, though text is a bit difficult.

————. "Fishing in the Whirlpool of Charybdis," *National Geographic*, CIV (November, 1953), pp. 579-618. Story and pictures of deep sea life brought up by the upwelling of the Mediterranean waters—excellent.

Pamphlets

Director of Fish and Wildlife Service
U. S. Department of Interior
Washington 25, D. C.
(Information about fish and their habits; much of the information is rather technical.)

Director of Coast and Geodetic Survey
U. S. Department of Commerce
Washington 25, D. C.
(Information about charting and measuring the seas plus data on tides and currents—this is rather technical.)

The Marine Library
The University of Miami
Coral Gables (University Branch) 46, Florida
Att.: Librarian
(A list of pamphlets and booklets on many phases of marine prob-

lems in and around Florida—many of these are free. However, the material is beyond all but the best Junior-high students.)

Subject-matter in the Unit. The major objectives of the unit, coupled with pupil questions, frame the subject-matter content, and yet, in the problem approach, there is ample opportunity for individuals to penetrate deeply into any phase of the unit. This unit abounds in science material; that is obvious. Social studies was integrated into the unit by discussing current events involving the sea, reviewing the seafaring history of America, referring to the early exploration and settlement of the New World, and in countless other ways.

English skills were more than accessories in this unit. Opportunities for writing abounded, and the students practiced such skills as note-taking, theme writing, letter writing, and many others. Spelling of unit words was integrated with the regular program following the state-adopted text. Vocabularies of the pupils were enlarged. The opportunities for reading were numerous. Since the library contained materials for all reading levels, individual differences could be met. Functional grammar study was possible since pupil papers contained the usual proportion of errors in verb-subject agreement, punctuation, misplaced modifiers, and the like. This gave additional motivation for the program of grammar review being carried on independently.

The mathematics teacher cooperated in utilizing many opportunities to integrate his program with the unit. Pupils worked problems using fathoms, nautical miles, degrees of longitude and latitude, and discussed the function of mathematics in charting the depths of the seas. This work was carried on concurrently with the regular mathematics program.

In arts and crafts, and industrial arts, the teachers provided pupils with materials and helped in developing their creative projects. In many instances, pupils went to the shop and art room during their Basic Education period in addition to going at their regularly scheduled time. The home living teacher assisted pupils by discussing the contribution of the seas to our diets. This kind of cooperation was a direct result of consultation carried on during the planning of the unit.

The music teacher helped pupils learn songs of the seas and played several musical selections with the sea as a theme. In speech class the pupils had opportunity to improve their techniques of oral delivery, thus making possible a closer relation between the speech and Basic Education classes. Even though it may not be on the grade-staff level but a matter of a few conferences before and after school, planning is essential in achieving integration. No attempt was made to coordinate physical education with the unit.

Throughout the study the mastery of subject matter *per se* was far from the major objective. Yet in the course of the unit, opportunities for making factual data a functional tool to learning were countless.

Teacher Evaluation and Comment. From initial planning to final evaluation, the unit involved thirteen weeks of strenuous study and learning. This is a long time to devote to developing one unit, but my considered opinion is that the effort was fairly successful. Parents, pupils and other teachers have shared this conclusion.

In several instances opportunities for learning were overlooked. We did not utilize any people in the community as speakers or resource people. We might have secured a better selection of films, and a field trip to the beach could have been rewarding. Pupils should have been led into a wider selection of individual projects. In preparing reports, too many pupils tended to copy information.

There seem to be several outstanding advantages in this kind of unit. The interest level it generates is extremely high. Material on all levels is almost unlimited. Pupils must depend on research since text-books do not cover the scope of such a unit. The opportunities for stimulating writing and reading are many, and individual projects can be planned on a very broad basis. In summary I might say that I consider this the most successful unit I have ever taught.

CHARACTERISTICS OF THE CORE PROGRAM

The following chart is designed to summarize the chapter and to point up the characteristics of the core program in action, as revealed by the two learning units described above.[3]

Characteristics of the Core Program in Action

What Are the Major Problems Facing American Education Today?	*The Seas Around Us*
I. Long block of time	
8½ hours per week; 2½ hour block on Monday and 1½ hour block, Tuesday through Friday.	12½ hours per week: 2½ hour block, Monday through Friday.

[3] See Chapter II for an elaboration of the characteristics which identify the core program in action.

Characteristics of the Core Program in Action

| *What Are the Major Problems Facing American Education Today?* | *The Seas Around Us* |

II. Cooperative planning: teacher-pupil, teacher-teacher, and pupil-pupil

Teacher-pupil planning

a. Drawing learning unit from problem area
   Discussion of previous learning units and experiences
   Discussion of approach to be used in selecting unit
   Setting up criteria
   Suggesting possible learning units
   Selection of the learning unit
b. Organization of learning unit
   Definition of scope
   Formulation of plan of attack
c. Development of learning unit
   Total group activities
   Small group activities
   Individual projects
d. Evaluation of learning unit
   Clarification of goals
   Teacher-pupil developed techniques
e. Planning activities apart from learning unit
   Class dance

Teacher-teacher planning

Consultation with staff members representing various fields of knowledge and with librarian

Pupil-pupil planning

Small group responsible for:
   Investigation of unit problems and reporting their findings to the class
   Preparation of bulletin board displays
   Jobs connected with planning and giving a class dance

Teacher-pupil planning

a. Choosing the learning unit
   Consideration of problem areas appropriate for grades 7 and 8
   Discussion of previous learning units
   Consideration of high-school academic program
   Development of set of criteria
   Suggestion of possible learning units
   Selection of the learning unit
b. Organization of learning unit
   Definition of scope
   Formulation of plan of attack
c. Development of learning unit
   Total group activities
   Small group activities
   Individual projects
d. Evaluation of learning unit
   Clarification of goals
   Teacher-pupil developed techniques

Teacher-teacher planning

a. Broad problem areas preplanned by staff
b. Work of various classes integrated with unit study

Pupil-pupil planning

Small groups responsible for:
   Investigation of unit problems and reporting their findings to the class
   Preparation of bulletin board displays
   Collection of resource material
   Preparation of list of activities
   Suggestions of field trips and visual aids
   Suggestions of references in science, history, and literature textbooks
   Securement of art supplies
   Ordering of research materials
   Preparation of display for PTA "Back to School" Night
   Making of a mural, a map, and a class scrapbook

Characteristics of the Core Program in Action

What Are the Major Problems Facing American Education Today?	*The Seas Around Us*

III. Problem-solving approach

a. Real problems dealt with in the learning unit
b. Clarification of what is to be achieved
   Definition of goals
   Definition of problems to be investigated
c. Formulation of plan of attack
d. Putting plan into action
   Development of unit
e. Evaluation of products and processes
f. Clarification of what has been achieved
   Statements of generalizations reached

Final discussion

a. Real problems dealt with in the unit
b. Clarification of what is to be achieved
   Definition of problems to be investigated
c. Clarification of plan of attack
d. Putting plan into action
   Development of unit
e. Evaluation of products and processes
f. Clarification of what has been achieved
   Construction of Scrapbook summarizing work of class
   Compilation of individual folders of materials related to unit study
Final discussion

IV. Scope based on common needs, problems, and interests of adolescents

a. Concerned with contemporary problems, personal-social in character
b. Drawn from *Problems of Education in American Democracy*

a. Concerned with contemporary problems, personal-social in character
b. Drawn from *Development and Conservation of Natural Resources and Science and Technology*

V. Utilizes subject matter which cuts across fields of knowledge

Subject matter cuts across several fields of knowledge

a. History and social studies
   History and development of education in America
   Effect of social, economic, and geographic conditions on education
   Influence of European education on American schools
   Social backgrounds and ideals of our culture reflected in our schools
   Social problems, e.g., inequalities in education
   Learning unit drawn from area which is primarily social studies in content

Subject matter cuts across several fields of knowledge

a. History and social studies
   Early exploration and settlement of the new world
   America's sea-faring history
   Current events involving the seas
   Geography
   Specific assignments in social studies textbook

Characteristics of the Core Program in Action

What Are the Major Problems Facing   The Seas Around Us
American Education Today?

V. Utilizes subject matter which cuts across fields of knowledge

b. Related arts
   Bulletin board displays
   Scrapbook
   Graphs and charts
   School building design and its contribution to a school program

c. Mathematics
   Graphs and charts
   Tabulation of data
   Simple computation—average, percentage, etc.
   Sampling techniques

d. Language arts
   Papers
   Oral and written reports
   Unit reading and research
   Free reading
   Word study (spelling)
   Note-taking and outlining
   English skills (grammar study)
   Class discussion
   Oral and written evaluation of unit work
   Paper and pencil tests
   Role-playing

b. Related arts
   Bulletin board displays
   Scrapbook
   Maps and charts
   Mobiles
   Mural
   Trip to shell shop
   Trip to museum of art

c. Mathematics
   Charting the depth of the seas
   Problems involving fathoms, nautical miles, degrees of longitude and latitude

d. Language arts
   Papers
   Oral and written reports
   Unit reading and research
   Free reading
   Word study (spelling)
   Note-taking and outlining
   English skills (grammar study)
   Class discussions
   Oral and written evaluation of unit work
   Paper and pencil tests
   Letter writing
   Specific assignments in literature book

e. Science
   Learning unit primarily science in content
   Specific assignments in science textbook

f. Music
   Singing songs of the sea
   Listening to recordings

g. Home living
   The contribution of the seas

VI. Required of all

Required of all   Required of all

Characteristics of the Core Program in Action

What Are the Major Problems Facing   *The Seas Around Us*
American Education Today?

VII. Individual and group guidance

Individual guidance

Individual conferences: to help pupil select materials appropriate for his interest and ability level; to encourage pupil to work on problems of special concern to him; to help pupil select problem to be investigated in small group; to help pupil evaluate his progress both in relation to the study of the unit and the group processes involved; to help pupil solve his personal problems

Group guidance

a. Learning units drawn from areas defined in terms of the personal-social needs, problems, and interests of adolescents in this society
b. Setting up of criteria and selection of the learning unit
c. Organization, development, and evaluation of the learning unit
d. Activities other than core unit
    Discussions of happenings around school
    Discussion of problems of concern to group
    Suggestions for creative writing and free reading

Individual guidance

Individual conferences: to help pupil select materials appropriate for his interest and ability level; to encourage pupil to work on problems of special concern to him; to help pupil select problem to be investigated in small group; to help pupil evaluate his progress both in relation to the study of the unit and the group processes involved; to help pupil solve his personal problems

Group guidance

a. Learning units drawn from areas defined in terms of the personal-social needs, problems, and interests of adolescents in the society
b. Setting up of criteria and selection of the learning unit
c. Organization, development, and evaluation of the learning unit
d. Activities other than core unit
    Discussions of happenings around school
    Discussion of problems of concern to the group
    Suggestions for creative writing and free reading

VIII. Evaluation—cooperative, continuous, creative

a. Continuous from time learning unit was selected until succeeding unit was undertaken
b. Utilized a wide variety of techniques
    Observation of pupil in total and small group situations
    Informal oral evaluation of committee reports
    Brief written evaluation of techniques used in the unit study
    Paper and pencil tests
    Reading records
    Individual projects and research papers
    Individual conferences

a. Continuous from time learning unit was selected until suceeding unit was undertaken
b. Utilizes a wide variety of techniques
    Observation of pupil in total and small group situations
    Informal oral evaluation of committee reports
    Brief written evaluation of techniques used in the unit study
    Paper and pencil tests
    Reading reports
    Individual projects and research papers
    Individual conferences

Characteristics of the Core Program in Action

What Are the Major Problems Facing American Education Today?	*The Seas Around Us*

VIII. Evaluation—cooperative, continuous, creative

Individual folders	Individual folders
Pupil self-evaluation	Pupil self-evaluation
Final discussion of learning unit	Final discussion of learning unit
List of generalizations	Summary of activities and projects undertaken by individual pupils

IX. Fundamental skills taught in terms of use made of them

a. Reading
  Unit reading: books, pamphlets, periodicals, newspapers
  Free reading
  Reading records kept

a. Reading
  Unit reading: books, pamphlets, periodicals, newspapers
  Textbooks
  Free reading
  Reading records kept

b. Written communication
  Themes
  Research papers
  Creative writing
  Written evaluations
  Paper and pencil tests
  Note-taking
  Outlining
  Vocabulary study

b. Written communication
  Themes
  Research papers
  Creative writing
  Written examinations
  Paper and pencil tests
  Note-taking
  Outlining
  Vocabulary study
  Summary of committee findings
  Letter writing

c. Oral communication
  Planning sessions
  Discussion and evaluation sessions
  Reports to the class
  Interviewing resource persons

c. Oral communication
  Planning sessions
  Discussions and evaluation sessions
  Reports to the class

d. Number skills
  Making graphs and charts
  Keeping class accounts
  Sampling techniques
  Tabulating poll results

d. Number skills
  Making graphs and charts
  Keeping class accounts
  Solving problems related to unit, e.g., charting depths of the seas

e. Relationships
  Many opportunities for participation in and evaluation of group processes
  Discussions and other total group activities
  Committee work

e. Relationships
  Many opportunities for participation in and evaluation of group processes
  Discussions and other total group activities
  Committee work

Characteristics of the Core Program in Action

| *What Are the Major Problems Facing American Education Today?* | *The Seas Around Us* |

X. Many uses of wide variety of resources

a. Persons
   Members of the class
   Staff members representing various fields
   Librarian
   Director of the school
   Teacher of boys' physical education
   High school guidance counselor
   Principal of a public high school
   College student from Mexico
   Two high-school students who visited the class
   Member of the State Department of Education
b. Materials
   Resources in library: books, newspapers and clippings, pamphlets, periodicals, charts, and pictures
   Films

c. Techniques
   Problem solving approach utilized
   Attention given to how to gather, tabulate, organize, and present information
   Field trips
   Interviews

a. Persons
   Members of the class
   Staff members representing various fields
   Librarian
   Owner of a shell shop
   Guide at museum of art

b. Materials
   Resources in library: books, newspapers and clippings, charts and pictures
   Maps, globes and atlases
   Films
   Filmstrip
   Textbooks
c. Techniques
   Problem-solving approach utilized
   Attention given to how to gather, tabulate, organize and present information
   Field trips

XI. Based on democratic values

a. Concern for optimal development of the individual
   See Individual and Group Guidance, above
   See Scope, above
b. Cooperative process emphasized
   See Cooperative planning, above
c. Problem-solving approach basic
   See above

a. Concern for optimal development of the individual
   See Individual and Group Guidance, above

b. Cooperative process emphasized
   See Cooperative Planning, above
c. Problem-solving approach basic
   See above

VII

THE ROLE OF THE SPECIAL-INTEREST AREAS IN THE CORE PROGRAM

One of the major blocks to the development of the core program is the confusion as to the role of the special-interest-area teacher in such development. When the well-established, logically organized subject-matter pattern of general education is replaced by the core program which deals with the common needs, problems, and interests of youth without regard to subject-matter lines, many teachers feel insecure concerning their particular contribution to this program and may even oppose it.

Problems dealt with in the core, if adequately handled, do cut across traditional subject-matter lines. This is far, however, from saying that the core group plans, executes, and evaluates in a vacuum. The rich offerings of the subject-fields are utilized in the core as they have a particular bearing on the problem at hand.

It is the view of the writers that all special-interest areas can make a significant contribution to the core, but it is only as the problem is thoughtfully studied by all concerned that the value of the special-interest areas in this framework will be fully realized. This problem must be explored further before any widespread reorganization of general education on the basis of a core program can be expected.

In the previous chapter, two descriptions of core classes in action were presented and then analyzed in terms of the characteristics of core. This analysis indicated that the various special-interest areas made significant contributions to the learning units described. The purpose of this chapter is to explore in more detail the role of the special-interest-area teacher in core program development.

Some Guiding Principles for Participation of Special-Interest-Area Teachers in the Core

The following general principles should be kept in mind by core teachers and special-interest-area teachers as the latter endeavor to make a significant contribution to the core program. Generally speaking, the special-interest-area teacher must understand the philosophy of education and psychology of learning underlying the core and be able to implement these through a specific area. Ideally, each special-interest area should be represented on each core staff. This implies that the special-interest-area teacher:

1. Understands how children grow and develop.

2. Can bring subject matter to bear upon the broad problems of a personal-social nature common to most adolescents.

3. Has a rich variety of resources to draw upon in men, materials, and techniques.

4. Has worked with core teachers in setting up the problem areas and in developing materials such as resource guides.

5. Has been a participating member in the initial planning of the learning unit in the classroom when expected to make any kind of a contribution.

6. Works with the group not only in planning but in executing the plans and evaluating these learning activities.

7. Has a working knowledge of the principles of group dynamics.

8. Does not expect the core teacher to abdicate when a special-interest-area teacher contributes to the core.

9. Is willing to spend the time and energy necessary to help groups meet their needs, solve their problems, and extend their interests through working together.

10. Understands the unique contribution of a particular area to the problem at hand, yet sees possibilities for other areas to participate significantly in the solution of the problem.[1]

[1] Lucile L. Lurry, "The Contributions of Home Economics to Selected Problem Areas in the Core Curriculum of Secondary Schools." Unpublished Doctoral Dissertation, Columbus, Ohio, The Ohio State University, 1949, pp. 213-214.

The Role of the Special-Interest-Area Teacher in Core Program Development

In a core program, the special-interest-area teacher may participate at two levels:

1. The preplanning level
2. The action level

Preplanning Level. The writers have assumed that a more adequate core program can be developed through defining the basic curricular structure of the school in terms of broad, preplanned problem areas —areas set up by the entire faculty in terms of the common personal-social needs, problems, and interests of adolescents. This type of preplanning affords the special-interest-area teachers the opportunity to think through with those who teach in the core their contributions to meeting needs through the core program. The special-interest-area teachers can also make suggestions concerning resource materials and aid in their development when this type of preplanning is done. It should not be assumed, however, that the mere act of drawing the special-interest areas into the core produces a more adequate program. The basic consideration is to use subject matter in a more functional manner as it impinges on the needs, problems, and interests of the learner. The entire resources of the school are thus marshalled as the faculty works together in the educational program.

Several studies serve to clarify the role of the special-interest areas in core program development. One of the studies directed toward this end was that carried out by Lurry.[2] An hypothesis of this study was that the possible contributions of home economics to the core program could be clarified by relating such contributions to pre-planned problem areas. Hence, sixteen problem areas in which youth have common needs, problems, and interests were developed.[3] These were developed in relationship to a set of criteria, a review of the litera-

[2] *Ibid.*

[3] The reader will note that only fifteen of the problem areas developed by Lurry were presented in detail in Chapter III. *Problems of Critical Thinking* was omitted on the ground that it might be treated as an area of method rather than of content.

ture over a period of ten years (1938-48), and the judgment of thirty leaders in the field of core program development. The problem areas included: *(1)* problems of school living; *(2)* problems of self-understanding; *(3)* problems of finding the values by which we live; *(4)* problems of social relationships in a democracy; *(5)* problems of employment and vocations; *(6)* problems of conserving natural resources; *(7)* problems of education in American democracy; *(8)* problems of constructive use of leisure time; *(9)* problems of family living; *(10)* problems of communication; *(11)* problems of democratic government; *(12)* problems of personal and community health; *(13)* problems of economic relationship in a democracy; *(14)* problems of critical thinking; *(15)* problems of achieving peace in the atomic age; *(16)* problems of intercultural relations.

The scope of the contributions of home economics to the core program was determined by the sixteen problem areas developed. These were sent in questionnaire form to teacher educators in home economics, high-school teachers of home economics, and to general educators. The participants were asked to state in general terms what they believed home economics could contribute in each problem area to help youth deal with their common needs, problems, and interests. They were also asked to indicate how their suggested contributions might be made most effectively by judging whether the home economist could contribute to the core best as a: *(1)* core teacher; *(2)* core coordinator; *(3)* resource person; *(4)* service person in the laboratory; or *(5)* member of the initial planning group.

The conclusions reached were:

1. Home economics has a significant contribution to make in each problem area developed in this study. The extent of this contribution will be defined in each instance by the nature of the core learning unit.

2. The home-economics teacher should always be a member of the initial planning group. She cannot otherwise be expected to render a worthwhile contribution to the core.

3. The home-economics teacher, perhaps, should be the core teacher in learning units oriented in terms of family living.

4. The home-economics teacher could serve the core in a valuable

way by coordinating the experiences of those learning units which deal particularly with home-economics subject matter, for example, personal and community nutrition.

5. The home-economics teacher can help meet individual needs in any problem area as a service person in the laboratory.

6. In most cases the home-economics teacher can best serve the core as a resource person. In this capacity she would teach short units and suggest and direct use of certain resources as they relate to the core unit, for example, field trips, library research, audio-visual aids, consultant service, and discussion groups.

One of the most recent studies in this field was carried out in a cooperative research project dealing with the contributions of mathematics, business education, and science to the core program.[4] The investigators based their study upon Lurry's sixteen problem areas. In order to determine the contributions of their respective fields to the problem areas, it was necessary to determine the possible activities in which students might engage as they come to grips with problems in each of the areas. These activities were developed cooperatively in terms of a set of criteria and without reference to any field. Each of the investigators then proposed the contributions which he thought his field might make to the carrying out of the activity.

The contributions of mathematics to the core activities were defined in terms of the mathematical concepts essential to carrying them out. Business-education contributions were stated in the form of common business-understandings. Here business education was defined as that area of education that deals with the understanding, the appreciation, and the intelligent and effective performance of managing, recording, communicating, consuming, and distributing

---

[4] Elsie J. Stalzer (Alberty), "Contributions of Mathematics to a Proposal for Reorganizing General Education in Secondary Schools on the Basis of a Core Program." Unpublished Doctoral Dissertation, Columbus, Ohio, The Ohio State University, 1952; William E. Jennings, "Contributions of Business Education to Selected Problem Areas of General Education in the Secondary School," Unpublished Doctoral Dissertation, Columbus, Ohio, The Ohio State University, 1952; Monir Mikhail, "Contributions of Science to Selected Problem Areas Proposed for a Program of General Education in the Secondary School." Unpublished Doctoral Dissertation, Columbus, Ohio, The Ohio State University, 1952.

economic goods and services. The contributions of science to the core activities referred to those scientific facts, concepts, principles, instrumental and problem-solving skills, attitudes, appreciations, and interests that need to be used or developed in order that these activities may be carried out most effectively. Pertinent contributions were drawn from all sciences without regard to the arbitrary boundries that separate one science from another.

The following illustrates how mathematics, business education, and science might contribute to the problem area concerned with *Economic Relationships in a Democracy*. In dealing with this area, a core group might wish to investigate the problems of consumer advertising. While a complete investigation of this problem is likely to go beyond the realm of mathematics, business education, and science, these three fields can make a significant contribution to the solution of the problem. Following is one of the suggested activities related to consumer advertising and the contribution of mathematics, business education, and science to the activity.

Activity: Collect and analyze samples of false or misleading advertisements, honest advertisements, and advertisements containing exaggerated claims.

Mathematical Concepts

The concepts categorized under proof: deduction, induction, assumption, hypothesis, definition, undefined terms, relevance, reliability, and representativeness.

Business Understandings

1. Advertising is a medium of mass communication between producers and sellers and consumers—a medium needed by each of them. It is a source of facts and guidance which helps the intelligent shopper.

2. Individual business men, advertising agencies, and government have put forth efforts to raise the level of advertising by barring exaggerations and deceptions.

Science Understandings

1. A large number of advertisements contain false claims.

2. Claims in advertisements may be validated by checking them with recognized authorities.

3. Among the qualifications of an authority are: recognition and accord with other authorities, special competence and established credibility.

A detailed analysis of all the activities suggested as appropriate for the sixteen problem areas disclosed that mathematics made a contribution to each problem area. In all, fifty-three mathematical concepts classified under the headings of number, measurement, relationship, proof, operation, and symbolism were considered essential to carrying out the core activities. The problem areas most dependent upon mathematical concepts were *Social Relationships, Critical Thinking, Economic Relationships,* and *Personal and Community Health.* Problem areas in which the concepts were essential to relatively few activities were *Self-Understanding, Constructive Use of Leisure, Democratic Government, Achieving Peace,* and *Communication.*

Phases of business education were evident in fifteen of the problem areas. Business education did not seem to contribute to the area of *Self-Understanding.* There were forty-one business understandings classified in terms of finance, record keeping, communication, distribution, consumer education, organization and management, occupational information, and human relations in business situations involved in the core activities.

Science made a significant contribution to twelve of the problem areas. Science made little or no contribution to problems of *Employment and Vocation, Education in American Democracy,* and *Democratic Government.* The suggested science contributions included 523 different statements that were classified under eight major categories: health and safety; atomic energy; conservation; human growth and development; values and beliefs; communication; critical thinking; hobbies.

In each case the investigator concluded that the special-interest area involved (mathematics, business education, science) made a significant contribution to general education as defined in the study.

Several other studies provide clues to the contributions which the special-interest-area teacher might make to the core at the level of preplanning. A seminar group under the direction of Harold Alberty[5] developed the activity-analysis technique in relation to the

[5] Harold Alberty and others, *Utilizing Subject-Fields in Core Program Development* (Mimeo.). Columbus, Ohio, Ohio State University Press, 1950.

area of *Self-Understanding* as a means of illustrating the ways in which special-interest areas might contribute to the core. The technique developed by this group was used later, with modification, by the three investigators whose cooperative research project was described above. Kalman[6] also made use of this technique in making a study of the contributions of related arts to the area of *Problems of Conserving Natural Resources.*

Action Level. The following descriptions illustrate the role of the special-interest-area teacher in the on-going core program.

CONTRIBUTIONS OF RELATED ARTS TO A CORE LEARNING UNIT[7]

This is a description of how related arts contributed to a learning unit on natural resources. The unit was planned cooperatively by the teacher and students in a ninth-grade core class at The Ohio State University School.

The University School provides the core class (grades seven, eight, and nine) with a three-hour period in which to carry out various responsibilities. Some of these responsibilities are:

1. To provide continuous experiences through which students can come to understand and meet their needs, extend their interests, and solve life problems in a way consistent with democratic philosophy.
2. To develop learning units from problem areas designed to provide the above experiences.
3. To deal with immediate problems of group living.
4. To be responsible for a free reading and free writing program.[8]

The observer did not attempt to cover the free reading and writing programs. Since the contributions of related arts are readily recognized in relation to such activities as class dances and parties, only that aspect of the program that deals with the learning unit will be described here.

[6] Doris Kalman, "Contributions of Related Arts to a Selected Problem Area in the Core Program." Unpublished Master's Thesis, Columbus, The Ohio State University, 1953.

[7] Prepared by Doris Kalman, graduate student, The Ohio State University, Columbus, Ohio.

[8] *A proposal for a Core Curriculum in Grades Seven, Eight, and Nine,* Report of the Curriculum Committee, Faculty of the Ohio State University School. (Mimeographed) Columbus, The Ohio State University School, 1945. pp. 1-4.

The ninth grade core class was composed of thirty-one boys and girls; the age span was thirteen to fifteen years. Their experience within the related-arts area ranged from none to eight years' experience. Related arts, as used here, refers to those activities commonly thought of as Fine Arts plus those industrial-arts activities or crafts that may be accomplished with the use of hand tools. The core teacher had little or no experience in related arts and expressed a lack of knowledge and understanding within the area. The investigator, an arts specialist, served as a resource person in this field. She worked with the teacher and the class during the entire learning unit, her main function being to observe the frequency and evaluate the importance of related arts in the activities of the learning unit. The specialist did not initiate any of the activities, but helped students carry them out once they were started.

On the basis of a set of criteria developed cooperatively by the teacher and students, the class chose the learning unit "Natural Resources in Industry." This learning unit was worked out during a period of five months. The major topics outlined for consideration were:

1. Food production, shortage, and distribution throughout the world.
2. The earth—soil, water, air, their effect on each other and our lives, and man's affect on them.
3. Natural resources and their use—wood, coal, water, minerals, metals.

Not quite two months were spent on the first two topics, the rest of the time being devoted to the latter. In the opinion of the teacher and of the observer, the projects and activities undertaken by the class were directed toward achieving the purposes of the unit, not toward the study of any particular subject-matter area.

The teacher and students, together, set up a tentative list of activities to be carried out during the study of the unit. As an over-all project, it was decided that each student would keep a scrapbook as a record of the unit. The class also agreed that everyone should be responsible for carrying out an individual project.

The teacher planned movies, discussions and reading, and study periods in the library. Later, the students were asked to write a research paper on some phase of the unit. Several field trips were planned to local industrial plants. These extended the core study into the immediate community.

It was felt that the class should undertake some all-class project that not only would further their study of the unit but also be helpful to the school or community. This project took the form of a food conservation program in the school cafeteria.

The Contributions of Related Arts to the Core Activities. Related arts contributed richly to the unit study. A careful analysis of the activities carried out in the core learning unit showed that related arts made many different kinds of contributions to the activities. These contributions were organized in the following listing:

1. Understanding and clarifying the purpose of a visual presentation; recognizing the need for language supplementation, lettering of titles, captions, keys, and guides; appreciating the value of clarity, conciseness, neatness and organization.

2. Gaining understanding and skill in idea communication, interpretation, and symbolic representation.

3. Discovering and/or using new and varied sources of materials and/or ideas; recognizing cost and use of such materials within the realm of related arts.

4. Selecting and using methods, materials and tools in terms of appropriateness and suitability to the situation.

5. Gaining discrimination in selecting materials, tools, and methods.

6. Gaining understanding and skill in reproduction and/or scale construction; recognizing part-whole relationships; visualizing finished products.

7. Displaying materials to best advantage; organizing, presenting protecting, placing, and arranging in terms of the specific setting.

8. Appreciating work of classmates and others through personal and cooperative efforts and experiences; extending scope of general appreciation through related-arts projects and activities.

9. Expressing creatively an idea through related-arts media.

10. Understanding the relationship between the related arts and social development; recognizing the value and place of related arts and esthetic appreciation in present-day living.

Different contributions or combinations of contributions were found to have been used in carrying out the activities, depending on the nature of the activity. The total number of contributions to any one activity varied from one to eight.

The group activities to which related arts made contributions were:

1. Scrapbooks. Each student in the class compiled a personal scrapbook of materials related to the unit of study. Such things as articles, pictures, booklets, and sketches were included. The scrapbook was to be a personal record of the unit. At various points during the unit, the students gave brief progress reports to the class on their scrapbooks. At the end of the unit, each scrapbook was evaluated by two other members of the class.

2. Research Papers. The teacher requested that each student in the class write a research paper on some phase of the unit. This involved

selecting a topic, doing considerable research, writing an outline, and then writing a final paper. About half the students made extensive use of illustrations and diagrams. Some students designed covers for their papers.

3. Field Trips. The teacher arranged a surprise trip for the class to the Ohio State Archaeological Museum where there was a display of natural resources and industrial developments of the past decade. Each member of the class was to express his impression of something he saw at the museum in whatever medium he liked. The related arts teacher explained what materials would be available to them when they returned from the trip. They selected materials according to the appropriateness and suitability of the materials to their ideas. All but two students chose related arts materials (i.e., chalk, charcoal, oil-paint, clay, wood, ink, and miscellaneous materials). The work was then displayed in the classroom.

4. Class Project. The class project was to cut down food waste in the school lunchroom. One committee surveyed the amount of food waste and publicized the findings over the public address system, the weekly bulletin, and the school paper. Another committee wrote articles and poems for the weekly bulletin, the "radio news" on the public address system, and the school paper. A third committee met with the related arts teacher to develop a third type of program. They cut slogans from colored paper and strung them through the halls and in the lunchroom entrance. They printed slogans on cards and taped them on the lunchroom tables. They followed this up with a large, mural-type poster taped on the wall near the steamtable.

In planning the learning unit the class decided that each student should make an extensive study of some phase of the unit to be presented to the class in a form supplementatry to an oral report. The students worked as individuals or in groups of two, and did considerable work in the related-arts laboratory. A day was set up to share each project with others in the class. The individual projects to which related arts made contributions were:

1. Maps. Two students made maps of the United States depicting the main mineral resources, and farm and industrial products in each state. The mineral resources were shown in terms of real or simulated objects. For example, scraps of sterling silver were used to show sources of silver, scrap copper to show sources of copper. The farm and industrial products on the second map were shown in symbolic form.

Two students studied the state of Wyoming in terms of production and possession of natural resources. This included such things as oil, oil refineries, coal, rivers, parks, and minerals. They constructed a pictorial map of the state and depicted these various resources by using symbols.

One student constructed six, related salt-maps depicting the life of a river in various stages. These were painted and mounted on a large board. Typed explanations were displayed with the maps.

2. Collections. One student made a study of products of the sea. The student had previously acquired a small collection of shells and objects and wanted to find out more about them. He designed an attractive cover for the paper and mounted the shells for display.

One student made a study of several different kinds of wood and collected samples. These samples were cut, waxed, or shellacked and polished. They were then displayed on a board with written descriptions.

3. Models. Two students constructed a model oil well. The model was approximately two-feet high with an additional foot of cut-away earth showing layers of topsoil, clay, rock, water, gas, and oil. Materials used for this construction were an Erector Set with motor and drill-bit, a wooden box with a glass side that contained layers of clay, rock and dirt. A drawing and layout of the cross-section was made previous to the construction. A second model was constructed similar to the first, but utilizing lighter materials such as balsam wood instead of the Erector Set.

Two students constructed a model limestone quarry to show the various processes used in quarrying limestone. The wood frame was about 2 by 3 by 1 foot. The inside surface was constructed with chicken wire, clay, and plaster with limestone chips imbedded in the surface. The construction of buildings and equipment involved the use of cardboard, wood, metal, and miscellaneous material. The project was then painted to resemble a quarry and signs and guides were lettered to identify the processes and equipment.

4. Tests. One student set up a soil erosion test involving four samples of soil. One sample was unplanted, two samples were planted with beans (one in rows sloping downward, and one terraced), and one sample was planted with grass. The samples were placed on a wooden frame, slanting downward. Glass containers were placed at the foot of each sample to catch excess water and sediment from each sample. The wooden frame was finished with plaster board, and signs were made to identify the samples and explain the experiment.

One student made a study of the manufacture of soap. The student tested a home process of making soap and demonstrated this to the class. She also found samples of as many different kinds and types of soaps as she could in the stores in this vicinity and mounted them on a large cardboard for display along with her test.

5. Illustrations. One student made a study of trees—their leaves, growth, and uses in industry. He illustrated the study of each tree by tracing the shape of its leaf. The research paper contained some fifteen different tracings.

The teacher and the observer had frequent conferences during the course of the learning unit and a final conference at its conclusion. On the basis of the frequent use of related arts and its importance in carrying out the activities successfully, they concluded: (1) that related arts made a significant contribution to the learning unit; (2) that related arts can make an even greater and more functional contribution when the specialist participates in the planning of the learning unit.

HOME ECONOMICS IN A CORE PROGRAM[9]

This is a story of home economics in action in a core program. This action took place in a seventh grade core class in Florida State University High School. The participating staff included the core teacher, a member of the University staff in home-economics education, twenty-five seventh graders, and cooperating teachers from the following subject-matter areas: music, industrial arts, and home economics.

The contribution of the homemaking teacher in this core group can be clarified by describing the experiences suggested and supervised by this teacher in a learning unit dealing with *Self-Understanding*. The homemaking teacher was to act as a resource person. In this capacity she would teach short units and suggest and direct the use of certain resources as they related to the core unit. In the teacher-pupil planning sessions at the beginning of the unit the core teacher, the homemaking teacher and the students decided to explore four broad areas of self-understanding: (1) the feelings or emotional self, (2) the physical self, (3) the mental or thinking self, and (4) the spiritual self. With these broad areas set up it was easier for students and teachers to organize their thinking and set up more concrete objectives for the unit. These objectives were set up with the idea that they could be added to or otherwise changed as the group might decide.

After examining the objectives, the core teacher and the homemaking teacher decided that the latter could make her most valuable contribution by dealing with those specific objectives concerned with the care of the body, food, clothing, and getting along with others. It seemed necessary that the homemaking teacher take over the class for at least an hour each day. Although the homemaking teacher had been present each day, the unit on *Self-Understanding* had been in progress several weeks before she began the actual teaching of her short unit. Realizing that she needed to get at the more immediate needs, problems, and interests

[9] In the discussion which follows the writers have borrowed freely from an article by Lucile L. Lurry and Betty Alford entitled: "Home Economics in a Core Program," *Practical Home Economics*, XXIX, 222-223, 226, and 25((May, 1951).

of the students, the homemaking teacher set up centers of interest around the room to create concern and to suggest new ideas for further study.

These centers of interest were groupings of available materials—pamphlets, books, leaflets, charts, pictures, and magazine clippings in the areas of food, care of the body or grooming, and manners. A bulletin board was arranged on each of these subjects with a table under each bulletin board for books and pamphlets. The students were asked to examine the materials and to jot down on paper the topics they were interested in and would like to study. Movies and filmstrips were used to motivate greater interest.

From the lists of concerns handed in the first day, the homemaking teacher was much more capable of helping her students plan a unit to meet their needs. The immediate objectives summarized from these papers were:

1.   Through better health habits to improve (a) our teeth, (b) our skin, (c) our posture, and (d) our choice of food.

2.   To improve our personal appearance through (a) better care of clothes, (b) selecting becoming clothes, (c) selecting clothes for various occasions and (d) giving more attention to personal hygiene.

There was so much interest in foods that it was decided to have a week's unit in this area. Since the group was pressed for time, it was decided to leave the activities concerning getting-along-with-others until the next unit on *Problems of School Living.*

The problem now was to organize activities in which the students could accomplish their objectives. It was decided that the class would divide into groups of five or six students, and that each group would explore a certain problem and then share with the class what they had learned. A group was set up to explore each of the following areas: posture, body cleanliness, teeth, hair, and clothing. Each student was given a chance to join the group in which he was most interested.

To help the groups get started, the homemaking teacher suggested that the class as a whole make up a list of activities in which each group might engage. The list developed included such things as reading illustrative materials and books furnished by the homemaking teacher, using the library, interviewing specialists, using films, going on field trips, experimenting with rats, and the like.

The entire class was given a reading assignment on health habits, and five days were allowed for the groups to engage in their various activities and to plan ways of presenting their findings to the class. During this period the homemaking teacher worked with the groups each day, making suggestions as to activities and resource materials, helping them to see how what they were doing related to their purposes, and stressing the importance of everyone's participating in the group.

Below are examples of activities used to achieve the agreed-upon purposes:

Body Cleanliness Group

1. Made a large poster showing the structure of the skin and presented it to the class with explanations as to how the skin functions, the cause and prevention of blackheads, etc.
2. Made a report on the care of the skin which included a poster showing the necessary elements of skin care, such as certain foods, soap and water, sleep, etc.
3. Investigated the causes of body odor and arranged a display of deodorants, explaining their uses and comparing prices.
4. Arranged for a report and demonstration on hand care for boys and girls which included a display of the better known hand lotions, their prices and uses.
5. Showed and discussed the movie, *Care of the Skin.*

Teeth Group

1. Made a large chart showing the structure of teeth. Explained how decay occurs.
2. Made a report (presented with the chart) on dental cavities and ways of preventing them.
3. Demonstrated the proper method of brushing teeth and presented pictures of the various kinds of tooth brushes available.
4. Demonstrated how to make tooth-powder from baking soda and salt, and explained how to use it.
5. Made a report to the class on the new fluoride treatment for teeth.
6. Made a report on the new ammoniated toothpastes and powders.
7. Made a survey of the dental cavities of pupils in the room. Prepared a chart showing the average number of cavities and compared it with a report on dental cavities of a seventh grade group that had had the fluoride treatment.
8. Showed and discussed the movie, *Care of the Teeth.*

Posture Group

1. Photographed front and side views of three members of the class and made a poster comparing these pictures with some clipped from a magazine illustrating good, fair, and poor posture.
2. Investigated the causes of poor posture and reported these findings to the class.
3. Made a poster illustrating common posture-defects and explained possible causes and means of correction.
4. Gave a short skit entitled "Postures on Parade" in which one per-

son recited a short poem while another student illustrated the posture described in the poem.

5. Gave report on the part diet plays in developing posture and used food models to illustrate a typical nutritious meal.

Hair Group

1. Made charts showing how hair grows. Pointed out what makes hair curly, straight, oily, or dry and why brushing and washing are important.
2. Arranged a picture display of different types of shampoo.
3. Prepared a report on becoming hair styles for different-shaped faces.
4. Gave a report on cause and cure of dandruff.

Clothing Selection Group

1. Made a report on color harmony in clothes. Illustrated matching colors with swatches of cloth brought from home.
2. Made a report on the various colors becoming to the different color-types.
3. Made a poster illustrating proper methods of attire for teen-age boys and girls for various occasions.
4. Compiled a list of home cleaning methods which was mimeographed and presented to the class.
5. Had an oral quiz in which the committee arranged various swatches of cloth which the class discussed in relation to color harmony and design.

In the sharing period the student committees were kept "on their toes" trying to satisfy questions of *why* and *how* that were raised by their classmates. These reports, plus the discussions, often covered two-hour periods. The students were gaining an understanding both of the body and its care and of the social implications of such matters. In each group, particular emphasis was given to the relation of good food habits to personal appearance and physical fitness. Evidence collected in each learning unit indicated that these students had come to make wiser choices of food.

As one means of evaluation, the students and the homemaking teacher set up a check list regarding progress toward their goals. This list was checked over a period of weeks. In addition an application-of-principles test was given at the end of the unit. The most interesting method of evaluation used, however, was observation of the changed behavior of the students and the letter sent to the parents at the end of the unit. Noticing that Billy and Howell were beginning to keep their hair in place; seeing that Claudette changed her hairdo; noticing that girls and boys were shaping and cleaning their nails; hearing Sandy tell about mixing a week's supply of baking soda and salt for his family's teeth, and receiving letters from parents saying that they had observed other changes in behavior in these respects at home, gave the homemaking teacher a feeling that, indeed, the "seeds were falling on fertile ground."

In summary, the following generalizations might be made concerning the possible contributions of a homemaking teacher to the core program:

1.   The homemaking teacher has a valuable contribution to make to the core program in the areas of personal and family living. The effectiveness of this contribution is dependent in large degree upon:

   a.   Her ability to relate the field of home economics to the common needs, problems and interests of boys and girls.
   b.   Her willingness and her ability to plan resource units and learning units with the core teacher and the students.
   c.   Her ability to use skillfully a wide variety of resources in men, materials and techniques in the learning process.

2.   If the homemaking teacher is expected to make a significant contribution in a core program she must always be a member of the initial planning group as the learning unit is developed.

OUR ATOMIC WORLD[10]

The Setting

An interesting learning unit on "Our Atomic World" was developed by an eighth-grade core class at the Maryland Park Junior High School, Maryland Park, Maryland. The pupils in this core program spend thirteen 55-minute periods per week under the guidance of one teacher. In addition to the core they attend regular classes in general mathematics, music or art, physical education, and industrial arts or home economics.

There were forty-two pupils in this class. There is no homogeneous grouping of pupils in this school, hence the ability of the class covered an exceptionally wide range—the reading level of the group ranged from the fourth to the eleventh grade. This span of abilities in a single class is not unusual. This condition is common in core classes in Maryland Park Junior High School.

[10] Submitted by Horace Story, eighth-grade core teacher, Maryland Park Junior High School, Maryland Park, Maryland. *Note to the Reader:* This learning unit draws very heavily upon the science subject-matter field. This is an example of possible general education aspects of science which could be considered in a core program. The core teacher in this case had a sufficient background in science to proceed with only a limited use of the science teacher as a resource person.

The school is located in Prince George's County, one block from the eastern boundary of the District of Columbia. Proximity to Washington affords a wealth of resources to enrich the learning of pupils. The building is rather old, but aside from somewhat crowded conditions in the classroom, the equipment provided is adequate. Four elementary schools feed into this junior high school which has an enrollment of 860. The economic status of the families of this area varies from modest to poor; few extremes of social class are present.

A typical daily schedule of this eighth grade class would be as follows:

```
8:30        —arrive at school
8:50– 9:00—morning exercises
9:00– 9:55— ⎰
10:00–10:55— ⎱ —core
11:00–11:55—general mathematics
12:00–12:30—lunch
12:30– 1:25—art or music (or) industrial arts or home economics
1:30– 2:25—physical education
2:30– 3:25—core
```

The core program in this school is defined as that part of the curriculum required of all pupils because it deals with the common personal-social problems with which all people must come to grips in our society. These personal-social problems are grouped in broad, preplanned problem-areas and resource guides are developed through county-wide teacher workshops. Several problem areas are pegged at each grade level and several optional areas are also suggested. Teachers and pupils may choose learning units outside the preplanned problem-areas if there seems to be a real need for such divergence and if the problem meets the criteria of a good learning experience. Core in this school is further characterized by teacher-pupil planning of learning units. All problems defined call for the use of subject matter which cuts across traditional subject field lines. It should be noted that the learning unit described below draws heavily upon the general education aspects of the science field. It is the belief of our faculty that the science needed by the average citizen can be taught in the core class as pupils draw upon the science field to solve their common problems.

Organizing the Unit. The impact of atomic energy upon the lives of the youth of our country and the queries and genuine concerns of the pupils in this school seemed to call for the development of a learning unit on the atomic world in which we live. Nuclear energy has changed the lives of the peoples of the world. Adequate education in the atom is necessary to the future attitudes of our young citizens.

Pre-Planning Activities. Since there was no county resource guide available to the teacher which could serve as a point of departure, the preparation for the learning unit was unusually extensive. This preplanning on the part of the core teacher involved the following steps:

1. Gathering of printed materials from sources within the school, i.e., room library, central library, and the files of other teachers; contacting the materials center at the Board of Education; and searching through state and federal publications. From this information a sizable bibliography was prepared which was graded as to its readability and interest.

2. Planning periods with other teachers, supervisors and school administrators, e.g., science teacher, librarian, art teacher, science supervisor, and core supervisor as to the contributions various organized fields of knowledge could make in helping the pupils meet their needs.

3. Examining resource guides, learning units, and theses and dissertations of teachers who have either taught a similar unit or explored various approaches, techniques, or teaching skills which would be applicable to the particular learning situation.

4. Locating and examining various films, charts, and posters which pertained to the unit.

5. Preparing, with the assistance of the librarian and the art teacher, an attractive book exhibit and a colorful art display through which the pupils could browse for ideas.

6. Locating resource persons. This list included a civil defense administrator, an air raid warden, an Army team whose job it is to publicize the uses and power of the atom, and a science teacher.

On the basis of these materials and resources, the core teacher then listed what he considered to be the basic attitudes, understandings, and appreciations the pupils should develop during the course of this learning unit. These were:

a. to improve skills in communication, i.e., reading, writing, spelling, and speaking.
b. to understand the many peacetime uses as well as military applications of atomic energy.
c. to realize that the individual is still a vital part of our atomic world and that only through his cooperation with others can the world exist.
d. to understand how we can protect ourselves and our families from atomic weapons.
e. to develop, within the limits of the pupil's comprehension, scientific understandings and appreciations of nuclear energy.
f. to understand that our atomic program is based upon the contributions of men from many countries and that the scientists of

today have used the knowledge of the past as a key to better understandings both of the present and the future.

g.   to cooperate with the people of other lands who share the power of the atom. No one will win the next world war; we must live in tolerance and understanding of the many cultures of the world.

Initiatory Activities.   The pupils planned the unit during the week that the Navy's atomic submarine "Nautilus" was commissioned. The clippings found in newspapers and magazines made possible an exciting bulletin board in addition to the book exhibit and art display. Up until this point in the learning unit all of the preplanning had been done by the teachers and supervisors; the students were not as yet drawn into the building of the learning unit.

As a means of bringing the students into the unit a Navy film "Operation Crossroads" was shown. The film proved to be an excellent motivator; it vividly illustrated the preparation for and the results of the atomic tests at Eniwetok and Bikini. A general discussion by the group followed to determine the content of the unit. The teacher's contribution to this discussion was to stimulate the thinking of the class by discussing such pertinent points as:

1.   The teen-ager of today; the first atomic generation.
2.   Albert Einstein's view as to the weapons to be used in World War III.
3.   Taking an optimistic rather than a pessimistic approach to the uses of atomic energy.
4.   The distribution of our tax dollar with regard to the national defense.

The pupils, after considerable discussion, expressed their needs concerning the understanding of our atomic world in the form of seven questions:

1.   What are the peacetime uses of atomic energy?
2.   How can we protect ourselves against atomic weapons?
3.   What can we learn about atomic energy?
4.   What are the effects of an atomic explosion on a community?
5.   What is the future of atomic energy in the world today?
6.   Who should control the use of atomic weapons?
7.   How did the atomic energy program develop?

These questions served as a basis for the study of "Our Atomic World" and were used continuously as criteria for evaluation of the progress of the class.

Planning to Achieve Purposes. On the basis of these questions, the pupils and teacher developed a structural plan for the learning unit. The next step required the class to plan a series of activities which would allow them to arrive at a satisfactory answer to each of the seven questions.

Planning groups were established to investigate the various learning activities and areas the individual, as well as the group, might explore to meet and satisfy expressed needs. To understand better the scope of their problems, the group examined available information and conferred with subject-matter teachers whom they thought could assist them in developing the procedures necessary for the successful completion of their task.

Activities. Some of the learning experiences the core teacher and the pupils of the class evolved are listed below with a brief explanation as to the development and relationship of each.

1. An important part of the continued learning and interest of the class was the maintenance of a bulletin board. Sufficient materials were available so that the board could be changed often. The art teacher was consulted as to the best arrangement and balance of the materials. A group, the "Committee on Current Affairs," was charged with the responsibility of keeping the class posted as to what is new in our atomic world. All of the students in the class had an opportunity to serve on this committee.

2. Peace-time versus military uses of atomic energy posed a problem for the pupils. The uses of the atom were divided into two groups—"Uses for the Betterment of Man" and "Uses in the Defense of Our Country."

3. Peace-time applications of the atom were stressed by the students. An investigation was made of ways in which the medical profession has used atomic energy to make our world a better place in which to live. Interesting oral and written reports were presented to the group. How active isotopes are traced through the body with a geiger counter was illustrated by a student. He showed, through the use of a diagram of the body, how the active elements are traced and explained the purpose of the test.

4. The soil scientist's study of the use of radioactive isotopes in agricultural research, along with an illustrated explanation as to how a chain reaction can be converted into a usable source of energy in the home, provided clearer understandings of the many benefits which mankind can share. Two students prepared a blackboard illustration and gave an explanation as to how a chain reaction can be converted into steam, which in turn can be used for the propulsion of a craft such as the "Nautilus."

5. The group thought that the utility of the atom, with regard to the defense of our country, was so complex that the topic should be divided into the following areas for study:

    a.   One such area was scientific concepts about the atom; e.g., How does an atomic bomb work? Both the class and the core teacher recognized their shortcomings with regard to the recognitions of the importance of science to the development of atomic energy. Accordingly, a group of pupils worked directly with a science teacher to plan steps necessary to learn what they could about this important field. Simple demonstrations were cooperatively planned. Demonstrations and discussion centered around such topics as:

        (1)   What is a chain reaction?
        (2)   What is meant by "splitting an atom"?
        (3)   How is magnetism related to an understanding of the atom and its function?
        (4)   What is a molecule and why can we not see it?

    b.   The science and core teachers realized that these pupils would be handicapped by the new vocabulary needed in discussing the structure and function of the atom. Therefore, a word list was prepared, the spelling taught, and the meanings and usage discussed as to how each of the words related to the various discussions. A sample word list follows:

electricity	energy	cobalt
electron	hydrogen	magnetism
radioactive	radiation	uranium
molecule	neutron	nitrogen
proton	radium	oxygen

    c.   A study of the lives of men who have made contributions to the development of our atomic world was a project undertaken by one group of pupils. The contributions of such men as Einstein, Ferme, Oppenheimer, and Urey were reviewed.

    6.   The assistance of the art teacher was needed in helping the pupils find adequate means of expression through which they could best illustrate artistically the atomic world in which they live. A mural with the atom as its central theme was drawn; a diorama was constructed which showed the effects of an atomic blast; paper and cardboard models of the atom, a chain reaction, an atomic pile and the "Nautilus" were constructed and suspended as a gigantic mobile from the ceiling of the classroom.

    7.   One committee investigated the results of the destruction of Hiroshima and Nagasaki. Their report included a diagram of the varying effectiveness of the bomb.

    8.   A day-by-day history of nuclear energy developments provided topics for a continuing current events discussion on "What is new in our atomic world?" The U-bomb, President Eisenhower's Atoms for Peace Plan, and other contemporary happenings helped to make the learning unit more realistic.

9. The operation of the Strategic Air Command (SAC) and the Continental Air Defense were studied by the class.

10. At this point in the unit the class developed a piece of creative writing on the topic "The Future of Our Atomic World."

11. A panel of pupils led a discussion on the debatable issue "How can war be prevented?"

12. The development of the Atomic Energy Commission (AEC) was shown by a chart and some blackboard diagrams. This work led into the question as to who should control the use of the atomic bomb. A play, "Pilot Light of the Apocolypse" by Louis N. Ridenour provided excellent background from which to explore the problem of who should control atomic energy. A small group produced the play for the class.

13. A government film, "Protection from an Atomic Bomb," was shown. A discussion followed as to how the class could protect itself from an attack. An examination of the school's civil defense program disclosed a serious need for a revision. A culminating activity of the unit was the development by the class of new civil defense plan for the school. Various nearby government agencies contributed a wealth of information. The class used as a resource person the Supervisor of Maintenance of schools of Prince George's County, who is also a coordinator of a county-wide civil defense program. The plan was completed and a practice drill was coordinated by the class. This reorganized plan of defense may prove to be a major contribution to the future welfare and safety of all of the pupils in the school.

Evaluation.   The teacher and the pupils desired to measure their growth as a result of the learning unit. Evaluation, being a continuous process, was not confined to testing at the conclusion of the study; rather, the growth of the pupils was checked at various intervals during the study of "Our Atomic World."

Paper and pencil tests were used as one method of evaluation, but written answers to posed questions were not the only means by which the progress of the class was measured. Other evidences of growth were: the increase in interest shown by individual pupils concerning the problems with which our atomic world is faced; the growth in pupils' attitudes and appreciations of the complexity of living on top of a "keg of powder"; the progress shown by the class in understanding how to protect themselves from an atomic blast; and, the increase in cooperative living skills, in clearer self-understandings and in demonstrating competency in the use of basic language skills.

THE ROLE OF THE LANGUAGE ARTS IN THE
CORE PROGRAM[11]

What constitutes the language arts? Teachers at every grade level have come to understand the broad title of language arts as encompassing the skills and techniques of writing, reading, listening, and speaking necessary to acquire information and knowledge and to share such understandings with others. Still the definition is made more concrete by the common practice of including grammar, usage, spelling, theme writing, free reading, remedial reading, poetry and literature, library skills, and public speaking. In short, the language arts represent the basic tools for research, for recording, and for communicating information while at the same time providing, through the great literature of the past and present, a framework of values and an understanding of the drama of human life. Such an area of learning is an essential part of the education of all the children not only because of its inherent worth but because of its most practical use in everyday living.

By nature and use the language arts must occupy a foremost position in the curriculum whether it be of the more traditional type or is one developed from the philosophy and concepts of the core program. The role of the language arts in a core class is that of a tool of learning. This does not imply, however, that nothing about the language arts should be "studied." There is no incompatability in a core class between a learning unit selected through teacher-pupil planning and the learning of subject matter. It is axiomatic that children do not think in a vacuum; nor do they learn in a laboratory devoid of equipment. Subject matter becomes vital and necessary to the extent that it contributes to the solving of a problem of concern to pupils. This transfer of the position of subject-matter mastery from that of the end of learning to a concomitant part of the entire learning process in no way implies the rejection of subject-matter competency. Perhaps we may say that within a core class in which pupils and teachers are free to pursue their emerging interests and problems rather than follow a prescribed and dictated course of study, any subject area is enhanced to a position of tremendous importance in the learning process.

Although the skills of the language arts must be used by every teacher within the school, the core class, dedicated to helping children grow and develop in those areas of learning necessary to successful living in our society, should bear the major responsibility for instruction in this broad area. Some might question the advisability of placing the language arts

[11] Submitted by Jean V. Marani, Basic Education Teacher, Sarasota Junior High School, Sarasota, Florida.

in a core class. Why not segregate it into special classes to insure proper emphasis? The answer lies in the nature of the learning process in a core program. In a core class, a variety of learning experiences are carried on in connection with a broad unit, thus eliciting a need for a variety of language-arts skills. The core period, functioning as a laboratory for problem solving, provides time to develop and mature the skills of writing, reading, and research beyond the state of rote learning. Students have abundant opportunities to make language arts experiences a functioning part of every daily activity. Since a core unit generally cuts across traditional subject-matter lines, the use of the language arts become an integral part of every learning activity. English is no longer thought of as a separate subject in the curriculum. The longer block of time which accompanies most core classes provides a natural setting for individualized help and group drill. The odium once attached to grammar, spelling, literature, and other aspects of the language arts seems to dissolve when these areas are incorporated in the natural flow of problem solving. We may not claim for the core class a monopoly upon opportunities to teach the language arts, but we may proclaim its endless need for an effective mastery and functional use of those skills and understandings. When core extends to the senior high school, elective areas in the language arts are usually offered. Some of these electives are speech, journalism, and English and American literature. These meet the needs of certain pupils in vocational or avocational areas.

It would not seem necessary to reiterate the many ways in which the problem-solving approach of the core class demands wide reading, thorough research in the library, clear and meaningful writing, accurate spelling and grammar, and ease and skill in oral communication. The following list of language arts activities indicates some of the ways which seventh and eighth grade basic-education teachers of the Sarasota Junior High School, Sarasota, Florida, have found particularly effective with adolescent boys and girls. They have been grouped under broad headings according to the type of language arts experiences which are needed during various periods within a specific unit or within the school year.

Orientation. An orientation core unit provides many opportunities for students to write and tell about themselves as a part of the get-acquainted program. This natural interest helps the teacher and student identify skills in grammar which need either individual or group attention. Faulty speech habits appear as students talk about themselves and their interests. Spelling lists can be compiled easily from these early writing assignments. The point of major importance is that students can be guided to recognize their shortcomings in language skills through orientation activities. Individual and class goals become personalized through student understanding of why they should master certain techniques.

As an outgrowth of an orientation unit, one eighth-grade class developed a year-long project which was of service to the school and highly instructive and beneficial to themselves. This was the bimonthly "Bookworm News" which gave information about new books in the library, short book reports from students throughout the school, and other interesting book news. This project was enjoyed by the entire student body. Those working on the paper have developed many skills: compiling data, interviewing, writing, drawing cartoons, editing, but above all they have achieved a sense of responsibility and the rewards of a job well done.

Orientation led one class to write personality analyses. Adolescents are concerned about themselves and their rapport with fellow students. Study of good traits and pleasing personality development provided motivation for a serious writing project: critical self-analysis. The need for improved written expression was strong.

Choosing a Unit. Choosing a unit can provide leads to functional spelling, grammar, and usage drill. Students might be asked to write themes outlining their choice for a unit. Enthusiasm for this runs high and students write willingly when they know their arguments may influence the class to select their unit. Before themes are read, a period or more should be devoted to correcting the papers. Effective writing becomes important to students.

Developmental Activities. After a unit has been selected a committee can be organized to outline the scope of the unit; another group can prepare tentative bibliographies for class use. Here a natural setting arises for teaching the skills of outlining and for recording bibliographical data.

The keeping of a notebook of activities and notes pertaining to the unit creates another need for effective writing, outlining and note taking. Spelling words from the unit, meanings of difficult terms, and individual goals help students plan their work and evaluate their progress.

A unit developed around the city of Sarasota, Florida, provided a variety of language arts experiences: letter writing to governmental leaders, interviews with prospective speakers, and summarizations of trips. The culmination of the unit was the writing of a book about Sarsota. The students improved in spelling, handwriting, and the organization of data.

A unit on "Colonial and Frontier Life" inspired a variety of book reports. Books were read with the understanding that reports could be given in any form the pupil desired. One report on *Journey Cake* was made tangible with a journey cake which the students could taste. Original book-jackets were popular. Some of the girls in the class made rag dolls and dressed them as favorite book characters. Shadow boxes told of other books. A few reports were given in the form of experiments. Originality and creativity are major goals in the core.

Reading and Literature. Providing a period in core classes for the reading of library books opens up a vast field of opportunities for the improvement of reading. The teacher can guide students in wise book selections. Informal book talks, reports, and discussions introduce and conclude reading periods. If the teacher is also reading during this period, motivation is provided for the more mature students to read at a more advanced level. A few words from the teacher about a book she enjoyed from the school library places it in great demand. A free reading period is a significant inducement to wide reading.

Language arts often provide leads to wider experiences for children. In a seventh-grade class, students selected poems to read to the class and then made a water-color painting to illustrate their impressions of the poem. Imagery of word led to imagery in color and line.

The "Classics Club" is popular in one core class. Membership is open to those who have read one or more classics (opportunity to teach discrimination about types of literature). Most students reported orally to the class about their books. Twenty-five students read twenty different classics within a period of three weeks.

Interest in poetry came from a unit on America's Heritage. The teacher read some patriotic poems to the class with the remark that while not all people could sing, they could have a song in their hearts through a poem. This aroused curiosity, and the students embarked on a search for poems relating to people, places, and events that have made our country great. These were read and enjoyed by the class. The climax of the activity was the writing of original poems with a patriotic flavor. This seventh-grade class will never find poetry dull.

A committee composed of students and the teacher can prepare a list of references in the literature books which relate to the unit. In order to have an accurate list much prereading must be done by the committee. This elicits interest in the contents of the literature books. Students readily read stories selected by their classmates. This connection between literature and the learning unit makes reading such selections a part of the learning experiences of the unit. Assignments are thus made important, not just a series of stories to be read without purpose.

Improving Skills. A core class is not without drill in such areas as spelling and grammar: and the expanded time allotted to a core class facilitates the handling of such work in an individualized manner. After need for group effort in some area of grammar is identified, the kind of drill needed can be selected for the individual or for small groups. When a spelling book is used, it is particularly effective to allow students to progress at their own rate. Setting the goal for a passing grade to 92 or 96 seems to challenge all students. Failure to reach that level after two chances automatically moves the student to the next lesson.

The writing of friendly letters grew out of a class's desire to stimulate interest in reporting research findings. Each student selected a pen pal in the room and wrote him letters which contained information relating to the broad questions of the unit. The pen pal's letters were read to the class, and each student later placed his own letters in a notebook. In a unit on Latin-American Neighbors the theme of the letters was an imaginary trip into a South-American country. A similar activity was used effectively to summarize information pertaining to a unit on Our American Culture. The novelty of this activity appealed to children; their imaginations were stimulated, and the techniques of writing friendly letters took on real importance.

Mathematics in a basic-education class provided a lead to the study of advertisements as a media of the language arts. Students began to search for advertisements utilizing the mathematical concepts they had been studying. Some even wrote original advertisements. This led to an analysis of the writing of such materials and the importance of words and phrases in catching our interest.

Before committees reported in one core class they gave a preview in which the specialized vocabulary of the report was presented to the class. Words were written on the board, defined, and illustrated. Students copied the definitions in their notebooks. A list of such words was displayed on the bulletin board for several days. Evaluation indicated that students learned to spell these words and added many of them to their vocabularies.

Reporting. Reporting to the class demands much teaching in the area of spoken English. Students must be helped to plan good talks, they must be given time to rehearse, and they need assistance from the teacher in these areas before the report is given. Oral English skills are very functional when committees have a purpose for reporting and something instructive to say.

A successful technique to encourage writing is the mimeographing of committee reports after oral presentation. This writing assignment may be an entire committee's responsibility or it may be delegated to a superior student who needs such experience. A student editing committee decides upon the format for the written reports and with practice they can handle the final editing. Pride in seeing all the committee reports mimeographed and distributed to all students provides much incentive for improved writing.

Evaluation. To help students evaluate their year's growth in library research it is useful to give an assignment in note taking at the beginning of the year and then at the conclusion of the school term. Students can suggest topics to be "looked up" during library period; in this way they share in the assignment. A note of anticipation may be interjected by letting students draw a topic from the hat. This activity provides information about the level of library skills possessed by the students; improvement can be achieved by group or individual instruction. Again the learning of library skills seems a natural thing to do, for students realize that proficiency in the library is essential for successful problem solving in the core class. At the end of the year when the assignment is repeated, evaluation is easy.

Oral English combined with enjoyment of poetry provided a real lesson in evaluation for a seventh grade class. They tape-recorded their reading of poems relating to the unit being studied. After extensive work in improved speech habits, the same poems were reread. Tangible results could be heard, and the students were able to evaluate the success of their learning experience.[12]

These activities have illustrated some of the opportunities which are constantly provided in core classes to further student proficiency in the language arts. There are no doubt some teachers who would be quick to point out that the core does not possess a definite content; that spelling, grammar, and literature instruction are left to chance. In an effective core program something beside immediate student impulses and whims must provide continuity and growth in learning. Just as a faculty preplans certain problem areas and "pegs" them for particular grades so must the faculty outline the areas of learning in the language arts which should be experienced by all pupils at any particular level. Through teacher-pupil planning these preplanned areas are translated into class goals which are meaningful and real to children. There is sequence of learning in the core through preplanning, and there is vitality, keen interest, and high motivation for learning through teacher-pupil planning. The activities outlined above are valuable to the extent they develop in students an intelligent awareness of why they need to master certain techniques. This gives to any learning experience the zest which changes it from drudgery to fun.

Throughout this very brief consideration of the role of the language arts in the core has run a current of thought which implies that the core gives ample and varied opportunity for students to experience all phases of the language arts necessary for general education purposes. The opportunities for meaningful study seem to be more numerous than in a traditional English class because the scope of a unit in the core transcends

[12] The author is indebted to the following Basic Education teachers for contributing to the above list of activities: Alva Griffin, Mary Hicks, Kathryn Mims, Thelma Richmond, Marian Smallwood, Julia Snyder, Helen Tatum, and Carla Turner.

the restrictive limits of the usual English program. The lengthened core period enables activities to be continued, often to completion, without the disconcerting lapse of a day. The nature of learning in the core elevates subject matter to the position of a source of data and a method of research for the solving of real problems; it is not just something to be memorized. Wise preplanning of language arts experiences assures that necessary techniques will be part of the learning environment of students; equally wise teacher-pupil planning assures that these learnings will demonstrate to students the importance of such proficiency in their daily lives. The core provides the laboratory in which the language arts become vital equipment for the experiences of living.

SELECTED BIBLIOGRAPHY

Alberty, Elsie J., "The Role of Mathematics in Core Program Development," *The School Review.* **LXIV:** 300-306 (October, 1956).

Alberty, Harold, *Reorganizing the High School Curriculum.* New York, The Macmillan Company, 1953 (Revised), Chapter 7.

————, and others, *Utilizing Subject-Fields in High School Core-Program Development.* Columbus, Ohio, the Ohio State University Press, 1950.

————, *The Core Program in the High School—Its Implications for Business Education.* Fourteenth Annual Delta Pi Epsilon Lecture. Chicago, South-Western Publishing Company, 1956.

————, "A Sound Core Program," *Journal of the National Education Association.* **45:**20-22 (January, 1956).

Alford, Betty Jean, "The Contribution of Home Economics to Selected Problems Areas in the Core Program of the Seventh Grade of the Florida State University Demonstration School," Unpublished Master's Thesis, Tallahassee, Florida, The Florida State University, 1951.

Deans, H. E., "Language Arts Enrich the Core Program," *School Review.* **63:**220-227 (April, 1956).

Fawcett, H. P., "Mathematics and the Core Curriculum," *Bulletin of the National Association of Secondary School Principals.* **38:**71-80 (May, 1954).

Forsheit, Samuel, "Why Aren't Foreign Languages in the Core Curriculum?" *Modern Languages,* **38:**254-357 (November, 1954).

Jansen, H. S., "The Relation of Mathematics to the Core Curriculum," *Mathematics Teacher,* **45:**427-435 (October, 1952).

Jennings, William E., "Contributions of Business Education to Selected Problem Areas of General Education in the Secondary School,"

Unpublished Doctoral Disseration, Columbus, Ohio, The Ohio State University, 1952.

Kalman, Doris, "Contributions of Related Arts to a Selected Problem Area in the Core Program," Unpublished Master's Thesis, Columbus, Ohio, The Ohio State University, 1953.

Lurry, Lucile L., "The Contribution of Home Economics to Selected Problem Areas in the Core Curriculum of the Secondary School," Unpublished Doctoral Dissertation, Columbus, Ohio, The Ohio State University, 1949.

McCoy, Mary E., "Planning for Physical Education in the Core Curriculum," *Health, Physical Education, and Recreation*, **XXV**: 23-24 (December, 1954).

Mikhail, Monir Kamel, "Contributions of Science to Selected Problem Areas Proposed for a Program of General Education in the Secondary School," Unpublished Doctoral Dissertation, Columbus, Ohio, The Ohio State University, 1952.

Schmidt, Mildred C., "Language Arts in Core Programs," *Elementary English Journal*, **XXVIII**: 208-215 (April, 1951).

Schmieder, Frederick J., "An Evaluation of the Role of English in Selected Junior High School Core Programs," Unpublished Doctoral Dissertation, Columbus, Ohio, The Ohio State University, 1956.

Stalzer (Alberty), Elsie J., "Contributions of Mathematics to a Proposal for Reorganizing General Education in Secondary Schools on the Basis of a Core Program," Unpublished Doctoral Dissertation, Columbus, Ohio, The Ohio State University, 1952.

Stewart, L. Jane, Frieda M. Heller, and Elsie J. Alberty, *Improving Reading in the Junior High School—A Librarian and a Core Teacher Work Together*. New York, Appleton-Century-Crofts, Inc., 1957.

Wachwitz, M. B., and Lucile L. Lurry, "Art in an Evolving Core Program," *Art Education Today*. New York, Bureau of Publications, Teachers College, Columbia University, 1953, pp. 72-88.

What Shall the High Schools Teach? 1956 Yearbook of the Association for Supervision and Curriculum Development. Washington, D. C., National Education Association, 1956, Chapter VI.

VIII
WORKING TOGETHER TO DEVELOP A CORE PROGRAM

The foregoing chapters of this book have described in some detail the "how to do it" aspects of the core program. The reader, at this point, must be saying "Very well, but how do you get such a thoroughgoing reorganization of the curriculum on the road?" "Who does what?" "How do you get people concerned enough to do all of this work?" "What does this cost in consultant services, resources, time and the like?" "Are there schools or school systems with experience in developing a core program which might be contacted for suggestions?" "Where should we begin?" These and similar questions puzzle those administrators and teachers who would like to take a more creative approach to general education.

What Are the Tasks Involved?

Developing a core program should rarely be attempted in isolation with a few selected teachers and pupils involved. This is not to say that one teacher or a small group of teachers in a school should not experiment on their own with ideas to meet more adequately the needs of adolescents. If the leadership for a full-scale reorganization is lacking, to proceed on one's own perhaps is the only way to realize a sense of achievement. Further, total-school, curriculum development programs have been known to begin when more and more teachers catch the gleam in the eyes of a few adventuresome souls. However, a piecemeal approach is probably not the most promising one in curriculum development.

When a faculty begins in earnest to change its curriculum to help youth meet their needs, to solve their problems, and to extend their interests, several very definite tasks will need continuous thoughtful attention. Let us assume that an awareness of the need for change has been created. At this point it seems necessary for the group, as a whole, to set down its beliefs concerning the role of the school in American society. Some might call this statement the school's *philosophy and objectives*. When this has been accomplished a *problem area study* is in order. In addition to the identification of needs of youth, a major undertaking in this study is the *clarification of the role of the core program and the special-interest areas in relation to the total program*. Resource guides to be used in pre-planning for learning units must be developed. This takes time and careful planning. The development of resource guides will not solve the problem of resources. Some group must carry the load of *marshaling a wide variety of resources* in the community, in printed materials and in people who might be helpful in developing a more creative approach to education. This takes time, energy and organizational ability. Not the least of the jobs ahead is that of providing for time scheduled within the school day or on school time for this work to be done.

How Do We Get Started? Creating Awareness

Since a total reorganization is in order in all areas when school people begin to face squarely the task of meaningful curriculum development, it is the administrative staff—principal, supervisors, superintendent—who must create the awareness of need for a change and give leadership to effect an organization whereby the evolving process of change may begin. This is not to say that teachers and pupils and parents should not indicate or suggest problems and needed changes. Actually the most genuine change comes about when teachers, pupils, and parents begin to ask questions. Their questions often concern the content of the curriculum, the handling of pupils with severe personal-social problems, the type and range of activities offered, the scheduling processes of the school, the reporting practices, and the role of parents in curriculum making. Such manifestations as these are signs to those in status leadership positions that the *status* quo is inadequate and that a cooperative, curriculum-development program should be undertaken. On the other hand, if such spontaneous reactions fail to come from teachers, pupils, and parents, administrators are not hereby relieved of their responsibility to involve those concerned in a vital and ongoing program of curriculum improvement.

Some schools and/or school systems start rethinking the program when teachers, parents, and pupils begin to question existing practices. This is a realistic approach which usually manages to avoid the criticism of those who think that philosophical discussions are a waste of time. Inevitably, these discussions must push back to the beliefs of the participants concerning (1) the nature of the individual, (2) the nature of the learning process, (3) the nature of Democracy, and (4) the role of the school. It appears to the writers that the public schools have no other alternative than to interpret their program in the light of these four factors. Child study groups such as those fostered by the Institute of Child Study, University of Maryland, offer excellent opportunities for school people to analyze their curricular offerings in terms of what is known concerning human growth and development. The public-school systems of several states, particularly Maryland, have brought many promising practices into action as a result of teacher participation in such groups. Some faculties have made a real educational experience out of the process of achieving accreditation by the National Association of Secondary Schools and Colleges. The intelligent use of the *Evaluative Criteria, 1950 Edition,* has caused much reflection on the adequacy of the present program and some schools have made needed changes because of this self-evaluation. A few, too few, administrators feel that their major responsibility is one of fostering curriculum development. As a matter of course, the staff is organized in a continuous program year after year in light of the particular problems faced and the needs and understandings of the teachers. One such school has been in operation four years. In the first year of its being, the staff was organized in a total faculty group and in departmental groups to become better acquainted through cooperative solution of the many problems facing a new school. The staff organized itself in grade-level groups to become more skillful in preplanning for learning activities through presenting such plans for analysis and criticism to the group dealing with these pupils. In three successive years this staff has done a study of the needs of youth in this situation and has followed up with a problem area study. They attempted to arrive at some evaluative devices to be used in the area of demo-cratic values (cooperation, critical thinking, social sensitivity, tol-erance), and clarified considerably the role of general education and special-interest areas in the total school program. Out of such continuous attack on problems faced, curriculum change moves forward.

A large county school system involved its 1800 personnel in the development of a statement of "This We Believe." This study used as a springboard seventeen issues, cooperatively defined, which seemed to involve, most, questions from parents, laymen, and new personnel as to county policies. Since this was a rather unique procedure in that it involved a large number of people, the story of this development is presented here in a step-by-step account. It is hoped that readers may get ideas as to how such a basic study could be organized in their school systems.

DEVELOPING A COUNTY PHILOSOPHY[1]

Conditions indigenous to our times seemed to demand a clarification of the *modus operandi* of the county's public-school system. We found ourselves faced with such particular conditions as (1) Increased public consciousness of and interest in the schools because of crowded conditions, increased cost of public education and use of new educational terms and practices. (2) The existence of an emotional climate unfavorable to public schools featured by tension, fear, uncertainty and anxiety. (3) Teacher problems such as shortage, turnover and preparation. (4) Mobility of population. (5) Increase in population.

Accordingly, the superintendent of schools initiated a concerted effort to develop a County Philosophy of Education which would provide a frame of reference within which administrators, supervisors, and teachers could operate with a reasonable degree of consensus. It was hoped that

[1] Submitted by Dean Manifold, Supervisor of Secondary Education, Prince George's County, Maryland.

this consensus, in turn, would tend to lessen the misunderstandings and misinterpretations expressed by the public and thus provide a reasonable degree of security in the schools' program.

The original committee, designated to explore the development of a County Philosophy, was a group of the superintendent's professional staff. The immediate task of the group—ten in number—was (1) to identify some controversial issues, and (2) to provide for a democratic consideration of these issues by all school personnel in the county. The original committee identified ten issues; the professional staff as a whole contributed seven more. These seventeen issues were: (1) Relation of General to Special Interest Education, (2) Indoctrination, (3) Place of Fundamentals, (4) Controversial Issues (teaching of), (5) Moral and Spiritual Values, (6) Curriculum Development, (7) Role of School, Home and Community, (8) Content of the Curriculum, (9) Grouping, (10) Standards of Achievement, (11) Grading and Pupil Reporting, (12) Promotional Policies (Retention, Automatic Promotion, Acceleration), (13) Motivation for Learning (Readiness, Competition, and/or Cooperation), (14) Place of Parents in the School Program, (15) Homework, (16) Adjustment of the School Program to the Atypical Children, and (17) The Cost to Pupils of Free Public-Education.

With identification of issues having been completed, the democratic consideration of these issues became the immediate goal. The steps taken to do this were as follows:

1. All principals were oriented concerning both the project and the issues, by either the County Superintendent or the Chairman of the Committee.

2. Principals were requested to refer the issues to individual faculties in an open meeting. A school consensus on each issue became the task at hand.

3. The two Secondary Principals' Associations, the two Elementary School Principals' Associations, and the Professional Staff accepted the project as a professional challenge. Each group, through the medium of an editing committee, submitted what was considered to be a consensus of the beliefs on each issue as expressed by the individual schools and individuals within each of the five divisions. In reality, then, there were five separate and representative statements submitted for consideration to a Final Editing Committee.

4. The Final Editing Committee (presidents of the four Principal Associations, eight staff members, six teachers) reconciled the five separate statements (without identification) into one representative statement concerning each issue. In the process of editing and refining, the committee exercised constant care so that the meaning and intent of the statements submitted were not lost. The final product, however, reflects

each and every widely divergent point of view. In reality, the final statements represent the highest level of agreement that could be reached on each issue by the members of the final Editing Committee.

Upon completion of the statement of philosophy, it was printed with some embellishments, as a booklet. The superintendent, Mr. William S. Schmidt, added the following message prior to its dissemination on a countywide basis.

A Message from the Superintendent

IT IS IMPORTANT that a county school system, such as ours, has worked together to develop a statement of guiding principles based on our best understanding of the nature of the learner, the learning process, and the aims and purposes of education in our democracy. It is even more important that each person employed as a teacher or as an administrator in our schools shall act in terms of these principles, incorporating them in instructional procedures and administrative practices.

More than one thousand teachers, principals, and staff members contributed to the development of the statements included in "This We Believe." Already hundreds of new teachers have joined with them in the responsibility of implementing these principles. Through consistent and concerted effort we can achieve and maintain a better educational program for the children and youth of our county. As your Superintendent of Schools, I invite you to become familiar with this publication, the principles stated therein, and the practices implied. Let's use it to evaluate our current procedures, but let's, also, study it critically. It represents, at present, our highest level of consensus; it is subject to revision and amendment as new developments and further research may demand.

While creating an awareness of the need for change it is obvious that a good administrator is alert to all possibilities to initiate a faculty study. Total-faculty viewing of a film such as *Skippy and the R's* or *Passion for Life* might start the ball rolling. On the other hand, the simple technique of a rating device such as "Where Does Your High School Stand?"[2] might turn the trick. Further, the administrator must make available through the library, Materials Center, or like arrangement, current literature on promising curriculum trends. This task can easily be handled by a committee reporting

[2] Harold Alberty, *Reorganizing the High School Curriculum*. New York, The Macmillan Company, 1953, pp. 529-536.

suggestions to the librarian, curriculum coordinator, or a person designated by the group as chairman. If consultant services are needed and available, arrangements must be made. A consultant should be chosen by the total group, but one person or a small committee should make the initial contact and make clear the services expected, the time schedule, and the consultant's fee. Further, the administrator has the responsibility for the full use of any central-office personnel who could serve as a consultant. Time within the school day should be provided for curriculum improvement. It is certainly within the province of the administration to see that schedules are made flexible and that teacher loads warrant added responsibilities. A four o'clock consideration of the growth and development of children is perhaps when teacher growth and development is at its lowest ebb! There are, in addition to on-school time, such possibilities as postschool or preschool workshops in which the participants receive renewal and extension of teaching certificates or, at times, some remuneration for personal expenses in the workshop. One county system held its workshop once each week from 7:30-10:30 P.M. during a three month period of the regular school year. This schedule worked well because teachers felt they were receiving help on problems they were facing at that time.

Two items of the task involved in developing a core program have been discussed, i.e., *creating an awareness of the need for changing the curriculum and developing a basic philosophy or statement of objectives.* In the former, it has been suggested that all concerned should participate and suggest ideas, but that those in administrative positions must assume leadership for spearheading organization and coordination. The total-school personnel should be involved at all stages in the development of their philosophy of education. Each person may assume a leadership position from time to time as the study progresses. Data collected, published research, and readings may be presented by individuals, panels, forums, symposiums, recordings, and filmstrips. The statement of philosophy should reflect the highest level of consensus possible in the group and should provide the basis for intelligent change of the school's program.

Getting a Problem Area Study Underway

The tasks involved in making a problem area study were described in Chapter III. Chapter IV: Concrete examples of how such a study was made in two situations. The principal tasks involved here are (1) to identify the common personal-social problems of youth in our society, (2) to translate these into broad areas in which all youth of our society have problems, (3) to outline some possible problems, issues, tensions, or conflicts which might be considered the possible scope of each area, (4) to plan for continuity of learning experiences of a well-rounded nature from grades seven through twelve inclusive, and (5) to consider the role of the special-interest areas in relation to the core program and vice versa.

It would seem desirable to involve the total school faculty, parents, interested laymen, professional staff at the central office, pupils, and a wide variety of resource people in the problem area study. Each group has a different but vital role to play. It is very necesary that teachers from all areas of the school's program join in this effort in order that the respective functions of general education and special-interest education be clearly defined in a cooperative manner.

All of those involved at the professional, lay, and pupil levels should join in a study of the common, personal-social needs of youth. There is ample literature in the field to be drawn upon for this analysis and there is no reason why the accumulated experiences of teachers and parents in the group could not be heavily drawn upon. Pupils may participate through the use of interest inventories, problem check-lists, various sociometric scales and in discussions with adult groups. A coordinating committee might be appointed to collect materials, list topics, schedule meetings, and assemble data. This committee might include parents as well as teachers and administrators. Here each person might assume a leadership role of some nature. When common needs have been identified, a small group might be assigned the task of translating these into a tentative set of *problem areas* for consideration and modification by the total group. The whole group might develop a set of criteria for the choice of *problem areas* before the small group does its work. This procedure usually provides a more rewarding consideration of the committee's initial report. Both groups might find the literature on problem-area development helpful.[3] The problem-area committee should submit, along with each suggested *problem* area, a few illustrative problems to give ideas as to scope. The total group could then be called upon for additional suggestions in each *problem* area. At this point the group needs to be very careful in its classification as to what belongs in the core and what should be taken care of in a special-interest area. While it is true that a clear-cut line can seldom be drawn between general and special-interest-area education, it is well to recognize that core teachers are not specialists in all areas and that much learning requiring specialist competency belongs in areas outside the core. For example, the core class might well deal with the *importance* of exercises to correct posture defects. On the other hand, it is the business of the physical education teacher to teach pupils the proper way *to use* such exercises to correct poor posture.

When the needs-study has been completed, *problem* areas have been agreed upon by the total group, and a possible scope has been selected for each *problem* area, the task of providing for well-rounded learning experiences in the core faces the group. Continuity may be provided in several ways. Some schools and/or school systems *feel* that it is better to peg certain *problem* areas at each grade level, particularly in the initial stages of the program. For example, one county system pegs problem areas as follows: **Seventh Grade Core—** (1) Exploring Our Educational Opportunities, (2) Achieving Good Intercultural Relations, and (3) Keeping Physically Fit. **Eighth Grade Core—**(1) The Four Freedoms on the March, (2) Discovering Maryland as America in Miniature, (3) How Did the United States Become a World Power, and (4) Understanding and Improving Myself. **Ninth Grade Core—**(1) Democracy—A Balance Between Right and Responsibilities, (2) Living Together in Prince George's County, (3) Finding Our Place in the World at Work, and (4) Achieving Personal-Social Adjustment.

Another school uses the following plan to insure over-all continuity

[3] See: Selected bibliography, Chapter III.

in the program:[4] **Seventh Grade**—*(1)* Problems of School Living, *(2)* Problems of Personal and Community Health, *(3)* Problems of Intercultural Relations, and *(4)* Problems of Economic Relationships. **Eighth Grade**—*(1)* Problems of School Living, *(2)* Problems of Self-Understanding, *(3)* Problems of World Peace, *(4)* Problems of Conservation of Natural Resources, and *(5)* Problems of Home and Family Living. **Ninth Grade**—*(1)* Problems of School Living, *(2)* Problems of Finding Values by Which We Live, *(3)* Problems of Democratic Government (Processes and Development), *(4)* Problems of Communication in a Contemporary World, and *(5)* Problems of Vocations and employment. **Tenth Grade**—*(1)* Problems of School Living, *(2)* Problems of Personal and Community Health, *(3)* Problems of Intercultural Relations, and *(4)* Problems of Vocation and Employment. **Eleventh Grade**—*(1)* Problems of School Living, *(2)* Problems of Self-Understanding, *(3)* Problems of Democratic Government (Processes and Development), *(4)* Problems of Conservation of Natural Resources, *(5)* Problems of Communication in a Contemporary World, and *(6)* Problems of Home and Family Living. **Twelfth Grade**—*(1)* Problems of School Living, *(2)* Problems of Finding Values by Which We Live, *(3)* Problems of Achieving World Peace, and *(4)* Problems of Economic Relationships.

In the two examples cited, teacher-pupil initiative and creativeness is fostered. Each learning unit is developed through teacher-pupil planning. These plans tend to vary widely from core class to core class in any school at a given grade level. Teachers are urged to keep rather careful records of learning units as to purposes, activities, and outcomes. These are filed in a central place for reference when other core teachers plan with these pupils at another grade level. Teachers also are urged to deal with significant problems, undefined in the problem-area structure, as they arise in their day-to-day efforts with pupils. When *learning units* have been drawn from the pegged areas, teachers and pupils are free to choose any area to explore which meets their criteria for good learning units.

---

[4] Note that this school has thirteen *problem areas* and that a *learning unit* is drawn from each once in the junior high school and once in the senior high school.

Some schools and/or school systems find that pegging *problem areas* is not necessary. Careful records must, of necessity, be kept in this set-up in order to avoid needless repetition or to avoid obvious gaps in pupils' educational experiences. The tasks of pegging *problem areas*, the writers assume, belongs to the professional educator.

The roles of the core and special-interest areas in the total school program, the reader will note, have evolved as all of those concerned work together in defining the *problem area* structure for the core program. Each supplements and reinforces the other as people cooperate in curriculum development. Some groups have found a statement of the specific and concomitant functions of each area to be useful in curriculum construction work. At any rate, we tend to clarify further what we are willing to act upon when we attempt to put our ideas in writing. Attention, however, should be given to the possibility that lines between the core program and the special-interest areas can be too finely drawn, whereas our efforts should be directed toward a blurring of these lines.

Developing Resource Guides for Use in Preplanning for Learning Units in the Core Program

Chapter V dealt with the process of developing a *resource guide* and an example of such a guide around the *problem area, Problems of Education in American Democracy* was included. The task of developing resource guides can be done effectively by core teachers with special-interest-area teachers acting as consultants when they have a competency related to the topic at hand. For example, when core teachers develop a *resource guide* on *Problems of Personal and Community Health*, science, health, home economics, art, physical education, and other teachers should be helpful as consultants. Involving these people helps to coordinate the core program with the special-interest areas. Supervisors and principals, too, should be used as consultants and coordinators of the *resource guide* development efforts. Outside consultant services are often helpful if such services are not available on the central-office staff or if principals are unable to give necessary leadership.

In order to produce adequate resource guides many and varied materials are needed. It is helpful for a group to make a decision as soon as possible as to which problem areas are going to be used as a basis for resource guide development at a particular time. Librarians and materials centers can then be alerted to accumulate a variety of materials on each subject. County and city supervisors and state departments of education are useful sources of materials. The United States Office of Education is helpful in suggesting good materials of a free and/or inexpensive nature. The United States Office of Education also has an accumulation of current bibliographies on many subjects. At any rate, it is very important that an individual or a group be delegated the task of collecting and arranging in usable form adequate materials for resource guide development.

Resource guides are usually developed in workshops. A word of warning is due here. Often, groups attempt to develop such materials in too short a time—a two or three weeks period. In order to develop a document that will prove helpful to teachers in their preplanning for learning experiences, time is needed to consider many possibilities as to purposes, scope, learning activities, evaluative devices, and a wide variety of resources. One school system has a continuing workshop during the entire school year to develop materials. Another school system sets aside a ten week period during the mid-winter for development of materials. Teachers meet in a workshop situation once each week for three hours. The interim between scheduled meetings is used to consider new suggestions of the group, evaluate and refine previous group suggestions, and to edit materials for mimeographing. A certain high-school faculty has developed resource guides from thirteen problem areas over a three year period in summer workshops. In each case described above, the participants decided in which problem areas resource guides were most needed and set to work on those selected. Inexperienced core teachers are often able to draw learning units from a problem area such as *Problems of Democratic Government* without too much preplanning material. This is a field with which most well-informed people are familiar. On the other hand, even the most creative teachers might need help in preplanning for a learning unit drawn from the problem area, *Problems of Self-Understanding*.

In *resource guide* development there is no one pattern. It is important, however, for the group involved to decide early in its work on a plan for their guides which seems to offer most for them in terms of helpful materials. Individuals in the group may volunteer for specific tasks such as collecting evaluative instruments, but it is particularly important that the entire group give its considered judgment on every phase of the work. The group should work as a whole until the scope and purposes have been clearly identified. Those with responsibility for assembling learning activities and resources should give careful attention to individual differences in interests and reading levels.

While the number of *resource guides* undertaken in one workshop will depend largely upon the size of the group in attendance, it is unwise to attempt too much. Materials, coordination, and clerical services bog down in such cases. Perhaps it is safe to say that an average of ten to fifteen teachers can produce the most creative effort on one *resource guide*. Each small group needs a chairman to pull together group ideas, and a recorder to keep records of each group session. Each small group needs an editing committee so that its materials might be presented to the over-all editing committee in the best possible form. An over-all editing committee could very well include one member from each small group so that original ideas might be protected in the published product.

Parents and interested laymen have given valuable assistance in *resource guide* development particularly in the clarifying of scope and in the assembling of resources. Pupils should always be included in *resource guide* development when scope is being suggested. Their questions are perhaps the most significant data a group could use when attempting to bring personal-social needs into realistic play. It seems that *resource guide* development is the task of trained curriculum workers—teachers, administrators, and professional consultants in the area of method and evaluation.

At some point in the development of a core program, all teachers should engage in the process of working together on *resource guides*. Those who do make their teaching more meaningful. They somehow get a deeper insight into genuine teacher-pupil planning and the value of direct experiences in meaningful learning situations.

Working Together in Continuous In-Service Experiences to Develop An Adequate Core Program

The core program is not a static thing. Good leadership provides for continuous in-service experiences which serve to refine and evaluate constantly the group's best efforts. A program dedicated to a continuous attack on the personal-social problems of youth in this society will face the need for change—the need for revising *problem areas* in light of current, immediate, and wider community-needs and adolescent-concerns, and the need for bringing resource *guides* up-to-date as to issues, problems, tensions, conflicts and resources. Effectively evaluating a core program in action is something that has long needed the concerted efforts of creative minds. A valid evaluation-program could afford a group a stimulating and challenging endeavor. One faculty group devoted a year of its in-service program to a study of the matter of method in the core program. This study resulted in some definitive and helpful statements as to methods of teaching critical thinking. Whatever the in-service project, it should be a carefully planned set of experiences with the full participation of all those concerned. It should give a sense of continuity to the program by staying with a project until a basis for sound hypotheses to guide action is provided.

What are some ways to organize for a good in-service program for core teachers? Let us hasten to admit that there is no *best* way. Most on-going programs use a variety of techniques. Some have found their *grade-level* organizations one of their best devices for providing continuous experiences for pupils, exchanging ideas, and evaluating the effectiveness of their program. These *grade-level* organizations include not only core teachers but all of the teachers who have a group of pupils in class. Parent meetings are often organized around these grade-level groups rather than the *en masse* experience of some parent-teacher organizations. *Departmental* meetings are useful to study problems that pertain particularly to the core program. Care should be taken to minimize meetings, however, which tend to isolate departments within a compartmentalized or "my program" approach. Naturally, the total faculty should be involved in any plan to progressively evaluate the core. Evaluation procedures should be set up as experimentation evolves.

Workshop, institutes, and conferences have been used to supplement continuous, in-service experiences. Workshops often take the form of a two to three week affair with a variety of experiences offered. Institutes and conferences are often limited to a one to two day period and concentrate discussion on one particular topic such as *Evaluating the Core Program*. These efforts need designated leadership of the administration, but there should be teacher-planning committees working in all areas to help define problems, name consultants, assemble materials, plan social aspects, evaluate, and the like. Outside consultant services have often been used effectively in the initial stages of core program development. Such people, with a wide variety of successful experiences with problems at hand, are able to help novices avoid many pitfalls. Further, their confidence and enthusiasm lend courage to the convictions of those trying something new. From time to time outside consultant services are useful when some particular problem, e.g., evaluation, arises. For leadership in the on-going development of the program, local schools and/or school systems would do well to employ personnel in a supervisory capacity who have strong competencies in developing an adequate core program. While such expertness may seem to come high to those who employ, in the final analysis, money, time, and energy may be saved.

Nearby colleges and universities have often cooperated with schools in developing core programs. A closer working-together on the part of teacher-education institutions and public-school systems might well serve to spur the development of programs for the preservice education of core teachers. Even if a particular institution of higher education is not directly concerned with the education of core teachers there are usually staff members who have much insight into problems the public schools face in this development. These people are trained in research techinques and often have a knowledge of current materials and trends not readily available to most public-school personnel. When colleges and universities are able to place their student-teachers in good core situations in the public schools a reservoir of applicants is established on a firm foundation.

Groups of core teachers have widened their horizons by working for a period of time with special-interest areas where general competency is needed. For example, many core teachers seem to come to their jobs with a satisfactory background in English and the social studies but they are often insecure in drawing upon art and science. Core teachers have a real need to draw upon these areas in their general education aspects. Some school systems have provided workshop experiences in which contributions of these areas to the selected *problem areas* are explored. Core teachers are afforded direct experiences to help them understand and use effectively the facts of science in everyday living. Science teachers and central-office staff who understand the core program are glad to render this service. Art workshops are held in each school and on a system-wide basis to help core teachers gain some skill in the art media used most often in core classes—mobiles, murals, individual illustrations, lettering, and papier-mâché. Parents often enter into this aspect of the program and themselves gain insight into the place of the creative arts in everyday life. Art supervisors, art teachers, and talented classroom-teachers serve as consultants.

In the foregoing portion of this chapter, the writers have endeavored to point out that the development of an adequate core program induces people to work together in ways that are both stimulating and challenging. The task requires creative leadership by administrative personnel. It further requires the marshaling of all available resources in men, materials, and techniques. It has been stressed that developing a core program is a cooperative and continuous process, that the job never ends. Eternal vigilance is the price creative people pay for the significant aspects of life. It has been made explicit by both example and theory that the development of a good core program is inextricably interwoven with the more encompassing task of reorganizing the total secondary-school curriculum in light of what we know about the goals of Democracy, and the nature of the learner and of the learning process.

The remainder of this chapter provides several examples of *how* groups have worked together in specific situations to develop their core programs.

IN-SERVICE PROGRAM FOR BASIC EDUCATION[5]

Dade County Public Schools, Miami, Florida

The Basic Education program as developed in Dade County has had its greatest success in the in-service program for its teachers developed in the individual schools.

Kinloch Park Junior High School was one of the first schools to initiate a core program—followed by two other large junior high schools, Miami Edison and Ponce de Leon. These three schools set the pattern for the other schools that have since entered the program. There has been a continued growth of the Basic Education program and nearly all junior high schools in Dade County are adopting it.

The in-service program for teachers varies from school to school, but generally it has followed the pattern first adopted at Kinloch Park Junior High School. In this school a group of teachers volunteered to go into core work in the seventh grade. This group met and planned a program. The schedule was so arranged that these teachers were free to meet on school-time twice a week for conferences to discuss the common problems they were encountering. Theory is one aspect of changing the curriculum, but practice is another and in the actual teaching situation problems arose that were not anticipated and policy had to be developed. It soon became apparent that outside-building help was needed. We were fortunate in being able to call in as consultant, Dr. William Alexander of the University of Miami who helped us immeasurably. In order that teachers who would next take up the core program in the eighth grade might receive help in planning their work, we invited Dr. Alexander in to conduct a practicum for our faculty. The entire faculty participated in a weekly after-school meeting.

The second year, the two teachers who apparently had met with the greatest success in teaching the core the previous year were named chairmen. Each worked with a grade cycle. We found this method most satisfactory. This plan was carried into the third year with three chairmen for the three grade-cycles and one overall chairman for the entire program. We encouraged other members to go out and explain the program to other schools. In the meantime a county group, interested

---

[5] Mimeographed material prepared by Loren Sheely, formerly principal, Kinloch Junior High School, Dade County, Florida. The terms *core program* and *basic education*, in this context, are synonymous.

in the core program, was organized. Through this group, which met monthly, teachers exchanged ideas and units of work and worked up lists of resource material.

The county-wide program is starting its fourth year of operation. Each new school going into the program has available: a problems course in Basic Education as developed by the University of Miami; a curriculum bulletin on Basic Education; numerous resource guides, and the full cooperation of successful teachers who are available when needed to visit with other faculties as advisors and act as councilors. The in-service experiences of teachers in the core-plan-of-teaching has gone far in making the Basic Education program a success in Dade County.

The problem of recruiting new teachers who have not been in the school system is answered in part by the following methods. The University of Miami, Florida State University, Stetson University, and the University of Florida are sending-out students who are interning in the core methods. The intern program does not meet the need for teachers but it may be a sign that the program is proving its worth. Building principals are more selective in hiring teachers where they have started the Basic Education program or are contemplating doing so. We have found that teachers with experience in the elementary field who move into the core program tend to adapt themselves readily and are successful in the shortest time. We have also found that beginning-teachers who have not yet become *pattern-bound* with traditional teaching are easily led into a method of working that is sometimes difficult for experienced, traditional-subject teachers to follow. We have also found that experienced teachers who are dissatisfied with traditional methods have an outlet of new educational experiences awaiting them in a core-experience program.

It seems that in any program where there is a desire to do an excellent teaching job, teachers will band together in an in-service program where guidance, cooperation, and planning can take place. Only one element is necessary for a successful program other than excellent teachers, and that can be summed up in one word—leadership. It helps to have leadership shared at the county level and the building level.

In summary, our in-service program in the schools includes (1) Outside, expert help (Universities), (2) Practicum courses for university credit held in own buildings on local problems, (3) County organizational assistance—leadership, (4) Building organization—committees and scheduled meetings, (5) Sharing successes with other schools, and (6) A common philosophy of the needs of young adolescents with building-leadership to execute a plan for successful teaching.

HEALTH EDUCATION IN THE CORE PROGRAM[6]

It is felt very strongly by the Health Education Supervisor of Prince George's County that the core program offers the best opportunity that has yet been presented for effective health-teaching in the secondary school curriculum. This opinion is based on the understanding that action to effect desirable health-outcomes is involved with over-all attitudes as well as a knowledge of sound health principles. Attitudes are the result of developmental processes which take a long period of time and are affected by the total experiences of the individual. If this reasoning is sound, then it is readily apparent that the best opportunities for health teaching are going to be in a curriculum area where the approach is through common problems of students rather than through isolated subjects which deal primarily with knowledge.

Where health-interest studies have been made among secondary-school students it has been evident that health matters ought to be included in the *problem* areas of the core program. This was discussed fully with the participants in the 1952 June Workshop. The purpose of this workshop was to define the *problem* areas to be used in the core program on the junior high school level. The Denver Health Interest study was used primarily as the basis for this discussion. It was urged that the group consider the following *problem* areas used in the core program:

1. Maintaining Body Efficiency pegged at the seventh-grade level
2. Developing Self-Confidence pegged at the eighth-grade level
3. Improving Personality pegged at the ninth-grade level

Subsequently, the Health Education Supervisor was asked to meet with sessions of a Core Workshop in the 1953 winter meetings. These workshops were concerned with content, resources, and the development of resource guides. The three topics listed above were broken down in detail for the group so that they would have a clearer understanding of their scope. In addition, there was indicated a possible scope in health instruction for the senior high school so that there would be a more complete picture before them. Major emphases for one of the topics, Maintaining Body Efficiency, were discussed at this time as a guide for developing emphases for the other topics and in order to tie health in with the total study.

Resources were discussed at some length and bibliographies of materials for teacher and pupil use and library materials were distributed. These materials were on display at the time and were discussed at some length. In addition, a list of reliable resource agencies for health-education

[6] Submitted by Mary A. Thompson, Supervisor of Health Education, Prince George's County, Upper Marlboro, Maryland.

materials was distributed along with a sheet which indicated possible contributions of the Health Education staff of the Board of Education to future learning activities.

In a later session the workshop group had an opportunity to see a large exhibit of health resource-materials such as pamphlets, posters, and teachers' guides. These were discussed in detail and each person was given a checklist of these materials and informed that a full file was being set up in each school library. This file would be supplemented from time to time.

This workshop group later chose to include four phases under the topic Maintaining Body Efficiency. There were: (1) Determining of Personal Health Status, (2) How Adequate Nutrition Contributes to Body Efficiency, (3) Normal Structure and Function of the Body, and (4) Building Resistance to Disease.

The group adopted the scope suggested for the topics Developing Self-Confidence and Improving Personality and organized it in two *problem areas*: (1) Understanding and Improving Myself and (2) Maintaining Good Family Relationships.

Conferences have been held with the secondary-school supervisor responsible for the core program and with teachers in some of the schools relative to the health content of the core program in the senior high school. Areas suggested here were: (1) Marriage and Family Problems, (2) National and International Health Programs, and (3) Current Health Problems for Scientists.

As learning units began to be developed by teachers and pupils, the Health Education staff was called on in various ways: to help teachers further with direction and materials, to participate in classroom discussions, to confer with committees of pupils, and to suggest other resource personnel and places. The following are illustrations:

1.   A seventh-grade core group was concerned with studying personal-health status in connection with the problem of Maintaining Body Efficiency. One member of the Health Education staff not only discussed types of health records with the pupils but demonstrated vision-screening before the class. This provoked so much interest that an eye model and other materials were taken into the class and the class itself was given a special session with vision-screening by the vision technician.

2.   An eighth-grade core class was concerned with developing an understanding of growth problems and body changes in connection with the problem Understanding and Improving Myself. A member of the Health Education staff was invited by the pupil-program chairman to visit the class and to discuss questions that had been raised. The questions were listed in order of preference. A very spirited discussion resulted, particularly around the topic of Why Girls Mature Faster than Boys.

3. A conference was held with an eleventh-grade core teacher in regard to direction and materials for health insurance plans for a class studying Purchasing Health under the problem of Marriage and Family Problems.

4. A committee of pupils from a senior high school studying community health organizations under the twelfth-grade problem area of Other Health Problems made an appointment with and visited the Health Education Office to discuss the School Health Program.

5. When diabetes screening took place in the secondary schools in the fall of 1954 one of the volunteer ladies doing the screening was asked to demonstrate the testing procedure to a class of seventh-grade core pupils concerned with determining personal-health status.

6. A teacher of a tenth-grade core class concerned with community health problems was interested in obtaining the help of resource personnel, particularly in regard to alcoholic addiction as a special community problem. She was referred to the very able director of the Section on Alcohol Studies of the State Health Department who had expressed a willingness to visit classes interested in discussing this topic.

These examples could be added to extensively because the Health Education staff is called on constantly. This material is being written, for instance, during time scheduled originally for an appointment with the seventh-grade core teachers in one school. The appointment had to be cancelled because schools were closed due to snowy weather.

CORE TEACHERS AT WORK IN AN IN-SERVICE PROGRAM, PRINCE GEORGE'S COUNTY, MARYLAND[7]

The junior high schools in Prince George's County embarked upon the core program in 1947. At that time no teachers were prepared for this work other than those few who attended workshops sponsored by the State Department of Education the previous summer. Due to this fact, it was thought wise to begin with an English-social-studies-fusion concept of core. A junior-high-school supervisor devoted part of her time to in-service education of core teachers. Groups of teachers were brought into the Board of Education from time to time to develop resource units and several art workshops were conducted for core teachers by the art supervisor.

[7] For a further account of the in-service education of core teachers see Lucile L. Lurry, "In-service Education of Core Teachers," *Preparation of Core Teachers for Secondary Schools.* Committee on Preparation of Core Teachers, Association for Supervision and Curriculum Development. Washington, D. C., Natural Education Association, 1955, Chapter VI.

In 1951 the county employed a person to devote the major portion of her time to the development of the core curriculum. An in-service program was launched to help teachers develop compentencies needed in an approach designed to make a continuous attack upon, for the most part, the contemporary problems of junior-high-school youth. At least three problems faced the group: (1) How to get a better understanding of the core in theory and practice, (2) How to go about reorganizing the basic structure of the program to bring it more in line with the needs of youth, and (3) How to develop materials to give teacher help and security in this changing process. Naturally, the added problem of interpreting this program to parents and other laymen loomed large.

During the 1951-52 school term, efforts were made to acquaint faculty groups with the research in core program development through discussion groups and reading. A few people enrolled in a course offered at the University of Maryland dealing with teaching in the core program. Some of the useful publications in core program development and bibliographies of the same nature were made available to teachers and principals. A sizeable group of core teachers and a few principals were sent out-of-state to conferences and to observe in laboratory schools to further their insights into the problems facing them. The mid-winter conference for all secondary-school teachers emphasized the need for reorganizing general education in the high schools. Substitutes were made available by the Board of Education for core teachers to engage in inter-school visitation.

In June, 1952, a county-wide workshop for core teachers was held. The over-arching purpose of this enterprise was to clarify further a concept of the core program in action. During the 1951-52 school year, teachers' suggestions were taken by a planning committee for small and large-group activities, for consultant services, and for materials needed in the workshop. Principals, guidance workers, special-interest-area teachers and their supervisors were invited to participate. Each of the fifteen schools asked at least two parents to work with the teachers. Large-group sessions were organized around such problems as: (1) Reorganizing the basic structure of the core program, (2) Understanding the common personal-social needs of youth, (3) Interpreting the core program to the public, (4) Using the scientific method and understanding its implications for developing an adequate core program, and (5) Evaluating the core program. Small group sessions dealt with such matters as: (1) Analyzing materials of instruction, (2) Organizing for best use of the core block of time, and (3) Improving reading through the core program. All kinds of audio-visual equipment were provided for demonstration and use. While there were innumerable intangible outcomes of this experience, at least two concrete evidences of change and helpfulness can be listed. First, the basic structure was reorganized in terms of the common, personal-social problems of youth. Second, though no publication was attempted, suggestions for the organization and content of a handbook for core teachers were made. This publication was developed during the summer and circulated to each core teacher, principal and librarian in the fall. Third, a plan for quarterly meetings of core teachers on a professional and recreational basis during 1952-53 was promoted. Needless to say, the exchange of ideas among core teachers and the recognition that other teachers faced similar problems helped to make the workshop fruitful. It should be added that very tangible evidence of growth was apparent in the core program in action in the 1952-53 school year.

Due to increased enrollments and replacements, twenty-five new teachers came to the program in 1953-54. Few of these had attended teacher education institutions which prepare core teachers. On the recommendation of experienced teachers, a program of in-service preparation was designed especially for newcomers. Attempts were made to acquaint them with the philosophy, methods of instruction, materials of instruction and the community as a laboratory. Several means were used here: classroom observation and conferences, audio-visual aids,[8] small- and large-group conferences in which discussions were led by experienced teachers and the supervisor, field trips, and demonstrations. A definite attempt was made to deal with the expressed problems of teachers. Inter-class visitation and inter-school visitation were found to be a most helpful means of promoting understanding. Funds for substitutes in this program were allocated in the county school budget. Funds were also provided for consultant services and out-of-state conferences. In addition a sum, totaling twenty dollars per core teacher, was allocated for materials of instruction to be bought by the individual teacher. This was over and above the regular textbook allotment per pupil.

Only three quarterly meetings were held for the entire group because of poor planning for last-minute pressures in June. These county-wide conferences gave further stimulus to teachers in the exploration of the full meaning of the core program. The fall meeting was a get-acquainted session planned by teacher committees. Several publishers were invited to set up exhibits of materials felt to be useful in the core program. At the winter meeting, an effort was made through a panel discussion to improve

[8] The following audio-visual aids were found to be helpful: (a) *A Core Curriculum Class in Action*, Audio-visual Material Consultation Bureau, College of Education, Wayne University, Detroit 1, Michigan, (b) Harold Alberty, *The Core Program in the High School* (a recording), Educational Recording Services, Los Angeles 45, California. (c) H. H. Giles, *Techniques of Teacher-Pupil Planning* (a recording), Educational Recording Services, Los Angeles 45, California.

articulation between the core program in the junior high schools and the elementary and senior high schools of the county. Participants represented the three areas and the panel was moderated by a principal. A consultant was invited for the early spring meeting to help the group deal with how to teach for critical thinking. The planning for these meetings was done by the executive committee of the core teachers organization. A more representative group was designated as a planning committee for 1953-54. This group began at once to work on plans to explore a major concern in next year's program—evaluation of the core in terms of present status and proposed next steps.

Perhaps the most promising experience, in terms of the needs of the program in Prince George's County, was the mid-winter workshop. These sessions were held once each week from 7:30-10:30 P.M. The purpose of this workshop was to develop resource guides for use by teachers in planning learning units drawn from the basic structure proposed in the 1952 Summer Workshop. Participants included core teachers, supervisors for all areas, principals and vice-principals,, librarians and special-interest-area teachers in physical education, homemaking, mathematics, music, and art. An effort was made to develop resources consistent with what we know about the common developmental tasks of adolescents. To this end, we found the services of the Institute of Child Study, University of Maryland, most valuable. During and following this experience, it was felt that, at last, insight was being developed into the function of the core program in relation to the special-interest areas and the contributions of each to the other's enrichment.

One more technique is perhaps worth mentioning in this brief account. Periodically a newsletter to core teachers was issued from the central office. This mimeographed material described promising practices going on in each of the schools. It suggested useful, new materials and included bits of human interest about as many core teachers as possible. The teachers seemed to enjoy the newsletter and to find it useful. They have suggested that the publication be taken over next year by a representative group of teachers from each school.

The extension of the core upward has met with some success in Prince George's County. Two of the smaller, and one of the larger senior high schools have initiated the program since September, 1952. In each case, very careful preplanning included the entire school staff, parents, pupils, and supervisors.[9] In each case very careful evaluation took place. Consultant services were made available to these school groups for needs-studies, interpreting to the public, materials of instruction, and evaluation. Particularly in changing reporting practices, parents were brought into the basic policies. A group consisting of parents, pupils, administrators,

[9] See: Nicholas A. Adams, "Guidance—The Function of All School Personnel," *Educational Leadership*, X, 370-374 (March, 1953).

and teachers developed a letter to parents explaining the purposes of the core, the criteria used in evaluating and, therefore, the reason for changing the existing system.

High on the list of in-service experiences planned for 1953-54 were: (1) an advisory council to make recommendations for improving the program and to keep in closer touch with the 200 core classrooms where action takes place—the council might include pupils, parents, teachers, principals and supervisors, (2) a course for those people who substitute in the core program to help them better to understand its philosophy and purposes, and (3) a workshop in art and music for core teachers that they might provide more integrating experiences for pupils by drawing upon these areas.

This story is told all too briefly. There are many techniques not mentioned here which serve to make an in-service program meaningful. Perhaps the most to be said for the success of any in-service programs is the degree to which all who are affected have a share in decision making. The worth of the individual, a premium on the cooperative process and the method of intelligence are values to be held dearly here as in the classroom with pupils. The untiring effort and support of a sympathetic superintendent makes the task all the more worth the attempt.

THE IN-SERVICE PROGRAM IN THE FAIRMONT HEIGHTS HIGH SCHOOL, PRINCE GEORGE'S COUNTY, MARYLAND[10]

In September 1950, the new Fairmont Heights High School opened with 796 pupils and thirty-one teachers. The majority of the pupils came from widely scattered sections of Prince George's County which covers an area of 486.17 square miles. The school is located in the metropolitan section of the county but many of the pupils had come from schools in the rural areas to which they had developed strong loyalties. Many of the teachers had been transferred from other schools in the county while others were recently out of college without previous teaching experience. Consequently, instead of being a closely-knit group, there was an aggregation of individuals whose members were largely unfamiliar to each other.

The following needs became evident as we began to function together:

1. The need to develop a feeling of belongingness, of security, and of loyalty to the Fairmont Heights High School by being active participating members of the group.
2. The need to create a continuously evolving democratic school

[10] Submitted by G. James Gholson, Principal, Fairmont Heights Junior-Senior High School, Prince George's County, Maryland.

community in which the group could develop an awareness and an understanding of:

a. The dignity and worth of each individual.
b. The use of the method of intelligence in solving problems.
c. Co-operation in the solution of common problems.

3. The need to achieve mastery of techniques and data that make possible greater control of one's physical and social environment.

A major portion of the time of the 1950 pre-school conference was spent in discussing and summarizing what the faculty believed concerning:

1. The purpose of education.
2. The nature of the democratic society.
3. The nature of the learning process.
4. The nature of the individual.

The contributions of the faculty were discussed, recorded, and revised in subsequent meetings. These became the set of tentative goals which gave direction to our living and working together in the Fairmont Heights High School.

Three of the most important committees organized in the school were the grade-level groups. These groups have an elected chairman and secretary. They have met regularly since the opening of the school. The major activities of these groups have included identifying tensions, perplexities, issues, and problems of boys and girls, developing and collecting resource materials, and refining techniques and devices for helping boys and girls meet their problems.

Among the techniques and procedures used for defining problem areas were the *Ross L. Mooney Check List, Lucile Lurry's Suggested Problem Areas for a Core Program, Harold Alberty's Some Statements of Common Needs of Adolescents and Problem Areas Suitable for a Core Program,* standardized tests, conferences, surveys, and other relevant materials.

In an effort to get community reaction and help in the kind of program being developed the following letter was sent to parents.

Dear Parent:

In order for us to plan the type of program best suited to the needs of your child, we are requesting your help by asking you to list some of the understandings, skills, and ideals which you think a child should develop in order to become a wholesome citizen.

We feel that as an interested parent you would want to share in the planning of your child's program. Please list your ideas in the spaces below and return to the school by your child.

Very truly yours,
G. James Gholson
Principal

The response to the communication was gratifying. A summary of parents' suggestions, in order of rank, follows:

1. Learning to get along with other people.
2. Developing basic skills in reading, writing, and arithmetic.
3. Understanding and developing wholesome health habits.
4. Appreciating the "finer" things in life.
5. Developing a wholesome attitude towards sex.
6. Developing vocational skills.
7. Helping teen-agers meet their emotional problems.

As a follow up of this activity a subcommittee of the School's Community Relations Committee, composed of teachers and pupils, carried on a field project by visiting churches and homes in the school community. These pupils and teachers talked about the kind of program the school was trying to develop. These contacts proved very worthwhile as parents expressed themselves concerning the school and what we were attempting to do with their boys and girls.

The faculty of the school has deemed it wise from time to time to bring in consultants to help summarize experiences, clarify concepts, and suggest next steps. The Board of Education of Prince George's County has been very sympathetic to this procedure and has given generously of its funds in bringing outstanding individuals to the school.

One of the many consultants has been Dr. Harold B. Alberty, Professor of Education at the Ohio State University. He has worked with the staff on a continuing basis. During the school year 1951-52, Dr. Alberty helped the staff explore the following problem and the related aspects which had emerged out of group thinking:

Problem:

How Can We Further Refine the Framework and Experiences We Are Developing With Our Boys and Girls?

1. How adequate is our present framework?
2. Where should we make immediate improvements?
3. What help can we get in validating some of the important hypotheses upon which we are operating?
4. What are some suggestions for putting in more permanent form some of the experiences we are developing with our boys and girls?

The following suggestions grew out of the group thinking with Dr. Alberty:

1. That the total faculty re-examine the existing problem area framework, grades seven through twelve, in terms of the school's stated philosophy.

2. That a thorough analysis of the scope of each problem area be made with the total faculty participating.
3. That resource units be constructed on each problem area with the total faculty participating. These resource units would gradually replace the present policy of faculty construction of teaching units.
4. That consideration be given to extending the core to the senior high school.
5. That consideration be given to selecting core teachers who majored in mathematics and science.
6. That validation of the present educational hypotheses of this faculty concerning the teaching-learning situation:
   a. Be recognized as a long time process.
   b. Make use of carefully recorded observations of student behavior over an extended period of time.
   c. Make use of the parents of students insofar as possible.
   d. Experiments with the student interview technique.
7. That the experiences of the faculty-student groups be put in permanent form through use of:
   a. Library files
   b. Resource units
   c. Resource files
   d. Materials bureau.

Closely related to our in-service program during the regular school year has been the series of summer workshops sponsored by the Board of Education of Prince George's County. These workshops have been geared to the problems identified by the staff during the school year. Participation of teachers from other schools in the County has enriched these workshop experiences. It was felt from the very beginning in the Fairmont Heights High School that the scientific method—or the method of intelligence—is one of the chief means by which individuals thoughtfully meet their needs in their everyday environment. Accordingly, much stress has been placed on the thinking process. The first workshop, co-ordinated by Miss Bernice O'Briant, Supervisor of Secondary Education at Hampton Institute, accepted the challenge of making the thinking process functional for boys and girls in relationship to their day to day problems. We were stimulated to organize preliminary planning of subject matter content (concepts, attitudes and/or skills) and of activities for adolescents, relative to a selected problem or need. We were further challenged to develop procedures for planning jointly with adolescents.

The progression of workshops gives some idea of the growth in the thinking of the staff. Our first workshop (1951) helped teachers develop, according to the scientific method of thinking, the preplanning of a creative learning unit of some problem that seemed to be pertinent to the maturity of their pupils in their efforts to solve their problems. During the 1951-52 school year, we were assisted by Dr. Alberty to become aware of the challenges of the pertinent problems of youth in contemporary life in relation to a larger frame of reference which we later called Problem Areas of Living. We realized, during the summer of 1952, that if teenagers are to grow and to aid in the reconstruction of a better world in which to live, that we the teachers must be developing clearer understandings of the most demanding issues, tensions, and problems of present day living and keener appreciations of the variations and likenesses of the maturing of adolescents. That is, that teachers must be continually examining and redefining the specific aspects of the basic issues that are important in the society at any particular time, and that we must be studying the potentialities, the needs, and the interests of adolescents as living organisms, evolving in a complex culture. Our problem then was to analyze in the form of resource units certain selected problem areas into tentative aspects, suggested activities, and materials suitable for adolescents in order that they might function more intelligently in an emerging democratic society.

Planning for the workshop for 1953 was done with Dr. Lucile Lurry, Supervisor of Secondary Education in Prince George's County. In order to get ready for the workshop of 1953 we set certain tasks for ourselves. We developed the following criteria for evaluating our problem areas:

Fairmont Heights High School Criteria for Evaluating Problem Areas

A Problem Area Should:

1. Be a problem pertaining to needs and interests of boys and girls in this culture.
2. Cut across subject matter lines.
3. Provide opportunity for direct and vicarious experiences.
4. Have available resource materials.
5. Provide for democratic skills which will lead toward growth in tolerance, critical thinking, self-direction, cooperativeness, and aesthetic values.
6. Provide leads to other problems.
7. Provide opportunity for use of problem-solving techniques.
8. Provide opportunity for generalizations beyond the experiences of the group.
9. Provide a balance of over-all relationships between felt needs and the demands of society.
10. Provide opportunity for cooperative planning.

11. Should be so defined that learning units can be developed in terms of individual differences.
12. Provide for skills in such fundamentals as reading, writing, speaking, and listening.
13. Provide a balance of problems of a personal, personal-social and personal-social-economic nature.

In the spring of 1953, we revised our problem areas in terms of the criteria and an analyses of other pertinent studies in the field. The revised areas are:

1. Problems of School Living
2. Problems of Personal and Community Health
3. Problems of Finding Values by Which We Live
4. Problems of Communication in a Contemporary World
5. Problems of Economic Relationships
6. Problems of Intercultural Relationships
7. Problems of Home and Family Living
8. Problems of Democratic Government (Processes and Development)
9. Problems of Achieving World Peace
10. Problems of Self-Understanding
11. Problems of Vocations and Employment
12. Problems of Conservation of Natural Resources

We made the problem areas more definitive by developing scope for each of them. The job for the workshop of 1953 was a further definition of the significance of our problem areas and organizing materials and resources. The consultant for this workshop was Dr. Miles E. Cary, formerly Principal of McKinley High School, Honolulu, Hawaii.

It is significant that even though the emphases in these workshops have been on the general education program, teachers from all areas in the school have participated. Their active interest and participation have enriched the core program and have given all the teachers broader concepts of method in their various efforts with young people.

It can be seen from the description on the preceding pages that the core concept in the Fairmont Heights High School has been an evolving one. The faculty is generally agreed at this stage that core is that part of the curriculum which has to do with the understandings, skills, and attitudes that are basic for all pupils. These experiences cut across all conventional subject matter lines. The core is defined in terms of our broad, preplanned problem areas which have been set up by the faculty after an analysis of the common needs, problems, and interests of boys and girls in their school.

Developing the core program has been a stimulating and rewarding challenge. Through these experiences it is felt that we are helping our boys and girls meet intelligently and courageously the problems of living. Through shared experiences the entire school has grown and is growing as we re-define and re-interpret our goals in the day-to-day running of our school. These understandings are basic to our living together:

1. The development of significant personalities can best be achieved through mutual sharing of interests and purposes.
2. Fundamental to the development of democratic growth is the reliance upon the free play on intelligence.
3. Every individual has worth and dignity, and therefore should have the opportunity for optimum development.
4. Individuals function as a community when they develop concepts and skills related to their common interests and needs through shared activity.

A Summary Statement

This volume has taken as its major emphasis the practical phases of the reorganization of general education in the high school within the framework of a core program. In Chapter I the idea was developed that there is a real need to bring general education more into line with the research in how people learn, the nature of the individual, and the aspirations of a democratic society. The core program, as the writers see it, offers a promising approach to high school administrators and teachers who feel their responsibility to move ahead.

It was the belief of the writers that little progress has taken place in core program development, despite the fact that the research[11] points in this direction, because public school people have lacked concrete examples of "Know-How." Therefore, the major effort in this book has been to indicate the several tasks involved in developing a core program and to provide actual descriptions of practice in selected secondary schools. These tasks were considered to be: (1) Defining the core, (2) Designing the core program in terms of the problem area approach, (3) Developing resources for use in the core program, (4) Making core work in the classroom situation, (5) Relating the core program to the special interest areas, and (6) Organizing and carrying on a continuous in-service program for core

[11] See Chapter I for documentation.

teachers. Related to these tasks are such concomitant tasks as making a study of pupil needs, using effectively the core block-of-time, and developing related learning activities in each possible problem area.

We have intended throughout this volume to make clear our convictions concerning the needed reorganization of general education in the American secondary school. Such reorganization can be a challenging and rewarding process for public school people. Furthermore, we have tried to make clear that the job is not an easy one, that resourcefulness, creativeness and time are all needed. We have tried too to indicate that people—teachers, pupils, administrators, parents, and other laymen—are the most valuable resources in developing a core program. These are the people who will be affected by changes made in the curriculum. These are the people, therefore, who should chart the course of these changes.

And, finally, we have tried to make it clear that a school or a school system does not develop a core program overnight. A core program, developed on a sound basis, requires a continuous re-examination and perhaps even a re-defining as teachers, pupils, parents, and administrators work together. Citizens in a democracy see this tentativeness of mind as a happy habit. A continuous in-service program is a must. We have seen this habit serve us well in government, labor-management relations, technological development, and war and peace, to name few areas. Education has a most vital role to play in democracy. A lack of final answers should not discourage us. This can be a challenging prospect.

The writers of this volume have a firm conviction that the core program provides an effective way to put democracy into action in America's secondary schools.

SELECTED BIBLIOGRAPHY

Alberty, Harold, *Reorganizing the High School Curriculum.* New York, The Macmillan Company, 1953 (Revised), Chapter 14.

Faunce, Roland, and Nelson Bossing, *Developing the Core Curriculum.* New York, Prentice-Hall, Inc., 1951, Chapters 11 and 12.

Klohr, Paul, "An Upward Extension of Core," *Educational Leadership,* X, 489-494 (May, 1953).

Laughlin, Hugh, "A Study of the Curriculum Development Program of the Secondary Schools of Garrett County, Maryland," Unpublished Doctoral Dissertation, Columbus, Ohio, The Ohio State University, 1951.

Lurry, Lucile L., "The Contribution of Home Economics to Selected Problem Areas in the Core Curriculum of the Secondary School," Unpublished Doctoral Dissertation, Columbus, Ohio, The Ohio State University, 1949, Chapter 4.

————, "Core Program Development Through Action Research," *The School Review*, LXIII, 469-476 (December, 1955).

————, and James A. Fickes, "The Preparation of Core Teachers—A Joint Responsibility," *Educational Leadership*, XI, 99-105 (November, 1953).

————, and Mary Beth Wackwitz, "Art in an Evolving Core Program," *Art Education Today*. Bureau of Publications, Teachers College, Columbia University, 1953, Chapter 8.

Mudd, Dorothy, *A Core Program Grows*. Bel Air, Maryland, Board of Education, Harford County, 1949.

Noar, Gertrude, *Freedom to Live and Learn*. Philadelphia, The Franklin Press, 1948, Chapter 15.

Preparation of Core Teachers for Secondary Schools. Washington, D. C., Association for Supervision and Curriculum Development, 1955, Chapter 6.

Ovsiew, Leon, *Making the Core Work*. New York, Metropolitan School Study Council, 525 West 120th Street, 1951.

Wright, Grace S., *Core Curriculum Development Problems and Practices*. Bulletin 1952, No. 5. Washington, Office of Health, Education and Welfare, 1952.

Appendix One

RESOURCE MATERIALS RELATED TO THE FIFTEEN PROBLEM AREAS PRESENTED IN CHAPTER III[1]

I. Problems of School Living

A. *Objectives.* To help students:
1. Become familiar with school buildings, grounds, and equipment.
2. Become acquainted with the school personnel and their contributions to the life of the school.
3. Understand and make best use of the opportunities offered by the curriculum of the school.
4. Explore school activities that have potentialities for developing desirable personal characteristics.
5. Develop an awareness of their abilities, interests, needs, assets, and liabilities as a basis for a wise choice of activities.
6. Assume the responsibilities of school citizenship.
7. Become acquainted with school rules, regulations, and traditions.
8. Establish effective study habits.

B. *Scope.* Orienting students to:
1. Physical aspects of the school.
2. School personnel.
3. Curricular offerings and activities.
4. School rules, regulations, and traditions.
5. Effective study.

C. *Suggested Activities.*
1. Physical Aspects of the School.
   a. Make a tour of the school buildings and grounds. Locate classrooms, laboratories, shops, library, gymnasium, offices, bicycle racks, and football and baseball fields.
   b. Ask the librarian to show the class how to make the most of the library.

[1] This section draws upon the resource materials developed by Elsie J. Stalzer (Alberty), "Contributions of Mathematics to a Proposal for Reorganizing General Education in Secondary Schools on the Basis of a Core Program." Unpublished Doctoral Dissertation, Columbus, The Ohio State University, 1952; William E. Jennings, "Contributions of Business Education to Selected Problem Areas of General Education in the Secondary School." Unpublished Doctoral Dissertation, Columbus, The Ohio State University, 1952; and, Monir Kamel Mikhail, "Contributions of Science to Selected Problem Areas Proposed for a Program of General Education in the Secondary School." Unpublished Doctoral Dissertation, Columbus, The Ohio State University, 1952.

    c. Improve the appearance of the classroom by refinishing furniture, making drapes, painting murals, planting flowers, setting an aquarium, and building bookcases.

    d. Set up criteria for evaluating the use of the lunchroom and suggest possible improvements.

    e. Visit the health service room. Ask the school physician or nurse to explain the types of services offered to students and how to profit from them.

    f. Visit the school store. Find out how it operates, what supplies are available, and their cost.

2. School Personnel.

    a. Have a get-acquainted session in which each student introduces himself by telling his name, where he lives, the school from which he came, and any other facts about himself.

    b. Plan a social event for acquainting students with staff members.

    c. Make a "Who's Who" booklet of members of the staff and distribute to new students.

3. Curricular Offerings and Activities.

    a. Discuss problems basic to effective work in core periods: On what basis should a learning unit be chosen? What are sources of data that might contribute to the solving of problems? How can progress be evaluated?

    b. Visit various special interest classes. Ask the teacher for information on the nature of the area, who may elect it, and its possible contribution to vocational and avocational pursuits.

    c. Ask the president of the student council to lead a discussion on the objectives, organization, and scope of the council's activities and responsibilities. How may each student contribute to the success of the council?

    d. Make a calendar of events, including assemblies, musical programs, dramatic productions, dances, and athletic events. Post on the bulletin board.

4. School Rules, Regulations, Traditions.

    a. Prepare a handbook of school regulations. Include such items as: attendance and punctuality; permission to leave early; use of the library; schedule irregularities; fire and security drills.

    b. Interview upper classmen for information about the school traditions.

    c. Learn the school songs, yells, and colors.

   d. Develop a code of safety ethics for both the school building and grounds. Make plans for putting it into action.

5. Effective Study.
Formulate a set of guides to students for developing better and more effective study habits. Analyze habits of study and make suggestions for improvement.

II. Problems of Self-Understanding

A. *Objectives.* To help students: .
1. Study their physical, mental, social, and emotional development.
2. Recognize the relationship of physical and mental health.
3. Discover personal abilities, interests, aptitudes, and understand how to make the best use of them.
4. Find out the relationship between their abilities and achievements.
5. Gain an insight into their assets and liabilities and what can be done about them.
6. Formulate constructive plans for improving their personalities in the light of what has been learned about themselves.
7. Develop an understanding of the forces which shape individuals, including the influence of friends, family, and others.
8. Develop tolerance of the wide variations among people.
9. Understand the essentials to living successfully with others.
10. Appraise their goals, ideals, and values.

B. *Scope.* Understanding ourselves through:
1. Studying our growth and development.
2. Discovering our abilities, interests, aptitudes, and personality traits.
3. Studying our behavior.
4. Appraising our value-system.

C. *Suggested Activities.*
1. Studying Our Growth and Development.
   a. Examine critically the following beliefs:
     (1) Birthmarks and deformities are caused by shocks suffered by the child's mother.
     (2) Tuberculosis can be inherited.
     (3) Boys resemble their mothers more than their fathers, while girls resemble their fathers more than their mothers.
     (4) Children of criminals tend to be criminals.
     (5) Bright people usually have dull children.

    b. Visit a baby ward, nursery, or clinic to observe and study infants at various stages of growth and development.

    c. Illustrate graphically:

        (1) Average amount of sleep per day needed at various age levels.

        (2) Average height of boys and girls from birth to maturity.

        (3) Average weight of boys and girls from birth to maturity.

    d. Draw a series of cartoons to illustrate some milestones along the way to growing up.

    e. Prepare a checklist of problems of health and physical development that concern adolescents. Ask each member of the class to check those items that disturb him. The following list is suggestive: being underweight; being overweight; lack of muscular strength; tiring easily; physical changes; frequent illnesses; poor physique; poor complexion; frequent colds; poor teeth; too tall; too short. Discuss what should be done in each case.

    f. Invite the school physician to lead a discussion on physical changes in adolescent boys and girls.

2. Discovering Our Abilities, Interests, Aptitudes, and Personality Traits.

    a. List and discuss kinds of abilities, such as: physical—strength, endurance, and coordination; mental—reasoning, memory, imagination, and judgment; social—getting along with people, leadership; emotional—control of anger, fear, and jealousy. As a follow-up, discuss conditions which favor the development of abilities. Include some blocks to the development of potential abilities.

    b. Make a survey of the interests of the members of the class in the following areas: games and sports; radio and television programs; books and magazines; movies. What is the value of such interests? To what extent does the school provide for the development of these interests?

    c. List experiences you have had which illustrate the importance of adjusting to and understanding other people. What bearing does understanding other people have on one's personal success? What can one do to increase his understanding of other people?

    d. Consider the difference in aptitudes among members of the class, your friends, and acquaintances. How can these differences be accounted for?

    e. Invite a psychologist to discuss factors that affect the development of personality.

f. Prepare a list of things on: "What I Like about Myself"; "What I Like about Others"; "What I Dislike about Myself"; "What I Dislike about Others."

g. Work out a personality rating chart. Suggest that members of the class evaluate themselves and plan a program of self-improvement.

3. Studying Our Behavior.

a. Draw cartoons illustrating the behavior of persons who have difficulty in adjusting to a group. These might include: a timid person; an irritable person; an over-sympathetic or "soft" individual; a neurotic person, prone to self-pity; a meek, repentant person; a person with an inferiority complex; a person with a superiority complex; the self-satisfied, emotional egotist.

b. Set up some criteria for evaluating behavior in the classroom, in the halls, in the lunchroom, on the athletic field. How do you measure up to these standards?

4. Appraising Our Value System.

a. Define specific problems in this area. Suggest possible courses of action and reasons to support them. The following is illustrative: Jane has been invited to a party by one of her school friends. Her parents have told her that if she goes to the party she must be home by 10 o'clock. Jane thinks this is too early. What course of action do you think she should take in this situation?

b. Summarize and discuss the reactions of the class to issues such as the following:

(1) No matter what a teacher does, he should always be obeyed.

(2) Students should be encouraged to discuss opinions differing from those of the teacher.

(3) Students should make their own rules.

III. Problems of Finding Values by Which We Live

A. *Objectives.* To help students:

1. Explore the various sources of values.

2. Become aware of the way they have acquired their beliefs, prejudices, superstitions, and other ideas.

3. Use the method of intelligence as a guide for selecting values and establishing beliefs.

4. Learn how to judge the relative value of alternative courses of

action that are proposed to solve the problems arising within their day-by-day life.

5. Develop an open-minded attitude toward those who hold different values from their own, or from those of the group with which they are identified.
6. Become aware of the conflicting values in American culture.
7. Understand the impact of culture on values.
8. Work toward developing a satisfactory world picture and a workable philosophy of life.

B. *Scope.* Studying problems of developing values and beliefs in the area of:
1. Personal living.
2. Personal-social relationships.
3. Social-civic-economic relationships.

C. *Suggested Activities.*
1. Personal Living.
   a. Invite representatives from the various churches in the community to talk to the class about their religious beliefs and customs.
   b. Arrange to listen to some of the recordings from the Edward R. Murrow "This I Believe" Series.
   c. Make a list of moral values that would serve as a guide to behavior in a democratic society.
   d. Make a list of common practices which have to do with standards of right and wrong. Analyze each as to its real basis.
   e. Collect superstitions and make plans for testing some of them. For example, to test the belief that a person will have bad luck if he breaks a mirror, each member of the class might keep a record of his good and bad luck a week before and a week after deliberately breaking a mirror and compare both.
   f. Prepare a bulletin board display contrasting some superstitions and unfounded beliefs with scientific beliefs. The following plan is suggestive:

Superstitions say	*but*	**Science** says
Diseases are caused by evil spirits.		Diseases are caused by certain micro-organisms.

As a follow-up, discuss the nature of the scientific method of solving health problems.

2. Personal-Social Relationships
   a. Identify some of the viewpoints of adolescent boys and girls which may be in conflict with those of their parents. What are some of the reasons underlying these differences? How may such conflicts be resolved?
   b. Invite several parents to participate in a panel discussion on questions such as the following: What are the chief mistakes of young people today? What ideals would you recommend for modern youth?
   c. Invite various authorities such as a physician, marriage counselor, psychiatrist, priest or minister to discuss problems presented by the class on sex, courtship, and marriage.
3. Social-Civic-Economic Relationships.
   a. Discuss the major ideals of American democracy. Compare them with those of other social philosophies.
   b. Compile a list of contradictory values and beliefs about economic, political, and social questions. Ask a number of persons to respond to your list by indicating the statements with which they disagree. Try to determine the extent to which the respondents accept contradictory values. The following are illustrative:
      (1) Honesty is the best policy,
          But: Business is business, and a business man would fail if he showed all of his cards.
      (2) Public service is a fine thing,
          But: Of course, a man has to look out for himself.
   c. Discuss the effects of confusions in the value-system in America upon personality, social structure, and national unity.
   d. Examine critically the following beliefs:
      (1) The lower classes have innate defects or they would have made good.
      (2) Our pattern of institutions (i.e., Christianity, democracy, capitalistic economy, monogamy) is the best pattern ever devised, and would be good for other nations if they would only try it.
      (3) Negroes are naturally gifted in music and dancing.
      (4) The American people have more initiative, ambition, and energy than the people of other countries.
      (5) Free competition insures maximum efficiency in industry.
      (6) As time goes on, our economic system will inevitably become more socialistic no matter which political party is in power.

IV.   Problems of Social Relationships in a Democracy

A.   *Objectives.*   To help students:
1. Study the social effects of scientific and technological advances on society.
2. Recognize conflicts of value which underlie social decisions.
3. Realize the importance of scientific planning for social change.
4. Become sensitive to areas in which social change is desirable.
5. Understand the role of pressure groups in social conflicts.
6. Participate effectively in activities of social significance in the community.
7. Broaden their concepts of the structure and importance of social institutions.
8. Understand how social problems may be solved through the use of the method of intelligence.

B.   *Scope.*   Studying problems of social relationships in a democracy at the:
1. Community level
2. National level

C.   *Suggested Activities.*
1. Community Level
   a. Make a study of juvenile delinquency in the community. What age group includes the most frequent offenders? What types of delinquency are most prevalent? What are some probable causes? Make recommendations for a preventive program.
   b. Invite a judge from the criminal court to lead a discussion on the causes of crime and factors which have contributed to the rise of organized crime. As a follow-up, formulate a plan for attacking the crime problem in the community.
   c. Invite a member of the police department to talk about the chief functions of the police department, major problems of police administration, and the recruiting and training of policemen.
   d. Analyze reports of family welfare and counseling agencies for data on the sources of broken homes. Compare these data with those of ten years ago; twenty years ago. Are any trends apparent?
   e. Interview a judge of the Court of Domestic Relations to secure information concerning marriage and divorce laws.

Report your findings to the class. Discuss the adequacy of the present laws.

f. Invite a member of the local planning commission to talk about plans for attacking the housing problem in the community.

g. Make a survey of community health services. This might include the health department, medical and dental clinics, hospitals, and various agencies for promoting the health of citizens of the community. Are community health needs being met? Compare findings with information on conditions in other communities.

h. Take a tour of an industrial plant in the community. Ask the safety engineer to point out how plant conditions, condition of equipment, and guards on machines affect the accident rate. Interview the hygienist to find out the principal industrial causes of disease and how they contribute to absence, inefficiency and labor turnover.

2. National Level

a. Compare the direct per capita cost of crime with the costs of such public agencies as education, public health, public recreation, and poor relief.

b. Make a study of the extent of unemployment in the United States during the last twenty-five years. At what point was unemployment greatest? Least? What is the outlook for the future?

c. Make a graph showing the number of strikes in the United States during the period 1938-56. How do you account for any marked variation? What is the effect of strikes on the economy of the nation?

d. Report on the development, present status, and forms of labor unions in the United States.

e. Make charts showing the major provisions of the following: Social Security Act; Fair Labor Standards Act; Minimum Wage Law for Women and Minors; Child Labor Laws.

f. Discuss the social significance of health. How can ill health and its results be both a social problem and a cause of social problems.

g. Have a panel discussion on: "The Major Health Problems of the United States."

h. Compare various plans for meeting the health needs of the nation. Make a chart showing the major provisions of each plan.

i. Illustrate graphically the average length of life in the United

States at ten year intervals during the last fifty years. What trend is apparent? What social problems has this change in life expectancy created?

j. Invite several persons sixty-five years of age or older to participate in a panel discussion on the major problems of old age.

k. Invite a representative from a poor-relief organization or social agency to talk to the class on the major causes of poverty. Discuss the relation between poverty and crime; poverty and ill health; poverty and birth and mortality rates.

l. Make a graph showing the distribution of American families within various income groups. Compare these data with those of twenty years ago, thirty years ago. Is a trend discernible?

V. Problems of Employment and Vocation

A. *Objectives.* To help students:

1. Develop appropriate techniques for exploring opportunities in any job field.

2. Acquire some basic information about occupations in general, and about the job fields in which they are interested in particular.

3. Become aware of the vocational opportunities in the immediate and wider community.

4. Develop an understanding of interrelationships among occupations and the contribution of all forms of work to the welfare of society.

5. Understand and appreciate the dignity, satisfaction, and independence that employment brings.

6. Develop an understanding of the problems of workers, employers, and their interrelationships.

7. Understand the social, political, and economic implications of vocational choice.

8. Realize the importance of a wise selection of work in terms of life satisfaction and happiness.

9. Discover their interests, aptitudes, personality traits, abilities and understand how these are related to occupational adjustment.

B. *Scope.* Studying problems of employment and vocations through:

1. Exploring the world of work.

2. Planning for job choice.

C. *Suggested Activities.*
   1. Exploring the World of Work.
      a. Contrast employment practices and vocations of today with those of the period preceding the Industrial Revolution. What changes have occurred? How may such changes be accounted for?
      b. Poll the class to find out the occupations in which there is greatest interest. Discuss: What is likely to determine development, growth, and trends in each field? How would growth in each of the fields affect living and working conditions in the community?
      c. Consult the *United States Census Report* or the *Dictionary of Occupational Titles* in order to find out the number and variety of occupations in the United States. List the major occupational groups under a bulletin board caption, "Your Future, What Shall It Be?" Arrange to have a weekly display of books, pictures, clippings, and pamphlets on a different occupation.
      d. Invite a lawyer to trace legislative measures concerning employment from their beginnings to the present time.
      e. Visit the local office of the United States Employment Service. Find out what services are offered; what types of jobs are generally available, available to the handicapped, available on a part-time basis.
      f. Invite the managers of stores, factories, and small businesses in the community to serve on a panel to discuss the requirements and opportunities in their specific fields of work.
      g. Prepare bulletin-board displays showing the vocational possibilities of different school subjects. For example, develop displays titled: "Vocational Opportunities in Stenography," "Opportunities in the Arts," and "Vocational Outlets of Foreign Languages." Invite the cooperation of the teachers of the various subjects.
   2. Planning for Job Choice.
      a. Make a list of the leisure-time activities of the members of the class, and discuss the vocational significance of these interests. Consult Part IV of the *Dictionary of Occupational Titles* for a listing of hobbies and leisure-time activities in which vocational skills and interests may be developed.
      b. Interview a number of persons to find out how each chose his occupation. Would he make the same choice again? What advice would he give a high school student concerning preparation for employment?

c. List occupations whose principal activities or duties require: skill with the hands; strength and endurance; supervision of others; influencing of others; written expression of ideas; indoor work; outdoor work; the use of abstract ideas. Which of these would you enjoy? Give reasons for your choice.

d. Develop a self-rating sheet on which aptitudes, abilities, and interests can be appraised. Suggest that members of the class rate themselves and discuss the results individually with the teacher. Arrange to take a series of standardized tests which will help you discover your aptitudes, abilities, and interests.

e. Interview workers in three or four vocations that interest you. Following are some suggestive questions: What is your job? How did you prepare for it? What are the advantages and disadvantages? What is the average yearly salary for beginning workers? What are the opportunities for advancement? What advice would you give to those considering this kind of work? Make a "Career Book" based on the findings of the class.

VI. Problems of Using and Conserving Natural Resources

A. *Objectives.* To help students:
1. Develop an understanding of natural resources.
2. Study the effect of natural resources on human welfare.
3. Understand the interrelations and interdependencies among men, animals, plants, and the earth that supports them all.
4. Realize that many resources are exhaustible and that there is much evidence of resource waste.
5. Develop a social philosophy of rights and clarify the rights of society as they conflict with the desire of the individual or limited group to exploit resources.
6. Study the relation of science to conservation.
7. Become acquainted with the conservation work that is now being done.
8. Develop a sound philosophy of conservation.

B. *Scope.* Conserving natural resources at the:
1. Community level
2. State level
3. National level
4. World-wide level

C. *Suggested Activities.*
1. Community Level.
    a. Take a trip to places where the effects of erosion can be seen. Follow this with a trip to an erosion-control project. Prepare reports on the various methods of preventing or controlling erosion.
    b. Take a trip to a farm where a complete conservation farming program has been put into effect. Notice the relation of soil conservation to wildlife conservation. Ask the conservation specialist to explain the farm program.
    c. Take a trip to the filtration plant to observe the various processes involved in purifying water. Collect data on the source of the domestic water supply, problems in securing safe water, how water is distributed, the average amount of water consumed daily, and costs involved in purifying water.
    d. Find out what species of wildlife have become extinct or very rare in the locality. How do you account for this?
    e. Study the community to determine whether there are evidences of misuse, deterioration, or depletion of recreational resources. Discuss possible remedies.
2. State Level.
    a. Make a study of the state conservation program. What provisions have been made for forest conservation? Wildlife conservation?
    b. Make a poster showing the various causes of forest fires. Prepare other posters suitable for use in a campaign to educate the public to the dangers of forest fires.
    c. Make a survey of the present wildlife resources of your state.
    d. Survey the recreational resources of your state and classify them under such categories as physical, biotic, esthetic, scientific, or historic. Compare these resources with those of other states. To what extent are they adequate?
3. National Level.
    a. Enlarge two maps of the United States, one showing forest areas in 1620, the other showing present-day forest areas. What factors have contributed to the shrinkage of forest areas?
    b. Write to the National Park Service, Department of Interior, Washington, D. C. for copies of available booklets dealing with the national parks. Give reports to the class.
    c. On an outline map of the United States, show the areas in

which most of the soil either has been severely damaged or completely destroyed by erosion. Study the relation between the erosion of the areas and their prosperity.

d. Report on some Federal water projects such as the T.V.A., Boulder Dam, Grand Coulee Dam, and the Florida Ship Canal. As a follow-up, discuss the government's responsibility for the conservation of natural resources.

e. Show by means of a graph, the relative proportion of the world's minerals possessed by the United States. Discuss the economic implications.

f. Have a panel discussion on the topic, "Can Scientific Discoveries Compensate for the Exhaustion of Our Mineral Resources?"

4. World-Wide Level.

a. Study the relation of natural resources to the wealth and strength of a nation; for example, the lack of sufficient resources for the large populations of China and India and its effect on their standards of living and strength as world powers.

b. It has been said that wars are fought primarily for the control of natural resources. Discuss how far this saying is true in the light of what is known about past wars.

c. Make a chart showing the world production of petroleum for the last twenty years. Is the production increasing or decreasing? What are some of the economic implications?

d. Study and report on topics such as the following:

   (1) How long the land of the earth, at the present rate of exploitation, will continue to support its population.

   (2) The decline of commerce and industry in some communities or nations due to the depletion or exhaustion of natural resources.

   (3) The world distribution of mineral resources and its social-economic implications.

VII. Problems of Education in American Democracy[1]

VIII. Problems of Constructive Use of Leisure

A. *Objectives.* To help students:

1. Develop a feeling of personal success and satisfaction.

2. Cultivate hobbies they can enjoy and become aware of the opportunities which avocations hold for vocational pursuits.

[1] This problem area was used to develop a resource guide in Chapter V.

3. Develop skills and attitudes for the enjoyment of a wide variety of leisure-time experiences—physical, emotional, social, intellectual, and cultural.
4. Use their leisure time healthfully, safely, and enjoyably.
5. Plan for a rhythm of work, rest, and play.
6. Assume personal responsibility for solving leisure-time problems in the home, school, and community.
7. Get acquainted with available resources for leisure-time activities in the community, nation, and other lands, and make use of such resources.
8. Understand the historical development of recreation and the relationship of recreation to social standards.

B. *Scope.* Guiding students to constructive use of leisure by exploring:
 1. Hobbies.
 2. Available leisure resources.

C. *Suggested Activities.*
 1. Hobbies
    a. Poll the class to find out the hobbies in which there is greatest interest. Invite students and staff members who have similar interests to help the class explore possibilities in these areas.
    b. Make a series of bulletin board displays related to the hobbies of interest to the class. As a follow-up, discuss the importance of having a hobby.
    c. Make a study of the hobby in which you are most interested. Find out: how to get started; what materials are needed; how to become acquainted with other hobbyists; what books, pamphlets and periodicals are devoted to this hobby; what personal benefits might be realized.
    d. Have a "Hobby Fair." Invite students, faculty, and members of the community to put their hobbies on display.
 2. Available Leisure Resources.
    a. Explore possibilities for pursuing leisure-time activities in the school. Obtain information on requirements for participation as well as the time schedule for various activities.
    b. Survey students' interests in leisure-time activities. In what activities are students most interested? Least interested? Disinterested? On the basis of this information, make suggestions to the student council concerning the school's recreational program.
    c. Suggest a list of leisure-time activities that can be enjoyed

by the family. What equipment is necessary for carrying out such suggestions?

d. Make a study of community recreation. What facilities are available? How are they financed? How are supervision and instruction provided?

e. Compare the recreational facilities of your state with those of other states. What recommendations for the improvement of the state program can be made?

f. Display a large map of the United States, locating the National Parks and other points of interest.

IX. Problems of Family Living

A. *Objectives.*   To help students:
1. Gain an insight into the importance of the family as a basic unit in a democracy.
2. Understand the effect of technological development on family living.
3. Establish sound, wholesome relations with all members of the family.
4. Understand factors that may affect the success of a marriage.
5. Recognize the duties and responsibilities as well as the privileges and rights of family living.
6. Develop an understanding of the problems one faces in establishing and maintaining a satisfying home life.
7. Develop a cooperative attitude in solving family conflicts.
8. Become aware of the interacting influence of home and community and of the individual's responsibility for helping raise the standards of community life.

B. *Scope.*   Studying problems of family living in the:
1. Home.
2. Community.

C. *Suggested Activities.*
1. Home.
    a. Make a comparative study of the family of today and that of fifty years ago. Include size of the family, functions performed by the family unit, leisure time activities, family relationships, and material aspects of the home.
    b. Make a survey of parent opinion concerning such problems as use of the family car and dating on school nights. Form a panel of parents and students to lead a discussion on these problems.

c. Write short plays highlighting problems faced by a teenager in a modern home. Include dating, getting along with parents and brothers and sisters, and finance.

d. Make a survey of class reaction to the following: "going steady" during high school, getting married before completing a high school education, and the age at which young men and women should marry.

e. Invite a young married couple to lead a discussion on the role of the courtship period in determining the success of a marriage.

f. Interview the County Clerk to secure information regarding marriage and divorce laws, the procedure for obtaining a marriage license, the age of consent for marriage, the number of marriage licenses issued, and the number of divorces granted last year.

g. Invite a psychologist to lead a discussion on the major causes of divorce and family separation. What are the effects upon the couple, their children, and society?

h. Interview some parents to find out what responsibilities they expect their children to assume in relation to maintaining the home. Report your findings to the class.

i. List household duties which need to be performed daily, weekly, or occasionally. Plan a fair distribution of these duties among the family members.

2. Community.

a. Make a survey of recreational, social, and educational facilities in the community that are available to the family. What needs are not being met? Formulate a plan for action.

b. Arrange for a tour through various districts in the community. Take pictures representing the best homes, middle class homes, and the worst homes. Discuss the effects of inadequate homes on the individual, the family, and society.

c. Invite a city official to lead a discussion on the family's responsibility to the community in regard to law enforcement, proper treatment of public property, and participation in community programs.

X. Problems of Communication

A. *Objectives.* To help students:
1. Understand the role of communication in social life.
2. Develop an increasing awareness of the various media of communication.

3. Realize the importance of developing skills in the effective use of communication techniques and devices.
4. Appreciate the effect of technology on the growth and improvement of communication.
5. Understand the methods, dangers, and necessary controls of mass communication.
6. Understand the factors that enhance or hinder effective communication among individuals, groups, and nations.

B. *Scope.* Studying problems of:
   1. Inter-personal communication
   2. National mass communication
   3. International mass communication

C. *Suggested Activities.*
   入. Inter-Personal Communication
      a. Develop a set of criteria for evaluating the quality of a conversation. In light of these criteria, rate yourself as a conversationalist. At what points do you need to improve?
      b. Analyze the voice tone and speaking pattern of types such as the following: the villain in a dramatization; the crooner; the fashion editor; the "sob-sister"; the gossip reporter. What effects are achieved by the speakers? How are they achieved? Do these have any social significance?
      c. Report on the gestural language used by theater ushers, baseball umpires, football referees, and policemen. As a follow-up, discuss the role of physical expression in communication.
      d. Invite the English teacher to speak on common errors in writing and how they might be avoided.
      e. Discuss the role of dress, personal appearance, and cleanliness in communication.
   2. National Mass Communication
      a. Make a study of modern journalism. Find out how the news is gathered in papers like the *New York Times* and disseminated to people all over the United States.
      b. Survey the likes and dislikes of radio and television enthusiasts in the school. Analyze reasons for the popularity of certain programs.
      c. Develop some criteria for judging motion pictures. Include such points as the social values, story, direction, setting, scenery, costuming, acting, and the like. Keep a movie diary and share your judgments periodically.
      d. Have a panel discussion on: "Strengths and Weaknesses of

Commercial Radio and Television Programs"; "Censorship of Films"; "The Effect of the Press upon Public Opinion."

3. International Mass Communication

a. Make a study of modern technological improvements in the rapid, cheap, long-distance communication of words and images. Analyze their social and cultural effects.

b. Discuss the role of government and private agencies in stimulating understanding among peoples through the mass communication media.

c. Have a panel discussion on "The Effect of a Universal Language on International Understanding."

XI. Problems of Democratic Government

A. *Objectives.* To help students:

1. Understand their responsibilities and rights as citizens in a democratic society.

2. Acquire a sense of personal worth as participating members of a social-civic group and understand their role in contributing to better democratic living in the home, school, community, nation, and world.

3. Acquire the understandings, skills, and attitudes necessary for effective participation in group living.

4. Gain an understanding of and appreciation for democracy as a way of life.

5. Understand the organization and functions of local, state, and national governments.

6. Become aware of the importance of an effective and intelligently-informed public opinion in a democratic society.

7. Compare democratic with non-democratic patterns of life.

8. Become aware of the threats or barriers to democratic living and possible remedies.

9. Examine the possibility of establishing a democratic world government.

10. Understand possible contributions of the United States to furthering democratic ideals in the world.

11. Trace the development of democracy and consider its possible future.

B. *Scope.* Studying problems of Democratic Government at the:

1. Personal level

2. Community level

3. State and national levels

4. World-wide level

C. *Suggested Activities.*
   1. Personal Level.
      a. Invite a lawyer, a judge, or some other competent civic authority to speak on "Civil Liberties and the Individual." Ask the speaker to focus on the strengths and weaknesses of citizen participation and the duties a citizen should perform.
      b. Make a series of cartoons showing the growth and development of the rights and duties of the American citizen.
      c. Depict in mural form the crucial issues facing the American citizen in various historical periods.
   2. Community Level.
      a. Make a study of the structure, personnel, and functions of the local government. Follow this up with trips to the county courthouse and the municipal building. If possible, attend a jury trial and meetings of the city council.
      b. Make a graphic presentation of the local tax structure. Discuss: How are taxes levied? What is the basis for distribution? What services are provided by taxes?
      c. Prepare a speech in favor of a proposed levy, a candidate, or a proposed change in policy now under debate in the community.
   3. State and National Levels.
      a. Construct a "time and event" line showing people and events that have contributed to the development of the state, in their proper time placement.
      b. Make a pictograph showing the various officials, departments, and commissions of the state government.
      c. Make a chart comparing the division of powers between the states and the federal government. Discuss the general basis on which the powers are divided. As a follow-up, investigate current issues in which federal "control" is involved; for example, federal aid to education.
      d. Make a study of the organization and operation of a political party, tracing it in detail from the party worker to the national committee. From these data, make a chart for bulletin board display.
      e. Make a study of current instances of graft and corruption in government. How were these instances uncovered? What can be done to prevent such practices?
      f. Form small groups to study the three branches of government. What are the duties and powers of each branch? Make a bulletin board display illustrating the system of checks and balances.

g. Make a map of the United States showing the distribution of electoral votes as compared with the population. Discuss the proposed changes in the electoral system as it now exists.

h. Make a pictogram showing the steps in how a bill becomes a law.

i. Investigate a case currently being tried before the United States Supreme Court. What kind of cases come within the jurisdiction of the court?

4. World-Wide Level.

a. Make a comparative study of Democracy, Fascism, Communism, and Socialism. Give special attention to such points as: form of government; purpose of the state; relationship of the citizen to the state; public opinion and political parties.

b. Indicate, in color, on a world map, the areas of autocracy and democracy as they stood a century ago; as they stand today. How do you account for any changes?

c. Evaluate the foreign policy of the United States in terms of its democratic ideals. To what extent has the United States practiced democracy in its relations with Canada, and Mexico? Europe? Asia? The Middle East?

d. Plan a panel on the topic, "Should the United States Support a World Government?"

XII. Problems of Community and Personal Health

A. *Objectives.* To help students:

1. Develop desirable health understandings, attitudes, and habits.
2. Become acquainted with community agencies for health improvement and develop a desire and ability to cooperate with such agencies.
3. Eradicate health fallacies and develop a critical attitude toward health information and self medication.
4. Develop an understanding of the causes of accidents and ways of reducing or preventing them.
5. Develop skill in giving first aid treatment.
6. Understand the relation of nutrition to health and plan their own diets adequately.
7. Solve their sex problems and develop a wholesome attitude toward the different aspects of sex.
8. Gain some understanding of the functioning of the human body and how to maintain it in good condition.
9. Practice rules conducive to good mental and social hygiene.
10. Develop an understanding of the scientific bases of healthful living.

11.   Understand the influence of social and economic factors prevailing in a country on the health of its people.

B. *Scope.* Achieving and maintaining healthful living at the:
1. Personal level
2. Community level
3. National and International levels

C. *Suggested Activities.*
1. Personal Level.
    a. Take snapshots of members of the class (side and front views) while they are engaged in various activities. Discuss the extent to which sound habits of posture are being practiced.
    b. Set up a display of balanced meals, indicating the approximate cost of each. Artificial foods or pictures pasted on cardboard are suitable for such displays.
    c. Keep a record of your food intake each day for a period of a week. Study the record critically to determine whether the diet was balanced and whether it was suited to your particular health requirements.
    d. Make a study of problems related to being overweight or underweight; for example, how to determine "normal" weight; how to gain weight; how to lose weight; what causes people to be overweight or underweight.
    e. Invite the school physician to lead a panel discussion on such topics as: "The Relation of Tobacco to Health"; "The Effect of Alcohol on the Body."
    f. Prepare a tabular review of present knowledge concerning important communicable diseases, listing the name of the disease, the causative agent, the source of infection, the agent and mode of transmission, and methods of immunization and control.
    g. Form small groups to study the digestive, respiratory, circulatory, and nervous systems. Make bulletin board displays describing the systems and their functions.
    h. Invite the school nurse to demonstrate first aid treatment for various conditions.
    i. Invite the school physician to talk about the purpose, content, and use of health examinations. Arrange to have a complete health examination.
2. Community Level.
    a. Collect news items concerning accidental injuries in the

home or school. Analyze these in terms of the nature, causes, results, and possible prevention.

b. Take a trip to the health department in your city or county and study its organization and functions. Also visit the laboratories and clinics of this department.

c. Take a trip to a hospital and go through its laboratory, X-ray rooms, operating rooms, wards, and emergency room. Observe methods used to obtain asepsis and the precautions taken in the isolation ward to prevent the spread of communicable diseases.

d. Investigate community provisions for safe water and milk, pure food, sanitation, sewage and industrial waste disposal, rodent control, quarantine, and control of dust and fumes.

e. Take trips to: a dairy to observe pasteurization and handling of milk; a local water supply plant to observe steps in the purification of water; an industrial plant to study provisions for the protection of workmen on the job.

f. Obtain data from the police department on accidents occurring during the last ten years. Compare these data with the national figures. Is the number of accidents increasing or decreasing? Explain.

3. National and International Levels.

a. Illustrate graphically: average length of life during the last fifty years; infant mortality during the last fifty years; tuberculosis death rate; diphtheria death rate. What trends are evident? Explain.

b. Secure data on the health of draftees as evidenced by pre-induction examinations. To what extent do these data give a picture of the health status of the nation?

c. Compare the chief killers of today with those of fifty years ago. What do you deduce from such a comparison?

d. Have a panel discussion on, "The Adoption of a Program of Socialized Medicine in the United States."

e. Study the effect of educational, social, and economic conditions prevailing in a country on the health of its people. Discuss the effect of war on nutritional diseases.

XIII. Problems of Economic Relationships in a Democracy

A. Objectives. To help students:

1. Become intelligent consumers.
2. Understand how the consumer's welfare is protected through the activities of various agencies.

3. Learn to manage their personal financial affairs efficiently.
4. Become oriented to vocational living.
5. Study the national economy, its past, present, and probable future.
6. Study the impact of science and technology on economic living.
7. Understand the interrelationship of a nation's welfare and its economic strength.
8. Understand the interdependence of the economic, social, political, and cultural aspects of living.
9. Compare the major economic systems of the world.
10. Recognize the economic interdependence of the peoples of the world.

B. *Scope.* Studying problems of economic relationships at the:
1. Personal-family level
2. Community and national levels
3. International level

C. *Suggested Activities.*
1. Personal-Family Level.
   a. Collect a variety of advertisements. Check the factual accuracy of each advertisement against the best information you can find. Post on the bulletin board samples of false or misleading advertisements, honest advertisements, and advertisements containing exaggerated claims.
   b. Report on the provisions of the Federal Food, Drug, and Cosmetic Act. Discuss the role of government in protecting the consumer.
   c. As a class project write a booklet entitled "How to Get Your Money's Worth."
   d. Make a plan for apportioning your allowance among the activities and needs for which you are responsible.
   e. Choose some occupation in which you are interested and report on its past, present, and probable future.
2. Community and National Levels.
   a. Make graphs showing government income and expenditures at the local, state, and national levels for the last twenty years. What trends are apparent? What factors have contributed to this state of affairs?
   b. Make a list of materials in common use today which were unknown: in colonial days; in Civil War days; at the turn of the century; twenty years ago; ten years ago.
   c. Make a study of the extent of unemployment in the United States during the last twenty-five years. At what point was

unemployment greatest? least? What is the outlook for the future?

d. Have a panel discussion on, "The Increasing Use of Machinery in Industry and Its Effect on Employment."

e. Determine the relative prosperity of individuals in various states by comparing the number of automobiles, radios, telephones, and other products owned per hundred persons. Analyze the factors which contribute to any inequalities.

f. Study the extent of the depletion of natural resources in the United States. How long will the country's present resources in forests, coal, and oil last? Estimate the monetary cost of this depletion. As a follow-up, discuss the responsibility of the individual and of government for the conservation of natural resources.

3. International Level.

a. Make a chart showing the chief exports and imports of the United States, Russia, Great Britain, France, and Japan. How do these exports and imports affect the economy of the country involved?

b. Discuss the importance of international economic cooperation and the efforts launched in order to promote it. Include the work of the United Nations, the Economic and Social Council, the International Labor Organization, and the World Health Organization.

c. Locate the chief sources of the essential natural resources of the world. Discuss the relation between a nation's natural resources and its standard of living; its industrial development; its strength as a world power.

d. Make charts explaining the difference between private enterprise and collectivism, socialism and communism, communism and fascism.

XIV. Problems of Achieving World Peace in the Atomic Age

A. *Objectives.* To help students:

1. Explore some contemporary theories concerning the causes of war.

2. Study the various effects of war on human progress.

3. Study different proposals for establishing world peace.

4. Keep abreast of the work of the United Nations and of the United States Atomic Energy Commission and actively support them in their constructive actions.

5. Study problems resulting from the liberation of atomic energy.

6. Understand the consequences of an atomic war.
7. Explore present and probably future peace-time uses of atomic energy.
8. Study different proposals for controlling atomic energy on an international level.
9. Gain sufficient information about atomic energy, to participate intelligently as a citizen in the solution of current national and international problems.
10. Identify and understand those factors which will promote better understanding and cooperation among people.
11. Understand the foundations of lasting world peace.
12. Understand their role in contributing to world peace, and accept responsibility for translating their understandings into action.

B. *Scope.* Contributing to the achievement of world peace in the Atomic Age at the:
   1. Community level
   2. National level.
   3. International level

C. *Suggested Activities.*
   1. Community Level.
      a. Make a bulletin board display of pictures showing the results of the bombing of Hiroshima and Nagasaki. Discuss how an atomic blast would affect the community.
      b. Make a diagram showing the effect of the atomic bomb at varying distances from the site of the explosion. Discuss what one should do in the event of atomic attack.
      c. Find out what security measures have been taken in the community, what provisions have been made in the school. Set up a practice security drill.
   2. National Level.
      a. Discuss the political, social, and economic effects of a large-scale peace-time military program in the United States.
      b. Secure a copy of the Atomic Energy Act of 1946 and briefly summarize its provisions. Discuss recent proposals for the control of atomic energy.
      c. Investigate the probable peace-time uses of atomic energy. Organize your findings under headings such as: Industry, Medicine, The Farm.
      d. Make a scrapbook of current information (articles, editorials, pamphlets, photographs, and cartoons) concerning the atom bomb, nuclear energy, world government, and related matters.

3. International Level.
   a. Arrange for a panel discussion on the psychological, economic, and political theories concerning the causes of war.
   b. Give oral reports on the economic consequences of wars. Give specific illustrations of: destruction of human lives, destruction of natural resources and property, creation of debts and taxes. Follow this up with a discussion of the social and moral effects of war.
   c. Make a study of the various attempts to promote greater international understanding. Include the Hague Conference, The League of Nations, the Kellogg Plan, the International Food Conference, Bretton Woods, and the United Nations. Discuss the successes and failures of each.
   d. Have a panel discussion on: "Should the United States Support a World Government?"; "Foundations for Lasting Peace."

XV. Problems of Intercultural Relations

A. *Objectives.* To help students:
   1. Develop an awareness of intercultural conflicts in the immediate and wider communities and study their causes and effects.
   2. Develop a feeling of personal concern and responsibility for the solution of intercultural problems by democratic processes.
   3. Acquire knowledge of and appreciation for the contributions of all cultures to the welfare of mankind.
   4. Understand and appreciate the composite character of the American population and its consequent advantage to the American culture.
   5. Realize the conditions under which racial or minority groups live within our nation.
   6. Practice wholesome, friendly, mutually respectful human relationships in everyday living.
   7. Recognize and understand both the similarities and differences between various culture patterns.
   8. Examine the origin, prevalence, and persistence of existing beliefs and attitudes that influence intercultural relations and develop a willingness to modify those attitudes that are not based on facts.
   9. Evaluate intergroup relations in terms of the democratic ideals.

B. *Scope.* Studying problems of intercultural relations at the:
   1. Community level
   2. National level
   3. International level

C. *Suggested Activities.*

   1. Community Level.

      a. Make maps showing the concentrations of racial and national groups in the community. Why do these concentrations exist? What is their effect upon the total life of the community? The minority group?

      b. Invite a foreign-born parent to describe his adjustments to life in the community. What were some of his pleasant and unpleasant experiences? A vivid picture of his confusions and frustrations should help create sympathetic understandings of immigrant problems.

      c. Arrange a series of talks on "Basic Religious Beliefs" to be given by a Jewish rabbi, a Catholic priest, and a Protestant minister. If possible, attend services in their houses of worship.

      d. Arrange a tour through various districts in the community. Evaluate the houses in each district in terms of previously defined standards. Try to find out what groups live in below-standard houses. How do you account for this?

   2. National Level.

      a. Invite speakers from the National Association for the Advancement of Colored People (for the Negro) from the YMCA (for the Mongolian race), and from the Indian Bureau (for the American Indian) to lead a discussion on the major problems faced by each of these groups. What are possible solutions?

      b. Make a study of the Negro in American life.

      c. Present an assembly program based on the cultural gifts of the various nationality groups to the United States. Give special attention to groups which are important in the community.

      d. Prepare a panel discussion on one or more of the following topics: "The Class System in the United States"; "The Use of Minority Religious Groups as Scapegoats"; "Social Mobility in Our Society."

   3. International Level.

      a. Collect and list stereotypes regarding national or racial groups. Example: "Scotchmen are tight-fisted." Present evidence which would tend to prove or disprove the stereotype.

      b. Have a panel discussion on the topic, "The Effect of Racial Discrimination on World Peace and International Relations."

c. Make a comparative study of several cultures of the world. In what ways are they alike? different? How do you account for their similarities and differences? If possible, arrange to have representatives from different nationality groups who are living temporarily in the United States participate in an assembly on various cultures of the world.

d. Make a study of UNESCO and how it attempts to improve relations among nations. The following questions are suggestive: What is UNESCO? Who belongs to UNESCO? What is UNESCO's program?

Appendix Two

SUGGESTIONS FOR USE OF THE CORE BLOCK OF TIME

There are many ways to use effectively the two to three hour block-of-time allotted to the core program during the school day. A long block-of-time affords opportunity for the planning of class social functions, announcements and administrative details, individual and small group conferences, class business meetings, discussion of school problems, free reading, practice sessions on the "fundamentals," creative writing, and supervised study, in addition to work on the unit of study.

Following are several possible weekly plans for a core class.[1] These are purely hypothetical and are not to be construed as a pattern to be followed. Learning unit plans should be developed cooperatively by the teachers and pupils using them. They are intended to give further clues as to the types of experiences which are generally provided for in the core block-of-time. Plan I assumes that a learning unit is being initiated; Plan II, that a learning unit is in the developmental phase; Plan III, that a learning unit is in the culminating phase. Plans I and II assume a three-hour block of time; Plan III, a two-hour block of time.

[1] *Handbook for Core Teachers.* (Mimeographed), Prince George's County, Maryland; Board of Education, 1952. pp. 16-19.

Plan I

Initiatory Phase of Learning Unit (Some Aspect of Conservation)—Three-Hour Block-of-Time

Assumes criteria for choice of learning unit already set up cooperatively.

Monday	Tuesday	Wednesday	Thursday	Friday	Types of Experiences
8:30–8:45 Administrative routine. Home-room business.	8:30–8:45 Same as Monday.	8:30–9:00 Report from Student Council—Discussion.	8:30–8:45 Administrative routine. Homeroom business.	8:30–8:45 Administrative routine. Allocating Christmas Seal Sale.	1. Administrative routine.
8:45–9:30 Browsing—to gain ideas for exploration —Bulletin boards, books, exhibits.	8:45–9:30 1. Report from library committee. 2. Teacher talks about possibilities of unit.	9:00–9:45 Select the emphasis and, if possible, some significant problems for learning unit. Teacher-pupil planning with entire group.	8:45–9:15 Teacher presents block plan, gets class reaction — makes needed changes.	8:45–10:00 (1) Remedial work for small groups. (2) Group on field trip to nearby seed store. (3) Group doing library research. (4) Group setting up soil experiment. (5) Group plans.	2. Homeroom business. 3. Browsing in many different types of materials for ideas. 4. Entire group discussion. 5. Film.
9:30–10:05 (1) Discussion led by teacher to pull together questions to explore in unit. (2) Attitudes test on conservation.	9:30–10:05 Resource person from faculty drops in to point up significance of unit.	9:45–10:30 Excursion to school grounds to explore suggested group project for flower borders.	9:15–10:00 (1) Set plans in motion—form committees—make individual assignments —make all group assignments.		6. Individual conferences. 7. Free reading. 8. Committee work. 9. Planning group goals and how to achieve them.
10:05–10:30 Film—Audio-Visual Room. To raise more questions for exploration—Followed by brief discussion.	10:05–10:30 Reading assignment in common book for background. Provide for individual differences.	10:30–10:40 Break	10:00–10:35 Committees meet to make plans—Teacher guidance.	10:00–10:45 Lesson on business letter writing for entire group.	10. Planning individual goals. 11. Library research.
10:30–10:40 Break	10:30–10:40 Break	10:40–11:15 Entire group plans ways to achieve objectives. Teacher leads discussion. Get	10:35–10:45 Break	10:45–10:50 Break	12. Excursion — entire group. 13. Field trip—small group.
	10:40–11:15 Work in small groups to set down possible problems.		10:45–11:10 Supervised study— (1) Reading in sev-	10:50–11:10 Written lesson—spelling.	14. Supervised study. 15. Practice sessions.

291

Plan I (Continued)

Monday	Tuesday	Wednesday	Thursday	Friday	Types of Experiences
10:40–11:15 (1) Short individual conferences on development in certain skills as shown by last unit. (2) Free reading period. (3) A committee may be sent to check with librarian on materials for unit. 11:15–11:30 Specific plans for Tuesday.	(2) Each individual sets down some ways to improve himself in unit and some of his problems not likely to be listed by group. 11:15–11:30 Specific plans for Wednesday.	aspects of evaluation in at all times. 11:15–11:30 Specific plans for Thursday.	eral sources on unit —definite questions. (2) Working on spelling words. 11:10–11:30 Evaluate planning to date. Plan for Friday.	11:10–11:30 (1) Evaluation of week's work. (2) Generally— what needs to be done next week? (3) Specific plans for Monday.	16. Remedial work. 17. Bulletin board. 18. Setting up experiment. 19. Group and individual evaluation.

Plan II

Development Phase of Learning Unit (Some Aspect of Conservation)—Three Hour Block-of-Time for Core

Monday	Tuesday	Wednesday	Thursday	Friday	Types of Experiences
8:30–8:45 Administrative routine. Homeroom business. 8:45–9:00 Quick recoup on plans for week.	8:30–9:15 Administrative routine. Entire school assembly. 9:15–10:15 Directed reading activity in literature books — (unrelated	8:30–8:45 Administrative routine. Homeroom business. 8:45–10:00 Field trip with parent to his nearby farm to observe con-	8:30–9:00 Administrative routine. Homeroom business. Jr. High dance plans. 9:00–9:45 Science Teacher serves as resource	8:30–8:45 Administrative routine. Homeroom business. 8:45–9:15 Spelling lesson from Dolch list and unit words.	1. Administrative routine. 2. Socio-drama. 3. Homeroom business. 4. Directed reading activity. 5. Committee work.

Plan II (Continued)

293

Monday	Tuesday	Wednesday	Thursday	Friday	Types of Experiences
9:00–10:00 Socio-Drama—presented by small group—Shows several ways to deal with a real conservation problem—analysis and discussion by entire group. Pupil leads with teacher guidance. 10:00–10:10 Break 10:10–11:15 Work on individual and small group projects — Teacher checks progress with each group. 11:15–11:30 Makes plans for Tuesday.	to unit.) Probably need 3 groups in different levels. 10:15–10:25 Break 10:25–11:15 Work on individual and small group projects. (1) Group in library. (2) Group with science teacher. (3) Group on school ground working on project. (4) Teacher helps with group needing remedial work. 11:15–11:30 Evaluate and plan for Wednesday.	tour and strip farming effects. 10:00–10:30 Practice session on verb forms for large group. Difficulty observed in written and spoken communication. 10:30–11:00 Work with art teacher in small groups. Finger-painting to illustrate some conservation problems. 11:00–11:15 Teacher discusses new words from Dolch List. 11:15–11:30 Plans for Thursday.	person. Small group demonstrates soil types in community. 9:45–10:30 Entire group planning session—What have we done? What is left to do? Should we change the plan? Teacher leads. 10:30–10:40 Break 10:40–11:20 Teacher introduces some phase of grammar for which need is anticipated in next few days. Supervised study follows to check understanding. 11:20–11:30 Plans for Friday.	9:15–10:15 Panel of pupils—Followed by group discussion concerning conservation problems in and around school. Draw upon reading materials from various sources. 10:15–11:15 Supervised Study-Work on research papers (individual) concerned with some aspect of conservation. Teacher gives individual help. 11:15–11:30 Plans for next week.	6. Individual projects. 7. School assembly. 8. Construction activities. 9. Science activities. 10. Remedial work. 11. Evaluation — individual, committees, entire group. 12. Field trip—entire group. 13. Practice session. 14. Spelling words from recommended list. 15. Art experiences for all. 16. Demonstration. 17. Resource persons. 18. Supervised study. 19. Introduction to new skill. 20. Panel. 21. Group discussion — research papers.

Culminating Phase of Learning Unit (Some Aspect of Conservation)—Two-Hour Block-of-Time for Core

Monday	Tuesday	Wednesday	Thursday	Friday	Types of Experiences
8:30–8:45 Administrative routine. Homeroom.	8:30–8:45 Administrative routine. Homeroom.	8:30–8:45 Administrative routine. Homeroom.	8:30–8:45 Administrative routine. Homeroom.	8:30–8:45 Administrative routine. Homeroom.	1. Group planning (entire).
8:45–9:45 A. Group planning for culminating experiences — Use purposes here. B. Scheduling: 1. Individual and group reports. 2. Pencil and paper tests. 3. Individual and small group evaluation. 4. Entire group evaluation.	8:45–9:45 Directed reading activity—chosen from various sources. Essentially same content. Projects groups thinking into next steps beyond learning unit.	8:45–10:00 (1) Committee at work on final plans for Thursday, e.g., setting up exhibits, arranging bulletin boards, practicing skit, checking points of forum, etc. (2) Teacher conferences with individuals about research papers, readings, notebooks, etc.	8:45–10:30 (1) The plan and purposes of the unit explained to parents by pupils. (2) What has been accomplished is shown through reports, skit, forum exhibits, experiments, bulletin boards. (3) Parents ideas are thrown in for discussion.	8:45–9:15 Selected spelling list test.	2. Small group and individual planning.
9:45–10:30 A. Committees meet to bring plans together. B. Teacher works with each group. C. Committee writes letter to invite parents on Thursday.	9:45–10:00 Attitudes Test— same as given in beginning of learning unit.			9:15–10:15 Discussion of changed attitudes as shown by attitudes test—entire group.	3. Directed reading activity. 4. Tests for attitudes, thinking, spelling, organization, skill development in other phases of language arts.
	10:00–10:10 Break	10:00–10:30 (1) Plans for Thursday are presented. Suggested changes incorporated. (2) Pointed out that certain formal tests will occur on Friday and following week.		10:15–10:30 Plans for next week might include (1) certain other pencil and paper test for application of principle and interpretation of data. (2) Essay type questions to get at organization and language-art skills. (3) Evaluation discussion with entire group. (4) Evaluation discussion with individuals.	5. Organizing and presenting data for parents. This was done using many resources and techniques. 6. Evaluation with entire group, small groups, individuals, parents.
	10:10–10:30 Plans for Wednesday. Committee appointed to receive parents, and explain projects.				

INDEX

Adams, Nicholas A., 250
Adolescent behavior, discussion of, 21-22
Adolescent development, levels of, 20; characteristics of, 21-22
Adolescent needs, concept of, 18-19, 22; See Needs
Adolescent problems, concept of, 20; relation to determining scope of the core program, 33-34
Aikin, Wilford M., 6
Alberty, Harold, 2, 4, 5, 6, 7, 16, 17, 18, 23, 24, 26, 52, 56, 58, 61, 67, 75, 81, 84, 90, 144, 202, 225, 232, 258
Alexander, William M., 6, 7, 10, 24
Alford, Betty, 208, 225
Ames, Louise B., 20, 21, 24
Anderson, Archibald W., 39
Anderson, G. Lester, 8

Bell, Howard, 73
Benne, Kenneth D., 12
Block-of-time, in the core program, 29; scheduling of, 45-46, 48; use of, 46-52
Bode, Boyd H., 9, 24
Bossing, Nelson L., 6, 7, 53, 145, 258
Bostwick, Prudence, 58, 90
Bradford, Leland, 12

Caswell, Hollis L., 59, 89
Characteristics of the core program, discussion of, 30-43; analysis of, 189-195
Chotiner, Allan I., 45
Citizenship education, 5-12; See also General education in the high school, Core program
Committee on the Function of Science in General Education, 14, 18
Core class, appropriate activities in, 46-52; unit activities, 46-47; home room activities, 47; remedial work, 47-48; school and community projects, 49-50; creative writing; 50-51; free reading, 51; individual and group guidance, 51-52. See also Block-of-time

Core program, description of, 25-53; current concepts of, 25-27; defined, 27-28; purposes of, 28-29; characteristics of, 29-43; relation of to rest of curriculum, 44-45; sample daily schedules for, 45-46; use of the long block of time in, 46-52; basic structure of, 54-90
Corey, Stephen, 62

Dade County Public Schools, Miami, Florida, 243
Deans, H. E., 225
Democratic values, 13; implications for education, 13-17; as basis for the core program, 42-43
Developmental tasks, concept of, 19-20; classification of, 19
Dewey, John, 8, 24
Doane, Donald C., 68, 75, 79, 81
Dorsey, Mattie F., 10, 11, 21, 24

Eight-year Study, 6
Evaluation, as a characteristic of the core program, 37-38

Fairmont Heights Junior-Senior High School, Prince George's County, Maryland, 45, 91, 251
Faunce, Roland C., 6, 24, 53, 145, 258
Fawcett, H. P., 225
Florida State University Demonstration School, 208
Forsheit, Samuel, 225
Fundamentals, development of, in the core program, 39-40

Gesell, Arnold, 20, 21, 24
General education in the high school, 1-24; defined, 5, 16; changes in, 5-6; usual practice in, 7; appraisal of subject-centered programs of, 7-12; basis for reorganization of, 13-23; relation of to special interest education, 16-17; a proposal for the reorganization of, 25-53; See also Citizenship education, Core program
Gholson, G. James, 45, 91, 251

295